The Confederate Surren

Also by Robert M. Dunkerly
and from McFarland

*Redcoats on the Cape Fear:
The Revolutionary War in
Southeastern North Carolina*, rev. ed. (2012)

The Confederate Surrender at Greensboro

The Final Days of the Army of Tennessee, April 1865

ROBERT M. DUNKERLY

McFarland & Company, Inc., Publishers

Jefferson, North Carolina, and London

All photographs are by the author unless otherwise noted.

LIBRARY OF CONGRESS CATALOGUING-IN-PUBLICATION DATA

Dunkerly, Robert M.
 The Confederate surrender at Greensboro : the final days
of the Army of Tennessee, April 1865 / Robert M. Dunkerly.
  p.   cm.
 Includes bibliographical references and index.

 ISBN 978-0-7864-7362-5
 softcover : acid free paper ∞

 1. Sherman's March through the Carolinas.   2. Greensboro
(N.C.)—History, Military—19th century.   3. North Carolina—
History—Civil War, 1861–1865—Campaigns.   4. United
States—History—Civil War, 1861–1865—Campaigns.
 5. Confederate States of America. Army of Tennessee.   I. Title.
 E477.7.D86 2013
 973.7'468—dc23   2013017751

BRITISH LIBRARY CATALOGUING DATA ARE AVAILABLE

On the cover: artwork *Furling the Flag*, 1869, Richard Norris
Brooke (© 2013 PicturesNow)

Manufactured in the United States of America

McFarland & Company, Inc., Publishers
 Box 611, Jefferson, North Carolina 28640
  www.mcfarlandpub.com

Table of Contents

Acknowledgments

Many people generously shared their knowledge to assist me in this work and I sincerely thank each one of them: Don and Catherine Saunders of Greensboro for research help and great hospitality, researchers Mark Kirkman, Paul Mitchell, Tim Thompson, and Boyd Lamberth; John Guss, Jeremiah Degennaro, and Diane Smith of Bennett Place State Historic Site, Tom Belton of the North Carolina Museum of History, Jennifer Burns of the High Point Museum, Ed Martin of the Chapman Society in Greensboro: Linda Evans, Stephen Catlett, Elise Allison, and Jon Zachman of the Greensboro Historical Museum; Donny Taylor and the staff of Bentonville Battlefield State Historic Site; Ann Brownlee of the Trading Ford Historic District Preservation Association; Jeff Felton; researcher Mary Browning; Bill Moore, formerly of the Greensboro Historical Museum; Dr. Chris E. Fonvielle Jr. of the University of North Carolina-Wilmington, and Ed and Sue Curtis of the Salisbury Confederate Prison Association.

In Virginia, Dr. Barry Morris of the Appomattox County Public Library; Len Riedel, executive director of the Blue and Gray Education Society; Cathy Wright, Teresa Roane, and John Coski of the Museum of the Confederacy; Chris Bingham of Appomattox Court House National Historical Park, and James Broomall of Virginia Tech University, who generously shared his research. Sharon Wallen of the Cass County Library in Missouri tracked down a rare source for me. Kathleen Shoemaker of Emory University assisted with finding a resource in the university library. Thanks also to Ann Upton of Haverford University, Dr. Peter Carmichael of Gettysburg College, and Hal Jespersen for the great maps.

Special thanks go to Mark Bradley, who answered questions and whose research has paved the way for many investigating the North Carolina Campaign of 1865. Lastly, to Karen A. Smith, whose editorial skills are unmatched.

Introduction

The surrender of the Confederate Army of Northern Virginia at Appomattox has captured the imagination of Americans and remains the sole event most people associate with the ending of the Civil War. It is one of the defining moments of American history. The surrender of the Confederate Army of Tennessee at Greensboro, North Carolina, presents an equally fascinating and largely unknown story. Many histories merely end the war in the western theater with the Army of Tennessee's trouncing at Nashville. In fact, the Army of Tennessee was in the field for nearly six more months and covered more ground in that time than it had the entire war.

While the Army of Northern Virginia surrendered in a formal ceremony at Appomattox, no such event occurred at Greensboro. The dramatic march of Lee's army into the village to stack arms was the only such surrender ceremony during the ending of the war. Few studies have explored the details of the Army of Tennessee's surrender at Greensboro. Almost none have approached it from the point of view of the common soldier. Most histories that cover this topic focus, rightly so, on the meetings between Sherman and Johnston at the Bennitt house.

Yet, for the average soldier, the end of the war was very personal: stressful and chaotic. The men of the Army of Tennessee never saw the Bennitt house and most probably never even heard of it. Their war ended in small towns and campsites scattered around Greensboro. Their overriding concerns, clearly expressed in their letters and diaries, were for more immediate matters: the next meal, a place to get out of the rain. They were with the army to the bitter end. And the end was indeed bitter.

Perspective is important, and an event as large and complicated as the surrender of the Army of Tennessee in North Carolina cannot be captured easily. I have tried to include not just the extremes—the views of the generals and of the privates—but other voices as well. The observations of others in the chain of command, such as supply officers, couriers, staff officers, medical personnel and others help fill the gaps. I also made a conscious effort to blend in accounts by civilians: men, women, children, and slaves. Each provides a unique perspective, and more important, they all tie together. The sum is an overview of a large event that is actually a combination of small events.

The closing of the war in North Carolina is not a neat, compact story like that at Appomattox. The armies did not perform a formal surrender ceremony. The commanders are less well known. The procedures were not even carried out evenly: some units received paroles in the field, others not until they reached home. The armies were not even in contact. Events occurred at various, widespread locations and are not easy to follow. It was extremely chaotic.

The North Carolina surrender is also more complicated than that at Appomattox, in part because events did not happen in one place, as they did in the small Virginia town. Generals Sherman and Johnston negotiated at the Bennitt place near Durham. The Confederate army's camps were spread over a wide area, with the troops camped at High Point, New Salem, Jamestown, Salisbury, Trinity College, Bush Hill, and Greensboro. Union forces were over sixty miles away in Raleigh. The stacking of arms and issuing of paroles — the only tangible motions of surrender — took place at the various Confederate campsites, for the most part, with no Union troops in sight.

In fact, the surrender in North Carolina is more symbolic of how the war ended than the one in Virginia. Greensboro is truly representative because none of the other surrenders at the war's end featured the ceremonies and procedures that unfolded at Appomattox. Thus the popular view of the war's end at Appomattox, with mutual respect shown by both sides and the troops in contact, is in fact unique and somewhat misleading. The reality is that all the war's other final acts (Citronelle, Alabama; Jacksonboro, Arkansas; Galveston, Texas; and Doaksville, Oklahoma) were defined by confusion, uncertainty, delays, and tension. In these other cases the armies were not together but separated by many miles.

For those who experienced it, the war's end at Greensboro was tedious, fraught with rumors, and agonizingly slow. Speculation abounded. The fighting was suspended, then resumed, then called off again; it was simply maddening. Even accounts of the Greensboro surrender are confusing, for after the war Confederate veterans mention surrendering at various places like Salisbury or Greensboro (where in fact they may have been camped) or even Bentonville, site of the last battle (but over one hundred miles from their final bivouacs.) The scattered deployment, along with faded memories, account for these discrepancies.[1]

The Appomattox surrender is more famous for many reasons: it is a neat and tidy story that involves the big players on each side. The one in North Carolina, however, is in many ways more important. Appomattox was first, setting the precedent, but General Joseph E. Johnston, with an army larger than Lee's and room to maneuver, had the potential to continue the war, or at least to stall for more time. That he did not, and that he instead (and against orders) negotiated the surrender was crucial to the war's end. The removal of the second major Confederate army, with the largest number of available troops, was a critical turning point from which there was no going back.

Lastly, the settings were vastly different. The village of Appomattox Court House had perhaps 120 residents, many of whom had fled by April 9. Greensboro, on the other hand, was a city of 2,000 swollen by refugees, wartime workers, soldiers, and deserters. The events of Johnston's surrender took place in an urban environment, with warehouses, railroads, depots, and other facilities serving as key parts of the story. In a modern day reversal, Appomattox Court House has been meticulously preserved and researched, with over 50,000 visitors touring it a year, while Greensboro and the Triad region's role in the second surrender go largely unnoticed.

Military conflicts usually do not end easily. There is often great chaos, social upheaval, fear, and uncertainty, not to mention lingering bitterness. This war was no exception. Despite the neat and calm appearance Appomattox presents, there was indeed much turmoil across the South in April 1865. Uncertainty is a word that would accurately describe everyone's mindset: former Confederate soldiers, southern civilians, former slaves, and even Union soldiers alike.

The surrender negotiated at the Bennitt house in Durham, North Carolina, did much to bring about the end of the conflict. Yet it has been, and likely will remain, overshadowed by the meeting in Wilmer McLean's parlor in Appomattox. There are few visible reminders of the Civil War events that took place in and around Greensboro. One book about Guilford County even says, "The South surrendered ... at Appomattox."[2]

In the case of both surrenders (which occurred about 130 miles apart), Confederate troops were to turn in the implements of war: their weapons, ammunition, cannons, tools, military equipment, musical instruments, and flags. At Appomattox the Confederate forces marched in to formally surrender their accoutrements in front of a line of saluting Union troops.

The Army of Tennessee experienced a less humiliating procedure, for these men simply had to stack their weapons in camp, park their cannons, and begin the journey home. No formal ceremony took place as was conducted in Virginia. The Army of Tennessee fought in some of the greatest battles of the war: Shiloh, Perryville, Stones River, Vicksburg, Chickamauga, Chattanooga, Atlanta, Franklin, Nashville, and Bentonville. For them the ending of the war was sudden and anticlimactic. And it ended far from where it began in Kentucky and Tennessee; it ended in the North Carolina piedmont.

One last motivation for this project was to shed light on the neglected final months of the war in the piedmont of the Carolinas. This rapidly growing region, along today's Interstates 85 and 77 corridors, including Greensboro, Raleigh, Durham, Salisbury, Charlotte, Rock Hill, and Columbia, saw its fair share of the war. Today there are few tangible reminders of the places where armies marched, men camped, and troops fought. The end of the war in the Carolinas is largely a forgotten story, but fortunately several good studies have emerged over the last few years. This book focuses on the experience of the common soldiers who lived through those uncertain days of April and May 1865, yet strives to keep events in the larger context of the war. Thus this work explores the "other" surrender, one that is no less fascinating and no less important than the one much of the public recalls as ending the war. The men of the Army of Tennessee, and the civilians caught up in its demise, deserve to have their stories told.

Readers may notice that I use the spelling "Bennitt" when discussing the family and house where Generals Sherman and Johnston met. I use this as it was the contemporary spelling of their name. I also use the new regimental designations created on April 9, 1865, when I discuss events that took place after that date. Thus the 58th North Carolina Regiment will be thereafter referred to as the 58th North Carolina Consolidated, which included the remnants of the old 58th and 60th regiments.

Finally, I wish to thank everyone who contributed to this project. It was immensely satisfying to work on this research, but was made more so by the great people who assisted me in the libraries, museums, archives, city streets, woods, and swamps.

1

From Tennessee to North Carolina

The vivid differences between the Confederacy's two main armies, the Army of Northern Virginia, and the Army of Tennessee, have been well noted in Civil War scholarship. The Virginia army, under General Robert E. Lee, and the western army, under Generals Braxton Bragg, John Bell Hood, and Joseph E. Johnston, could not offer a more complete contrast.

While Lee's army spent the entire war successfully defending its namesake, the Army of Tennessee, which fought in the western theater, endured a long and difficult odyssey. Tennessee and North Carolina share a common border, but the journey taken by the Confederate army went through such bloody places as Shiloh, Perryville, Stones River, Chickamauga, Chattanooga, Atlanta, Franklin, Nashville, and finally Bentonville. From Tennessee, down to Mississippi, into Kentucky, to Georgia, back to Tennessee, and eventually to North Carolina, the Army of Tennessee did not enjoy the success of the Virginia army. Geography and generals were its enemy: the Cumberland and Tennessee rivers allowed Federal forces to penetrate southern territory easily, and the war's best Union commanders emerged here.

In 1864, as the war entered its third year, both sides redoubled their efforts to end the conflict. Having endured tremendous losses and suffering, both sides felt victory was close at hand. General Ulysses S. Grant, the overall Federal commander, intended to coordinate the movement of armies across the South to attack the Confederacy simultaneously. For the first time, the Union would apply its superior resources in a way that would effectively end the war. Grant focused his personal attention on coming to grips with Lee's army in Virginia. Another major part of that plan were the forces of General William T. Sherman in the western theater. The determined Sherman led his forces into northern Georgia, forcing General Joseph E. Johnston's Army of Tennessee back towards Atlanta. Sherman and Johnston maneuvered and skirmished in the mountains of northwest Georgia, but the Federals gradually drove Johnston's defenders back. Impatient at his lack of aggression, Jefferson Davis replaced Johnston with General John B. Hood, who would bring all the aggression the army could handle. Hood boldly attacked the encircling Union armies at Atlanta, but he failed to stop their progress. The city fell in September, and Hood withdrew to strike again. He pushed north into Tennessee, hoping to retake the state and draw Sherman after him. That Ohio-born general had his own plans, however, and with a sufficient force left behind to deal with Hood, he marched instead towards Savannah.

Hood's Tennessee campaign culminated in two disasters back to back: the battles of Franklin and Nashville. The Army of Tennessee was wrecked, and its remnants fell back to winter in northern Mississippi along the Natchez Trace, an ancient trading path. While the army fought well in North Carolina, in many ways it never recovered from the effects of the grueling winter campaign in Tennessee. As Sherman's forces struck out in early 1865 from Savannah and moved into South Carolina, the Army of Tennessee was recalled and brought east to meet its old foe again on new ground.

A variety of colorful figures headed the Army of Tennessee that spring. Joseph E. Johnston, a Virginian, remains one of the most controversial Civil War commanders. Johnston had great promise, commanding at the first major Confederate victory at Manassas in 1861. A veteran of the Mexican and Seminole wars, he was one of the few military officers with actual combat experience when the war broke out in 1861.[1] Lacking good diplomatic skills, Johnston ran afoul of President Jefferson Davis. Shuffled to various commands during the war, he had a lackluster performance, notably at Vicksburg and Atlanta. Finally, in early 1865, Davis appointed him to command of the Army of Tennessee again.

Johnston's corps commanders were an experienced group. At thirty-two years of age, General Stephen D. Lee was the youngest lieutenant general in the Confederate army. He rose to command having fought first in Virginia, then at Vicksburg and in the Department of Mississippi, Alabama, and East Louisiana. He took command of Hood's old corps during the Tennessee campaign of 1864. Lee was an able and accomplished general.[2]

General William J. Hardee was one of the most respected commanders on either side. Fifty years old in 1865, Hardee was born in Georgia and attended West Point. He composed a drill manual for training that both sides used — *Rifle and Light Infantry Tactics*.[3] Hardee fought as a corps commander at Shiloh and remained with the Army of Tennessee until General John B. Hood took command. Disagreement with Hood led to Hardee's requesting a transfer, and he left this army in 1864, taking command of troops in the path of Sherman's march. In early 1865 he commanded the small force that opposed Sherman in South Carolina.[4]

Forty-four years old, General Alexander P. Stewart was a native Tennessean who fought with the army in every major battle of its history. In 1864 he assumed command of General Lenodias Polk's corps after Polk was killed in action. Stewart temporarily commanded the army for a brief period prior to its reorganization in April 1865.[5]

Born in Nashville, Benjamin F. Cheatham was another Tennessean who fought with the army in all its major campaigns. Cheatham had Mexican War experience, but was known to be temperamental and to enjoy the bottle. He rose to corps command following the departure of General Hardee after the fall of Atlanta.[6]

Wade Hampton was a South Carolina planter who raised and outfitted his own legion at the start of the war. The forty-seven-year-old aristocrat was thought to be the wealthiest man in the state. Hampton spent most of the war in Virginia, transferring to the cavalry in 1862. He was wounded twice (at First Manassas and Gettysburg), and eventually rose to command all of Lee's cavalry following the death of General J.E.B. Stuart in 1864. Transferred to the Carolinas in January 1865, he fought with determination but had limited resources to stop the march of Sherman in his native state.[7]

Twenty-nine-year-old Joseph Wheeler was the long-time cavalry commander who had fought with the Army of Tennessee throughout its battles in Tennessee, Mississippi, and Georgia. He had attended West Point and initially fought with the infantry at Shiloh. Wheeler was an inspirational leader known for bold action. He was wounded three times during the war and had sixteen horses shot from under him in combat. From his service on the frontier before the war, he came to appreciate a force that could move rapidly to strike, fight dismounted, and ride off. He adeptly applied these tactics during the Civil War.[8]

With these generals of varying degrees of ability and a history of internal rivalries, and with their rugged veteran troops, Johnston did his best to organize a defense of eastern North Carolina. Union forces had already seized Wilmington and Fort Fisher, and Sherman's army was pushing into the state from his march across South Carolina. Federal forces would soon be overwhelming in numbers and resources.

January 1, 1865, found Sherman's Union forces in Savannah, which they had taken in December. These troops had been organized into wings: the Army of the Tennessee (named for the river) and the Army of Georgia (named after their successful march across the state). General William Hardee commanded the only force of Confederates in Sherman's path. His small corps was not enough to challenge the Federal troops. To defend the Carolinas, southerners had a mix of forces from various commands and Departments, but not a unified army under a single leader.[9] That began to change on February 22 when General Joseph E. Johnston was placed in command of the Army of Tennessee, and all the troops in the Carolinas. Johnston traveled to Smithfield, east of Raleigh, North Carolina, and made preparations to unite his scattered commands.[10] Wrote one Confederate officer upon hearing of Johnston's return, "Thank God he has been reinstated and I hope will be able to organize the army again, it is now a complete mob. I never have witnessed so much demoralization in my life."[11] A Louisiana cavalryman said of Johnston:

> No General at the head of any army was ever more alert, careful, cautious, present, divining, thinking out, and providing for every possible move of his adversary. It was a sight to see that old gray-haired old man, his body already scarred with eleven wounds, riding along his lines, through storms of shot and shell, to see if his officers and men were unduly exposing themselves, and making all such lie down and find shelter. Never in the whole war did he sacrifice a life uselessly, while utterly reckless of his own. He took no thought for himself, but all for his men and their safety.[12]

The challenge facing Johnston was uniting his scattered forces with a dilapidated infrastructure. Sherman's troops had wrecked many of the railroads in central Georgia and South Carolina. Some units came from as far as Mississippi and Alabama, as well as the Carolina coast and Georgia. General Wade Hampton noted, "It would scarcely have been possible to disperse a force more effectively."[13]

One historian observed, "The Confederate answer to Sherman was at first little more than a confused effort to get cotton and mill stores out of his way and to concentrate scattered military units against him."[14]

The rail lines that did exist were not only in poor shape but were not integrated. This was a common problem north and south, but during wartime it proved fatal to the Confederacy. The railroad from Chester, South Carolina, to Charlotte, North Carolina, was a five-foot gauge. However, from Charlotte to Salisbury, Raleigh, and Goldsboro the line was four feet, eight-and-a-half inches. Traffic could not flow through without changing trains, a time-consuming process.[15] The military leaders ordered the tracks above Charlotte widened as far as Salisbury, and work crews went out to enlarge the forty-three–mile stretch. Governor Vance of North Carolina, however, opposed the change and halted the work. Thus two problems that plagued the Confederacy all through its existence, poor rail connections and friction between state and national authority, manifested themselves in its last days.[16]

A strong storm hit the state in March, heavy rains saturating the ground and soaking men in blue and gray alike. Rivers like the Haw, Deep, Neuse, and Roanoke, along with numerous streams, overflowed their banks. The storm moved rapidly inland from the coast and retained enough force to do considerable damage in the piedmont of the state. Cattle and horses were swept up, dams and locks broke, mills and factories were damaged.[17] Nature can wreak havoc with the best-laid military plans, as well as the daily lives of civilians. In 1863 the state experienced a draught; now, two years later, it had all the water it could handle.[18]

General Beauregard initially planned for either Charlotte or Chester to be the southern army's concentration point. As the situation changed with Union advances, Beauregard adjusted his plans. By early March he settled on Greensboro, then shifted it back to Charlotte. As Federal intentions became clearer, he finally settled on Smithfield. This eastern town enabled the Confederates to protect Raleigh and was located along a major rail line.[19]

On March 8, Sherman's armies crossed into North Carolina, having moved across the Palmetto State with little opposition. Through the first two weeks of the month, Johnston continued to move his troops towards Smithfield. In the meantime, Hardee's force, now joined by cavalry under General Wade Hampton, attempted a delaying action against Sherman above Fayetteville.[20] The Battle of Averasboro, fought March 15–16, was a first step to slow Sherman down. The Confederates were unsure of his intentions: Raleigh, Wilmington, or Goldsboro. The fight at Averasboro gave them a chance to delay Sherman and continue regrouping their scattered forces.[21]

Hardee deployed his small corps, which consisted of infantry and artillerymen converted to musket-bearing soldiers, across the Raleigh Road north of Fayetteville. The Union troops of General Alpheus Williams's Twentieth Corps and General Jefferson C. Davis's (no relation to the Confederate president) Fourteenth Corps encountered them and slowly pushed them back.[22] The battle cost each side nearly equal losses: about 500 Confederates and 682 Federals. In delaying the Union forces, Hardee bought Johnston a little more time to assemble troops at Smithfield.[23]

The next week Johnston was ready to give what he hoped to be the knock-out blow at Bentonville, a small crossroads town not far from the modern junction of Interstates 95 and 40. Learning that the two wings of Sherman's forces were separated by several miles, Johnston attempted to crush the divided columns. He named his unwieldy force the Army of the South and sent them down the road towards Bentonville.[24]

Among the Confederates were many artillery units that had been converted to infantry regiments. The 3rd North Carolina Artillery Regiment, for example, had spent most of its existence garrisoned in the towns and forts of the North Carolina coast. Its various companies were scattered at places like Wilmington, New Bern, Goldsboro, Fort Fisher, and Fort Anderson. Upon the fall of Fort Fisher and Wilmington in January, these troops were pulled back and reunited, for the first time, as a unit. They fought as infantry at

Bentonville and were known as the "Red Infantry" due to the red trim on their artillery uniforms. They were not the only ones, as several coastal South Carolina artillery units were also hastily converted to riflemen after the loss of their forts and heavy guns.[25]

Fought among its sandy groves of pine trees, Bentonville would be the last major battle between these long-time adversaries, armies that had been fighting since the beginning of the war. The Confederate attack went well, cutting off a Union division at one point, before Federal reinforcements arrived. The Union troops were caught off guard, not expecting to encounter a large force or a major battle. General Henry W. Slocum commanded this force, the Army of Georgia, which consisted of the Union Fourteenth and Twentieth corps (the same troops who had fought at Averasboro).

As the fighting grew more intense, Slocum realized this was no delaying action; he was facing a large enemy force. He sent a note to Sherman requesting assistance. Sherman dispatched the troops of General Oliver O. Howard, who commanded the other Union wing, the Army of the Tennessee.[26] On the afternoon of March 19 Johnston's army launched what would be its last major charge, driving the outnumbered Union forces back. Fighting raged amid the marshes and piney woods broken by occasional fields and country lanes. At one point Union troops fought off savage attacks from both directions, an entire division being surrounded. But by day's end the Union line had held.[27]

The two subsequent days saw more fighting, but little maneuvering. In the end Johnston had to break off the fight, as both Union wings united to outnumber him. The chance to destroy one isolated piece of Sherman's army was gone, while heavy rains fell as the fighting died down.

Bentonville had only delayed Sherman and failed to permanently cripple his army or halt his progress. Linking up with other Union forces from Goldsboro and Wilmington, the Federals would be able to mount an overwhelming campaign against the southerners. Johnston withdrew his army from Bentonville over rain-swollen Mill Creek. The Confederates fell back to Smithfield, where they rested and refitted. Said private Henderson Dean of the 66th North Carolina, "I did thinke that Bentonville would Be our Last Battel." Sherman's forces converged at Goldsboro, rested, and received new supplies. Both sides knew this was a temporary lull before the next round. To the west, General P.G.T. Beauregard set up headquarters in Greensboro and oversaw the establishment of supply stations and forwarded troops and material.[28]

The war had now come to North Carolina, a state that had weathered Union invasions along the coast but was now faced with the prospect of major fighting in its interior. Civilians from Raleigh to Greensboro to Charlotte braced for what lay ahead.

Bentonville Battlefield. This area was the scene of heavy fighting on March 19, 1865, as Confederates drove Union troops back. Johnston's effort to destroy part of Sherman's army ultimately fell short.

As 1865 opened, these old antagonists, the Confederate Army of Tennessee and the Union Army of the Tennessee and of Georgia, faced off once again. It had been a long, hard, and crooked road from Tennessee to North Carolina.

The Old North State was ill-prepared to suddenly become the center of the war at this stage. Though there had been no major fighting here over the course of the conflict's four years, the state's resources had been gradually depleted over time. North Carolina's infrastructure, like that of other areas of the South, was also degraded. Now as spring dawned, unexpectedly the state faced the prospect of major armies crossing its territory and fighting there. The Confederates scrambled to get railroad facilities prepared, supply bases established, telegraph lines upgraded, and other logistical concerns addressed. As the Old North State's rail lines were occupied in transporting Johnston's troops, the regular supply lines used to feed General Lee's army at Petersburg, Virginia, were congested, further straining the Army of Northern Virginia. Different track gauges meant supplies had to change trains at critical junctions, and single-lane tracks prevented trains from returning promptly.[29]

At the start of the year, there were only garrison troops along the coast. By March, over 100,000 Union soldiers stood on North Carolina soil and roughly 50,000 southerners joined them. Supporting an army is a massive undertaking the state was ill prepared for. Each artillery battery, for example, had about 70 horses, each of which need roughly 20 pounds of food a day. The armies had thousands of wagons, caissons, ambulances, and other vehicles that needed repairs, and that were pulled by mules and horses. Each soldier needed food, ammunition, and other material. For years the Confederate Army of Tennessee had been supplied out of logistical bases in Mississippi, Alabama, and Georgia; now its operations had shifted to North Carolina, where there was no precedent for maintaining armies on such a scale.

The Carolinas Campaign has been largely overlooked by historians. It was relatively brief and did not feature any major battles on the scale of Shiloh, Antietam, or Gettysburg. Yet the armies maneuvered for three months in North Carolina, and one of the war's major surrenders occurred here. In the ranks, the common soldiers had seen much action over the course of these four years, and they now braced themselves as they saw the seriousness of the situation. An army is best understood by analyzing the feelings of the men in the ranks; their words will tell the story that follows.

2

Consolidation and Retreat

The Confederate army assembled by General Johnston that spring was a mix of troops from various Departments, including remnants of the Army of Tennessee, troops sent from the Army of Northern Virginia, units from the Department of the Carolinas, and North Carolina reserves. The collection was united and dubbed the Army of the South. Johnston's army included a host of officers who shared a mutual dislike for each other. The need to stop Sherman's march was urgent, and there was no time to integrate units and allow commanders to get familiar with their men. The army would fight with the disadvantage of not having worked together.

Johnston had an overabundance of officers as well, many of whom had been shuffled about from various commands and nearly all of whom harbored bitter feelings toward each other. The cast included General Pierre Gustave Toutant Beauregard, who had served with Johnston at the war's first major battle at Manassas; Wade Hampton; Joseph Wheeler; Braxton Bragg, who once commanded the very army he was now a part of; and General William Hardee, who had been detached from this army but whose independent command was now absorbed by it. It was an odd, cumbersome, and, likely, somewhat awkward situation. Johnston's motley Army of the South performed well at Bentonville, given the circumstances. Many troops were ill clad and not properly armed and equipped. At the front line level, the army consisted of units and officers from various commands, many of whom had not served together. There is no greater test of cohesion than combat itself, and these troops performed adequately at Bentonville.

Despite stalling Sherman's march, Johnston had ultimately failed in his objective of destroying a significant portion of the Union army. On March 22, Johnston withdrew the Army of the South to Smithfield. At this point he reorganized the army on the twenty-sixth, consolidating many understrength regiments, and renaming the entire force the Army of Tennessee. He made his headquarters at the home of Pharaoh Richardson.[1]

The number of troops present on March 31 was 25,011. Desperately over the next few weeks Johnston tried to get all of the detached troops who were in the Carolinas, Mississippi, Alabama, and Georgia forwarded to join his command. He also reallocated the distribution of the army's wagons and transport and took stock of supplies. Over 1,500 men, for example, had no shoes.[2] Among other things, Johnston contacted state governors requesting their assistance in bringing in stragglers, sent orders for garrison troops to take the field, replacing them with home guard units, and demanded troops from his army who had been detached to other commands.[3] The 1st South Carolina Artillery, for example, left Charleston and took the field as infantry. These artillerymen fought at Averaysboro and Bentonville with rifles, as did displaced North Carolina artillerymen from the Wilmington area.[4] Officers saw to the refitting and reorganization of their forces. General Robert F. Hoke dispatched General Johnson Hagood to South Carolina to recruit men for his depleted Palmetto brigade.[5]

After Sherman's Union forces united with those of General John Schofield at Goldsboro, they stopped to rest. Johnston wrote, "This pause was advantageous to us too; for it gave time for the arrival of several thousand men of the Army of Tennessee coming along the route through Georgia in detachments, to rejoin their corps. Many, indeed the greater number of these veterans, were unarmed...."[6] Sumner A. Cunningham of the 41st Tennessee wrote of the time spent at Smithfield:

> We were near the Neuse river in the pine woods of North Carolina. For a while we found the situation rather unpleasant. We had no wood to burn except the pine which produced so much smoke and soot that we were soon as black as negroes. It was no use to wash, for we would in a few minutes be as black as ever. The soldiers generally had a happy faculty of taking everything easy, so it soon became a source of mirth. We were getting good rations, and some of the commands were faring sumptuously upon fish. It was the shad season, and several Generals "pressed" some of the numerous fisheries that line the Neuse river, and detailed men to operate them, and issued out the fish as rations to their men. General Ripley came in for a good supply of abuse for not furnishing his command also.[7]

One gunner, D.E. Huger Smith of Charleston, South Carolina, serving in Parker's Battery, wrote of their camp at Smithfield:

> We parked our guns in a corn-field and "took" the rain. Heavens, how it rained! And how deep the mud where we had to sleep! I remember getting a half-dozen rails from the fence, one which I rested on end of these rails with the other in the mud. Thus I slept, wet to be sure and finding my bed a little ridgy, but at least I escaped being smothered in mud.... The whole afternoon the driving rain fell and the driven men marched! The whole night we splashed along, only stopping

once in a way to pull out of his harness a broken-down horse and to put in another. I never heard how many horses we left on the road that night.... You see for days the poor creatures had been without forage and only with reduced rations of corn, so it was not surprising that so many succumbed to the misery of that forced march and fell by the way.[8]

Lieutenant Colonel Walter Clark of North Carolina wrote a letter to his mother saying, "While I am able for service I intend to stand by the cause while a banner floats to tell where Freedom and freedom's sons still support her cause."[9]

Following the battle of Bentonville both forces took a breathing spell among the sandy fields of eastern North Carolina. On April 3 Governor Zebulon Vance of North Carolina and General Johnston reviewed Hardee's Corps. The next day they reviewed the whole army.[10]

While General Johnston dutifully obeyed his orders to reunite and refit the army, he was becoming increasingly disillusioned. General Thomas Clingman visited him at this time and insisted that the army fight until the end, saying, "Sir, much has been said about dying in the last ditch. You have left with you here thirty thousand of as brave men as the sun ever shone upon. Let us take our stand here and fight the two armies of Grant and Sherman to the end, and thus show to the world how far we can surpass the Thermopylae of the Greeks." Unmoved, Johnston replied, "I'm not in the Thermopylae business."[11]

William H. Andrews of the 1st Georgia Regulars recorded this in his diary: "Rations are getting extremely scarce. For instance, since beginning in this camp I have paid one dollar per ear for corn to parch, and thought I was extremely lucky to get it for that. At the same time, knew it had been stolen from some poor old horse that needed it as bad as I did, but hunger does not make a man feel very charitably indeed."[12] That same day in their camp, members of General Hume's cavalry division prepared a resolution. They announced their continued confidence in General Joseph Wheeler, and stated that they were "full of confidence in the ultimate triumph of our struggle," were and "more determined to faithfully discharge" their duty. It was evidence of the fighting spirit that still prevailed in the army.[13]

On April 4 Benjamin L. Ridley wrote about the army's days at Smithfield. In particular, the review that day struck him. He recorded the following:

I witnessed today the saddest spectacle of my life, the review of the skeleton of the Army of Tennessee, that but one year ago was replete with men, and now filled by men with tattered garments, worn out shoes, barefooted, and ranks so depleted that each color was supported by only thirty or forty men. Desertion, sickness, deaths, hardships, perils, and vicissitudes demonstrated themselves too plainly upon that old army not to recover.... The march of the remnant was so slow—colors tattered and town with bullets—it looked like a funeral procession.[14]

Others saw hope with the growing strength of the army. During this review a South Carolina soldier wrote that the army was "jolly and full of life." He recalled horse races among the troops of the Carolinas, Tennessee, Kentucky, and Georgia, with a great deal of betting. Local women turned out to watch and see the army.[15] Other soldiers wrote that the army "once more ... began to look like soldiers," and "the army presented a fine appearance and the men were in excellent spirits."[16]

The review took place in front of the Stevens house, a plantation home near Selma, just north of Smithfield. Archer Anderson, Johnston's aide, sent an order: "The Army will move to-morrow morning by the Lewisburg road ... two or three miles the other side of the railroad depot. Corps commanders will send staff officers ahead to communicate with Major John Johnson ... at Steven's House by 10 A.M., and learn the ground intended for their troops."[17] Captain William Calhoun of the 42nd Georgia wrote of the review: "General Johnston had a review of the army, and once more we began to look like soldiers. I remember how he looked as he sat on his war horse. He seemed from that piercing look to give each soldier as he passed a most scrutinizing look."[18]

The army held several reviews during these days of early April. One soldier recalled that during one, "the generals and their staffs make a fine display in their new and flashy uniforms, but the poor soldier boys in their rags don't cut much of a shine."[19] Captain W.H. Andrews of Georgia agreed, noting, "The generals with their staffs had on their Sunday go-to-meeting clothes, and looked as gay as rice birds, mounted on their splendid chargers." It was no secret that the army was officer-heavy.[20] Lieutenant Colonel James W. Brown of North Carolina recalled these days in his diary. On the 7th he wrote:

> This has been a notable day in my field experience, for Gov. Vance brought about 25 ladies from Raleigh to review our Corps. I thought it rather too much of a good thing to be paraded twice in a week, but the sight of the girls soon drove such unsoldierly thoughts away. This Review was more creditable than the first, & our Brig. was noticed. This shows what drilling will effect. After the Review, the Brig. commanders were invited to Corps Hdgrs to meet the ladies, & after regaling upon Ham & biscuit and ginger cakes in the eating line, brandy & ice was handed. About 3 P.M. the party went to Genl. Hoke's Hdgrs where the Gov. spoke to the Junior Reserves. His remarks were most encouraging & no doubt did much good. Fortunately it did rain but little. At dark this pleasant scene was ended.[21]

While some may have been optimistic, the mood of everyone soon changed. The next day the army received mind-boggling news: Richmond

The Stevens house, near Selma, North Carolina. In front of this home took place the last review of the Army of Tennessee.

had fallen. The city had resisted Union capture for four years but was now in enemy hands.[22] Major John Johnson of the Engineers wrote in his diary that the unit's glee club sang that night, despite hearing of the capital's fall. "*Bad news from Richmond!,*" he wrote in his diary.[23] At this time General John Kennedy's South Carolina brigade was reorganized, with the regiments being consolidated. Apparently Kennedy himself was allowed to decide how best to combine his understrenght units. The 8th South Carolina, for example, had only sixty-two men.[24]

Governor Zebulon Vance of North Carolina again reviewed the army on April 6. Captain W.H.S. Burgwin of Clingman's Brigade wrote that "many ladies and civilians from Raleigh ... and officers of the state and Confederate Government were present.... The army presented a fine appearance and the men were in excelled spirits.... It was a splendid body of American Soldiers, survivors of one hundred battlefields.... [T]hey marched proudly in review before their general."[25] David T. Copeland of the 3rd South Carolina wrote, "Our Army was reviewed by Gen. Johnston yesterday and today I think a great many of our men are low in spirits for the Army of Tennessee is in bad condition...." He added, "I think myself things look a little gloomy at present but we must not discourage."[26]

Site of the last review. In these fields the Army of Tennessee paraded for General Johnston and Governor Vance.

Captain William Dixon of the 1st Georgia noted, "All the men were in
the best of spirits." Cornelius Walker of the 10th South Carolina agreed, writing that the army was "confident" and the men were anxious to fight on for
their ultimate goal, Southern independence. He urged his wife at home to
"keep up a noble spirit."[27]

April 9, Palm Sunday that year, was described as "clear and pleasant" by
Alfred Tyler Fielder of the 12th Tennessee. The men speculated "a good deal"
about the consolidation, chiefly "who would be retained as officers and who
would be relieved."[28] An officer with the North Carolina Junior Reserves
wrote that after the day's review, "Governor Vance made a stirring speech to
the North Carolina Troops, which by its eloquence aroused enthusiasm and
caused fire of patriotism to burn more brightly in our hearts." Among other
things, Vance urged the army to fight "till hell freezes over."[29]

Unknown to Johnston, Vance, or anyone else in North Carolina, on April
8 advanced units of the Army of Northern Virginia reached Appomattox Station and Appomattox Court House in Virginia. Their war would soon be ending. About 125 miles to the south, near Weldon, General Braxton Bragg
reported that 1,000 stragglers from Lee's army were "marauding and plundering." This would only increase over the next few weeks, and its impact on

the Army of Tennessee was devastating.[30] Dominating General Johnston's thinking at this time was a junction with Lee's forces. He did not know where or when he would link up with Lee, but he tried to communicate with his counterpart in Virginia and issued orders for the army to be ready to move northeast to meet Lee.[31]

Johnston also took steps to improve his supply lines, working with officers to stockpile goods and ensure rail lines were running to the west and south. By the end of March supplies were flowing and order had been imposed on the rail line running from Charlotte, North Carolina, to Washington, Georgia.[32] The supply situation did not improve fast enough, however, as noted by observers, from privates to generals. Many animals with the artillery were "utterly worthless" and there was little forage in the region, it being "pretty well eaten out." General Lafayette McLaws agreed, noting "forage very scarce." A Georgia soldier wrote, "Rations are getting extremely scarce."[33] Charles Jones with the Chatham Artillery (GA) described the situation facing his unit stationed near Hillsborough: "It was a most difficult matter at this point to secure either rations for the men, or forage for the battery animals. The country for miles around was scrounged for corn, and there was but one mill in the neighborhood where this could be ground. At times the mill could not run on account of the high water, and then the corn was issued to the men who were compelled to shell and parch it in their camps as the only means of substinence. Of meat, there was little, and often none at all."[34]

The Confederates, many of whom had marched or traveled for weeks and then fought a major battle at Bentonville, were in poor shape. Many troops lacked basic equipment like shoes and rifles. Food was also in short supply. General Johnston spent much of his time in late March and early April dealing with these issues.[35] By now the army's strength had risen from 25,000 to over 30,000. Stragglers from Bentonville and the arrival of reinforcements account for this increase.[36]

The correspondence of Johnston and Davis is fascinating for its insights, both being out of touch with Lee in Virginia. General Johnston remained focused on joining forces with Lee somewhere in upper North Carolina, as he had no idea of the true nature of the situation in southside Virginia. Johnston wrote "there was nothing ... to suggest the idea that General Lee had been *driven* from the position held many months with so much skill and resolution." For all Johnston knew, Lee had simply "evacuated" the capital, but he would soon be rudely broken of that notion.[37]

The next day, April 9, the same day that Lee met with General Grant in the parlor of the McLean house at Appomattox Court House, General Johnston reorganized his force again and renamed his command the Army of Tennessee. He ordered that the administrative work proceed "with all possible speed, Sherman will not give us much rest." In another order he wrote that consolidation should begin "without delay."[38]

The army had seen consolidations before, but this was a much more thorough house cleaning. There were too many understrength regiments and too many general officers. Many regiments were combined into new "Consolidated" regiments. The effect on morale was largely negative.[39] This was the most radical reorganization of any army during the entire war and deserves a detailed look. It far exceeds the depth of changes seen when Lee expanded his Army of Northern Virginia from two to three corps after the 1863 battle of Chancellorsville, or when the Army of the Potomac merged the First and Third corps into the Second and Fifth after the Gettysburg campaign. Not only were corps and divisions reorganized at Smithfield, but entire regiments, the backbone of the army, were also restructured.

Consolidating corps is one thing, but breaking up and reconstituting infantry regiments and artillery batteries is quite another. For the common soldier, a change in corps or division structure often has little impact on him. Consolidating his regiment or battery, however, is a very real and very powerful change. The smallest subsets of organization that the men had been fighting under for several years had been irreparably altered. These units were often raised in one particular town or county, and had a tremendous amount of local pride. In addition, through years of hard service, they had developed a sense of unit esprit de corps and self-reliance. It was often at the local unit level — the regiment — upon which success or failure in combat hinged. Civil War armies were large, unwieldy organizations difficult for commanders to manage. Yet the individual regiment was often a source of stability in battle.[40] Excess officers were assigned to other Departments, sent home to recruit, or transferred to other assignments. A few hoped to command newly raised troops, including controversial African-American units that the Confederate congress had recently authorized. As events turned out, however, none would be organized outside of Virginia.[41]

William Dixon of the 1st Georgia wrote, "All the officers are now anxious about the consolidation which is to take place in a few days, as the most of us will be thrown out, the regiment not being more than large enough to make one company or two at the most. My company is now the largest in the regiment and it only numbers fourteen men and four officers." A full strength company was to be 100 men.[42] Tennessee private Thomas L. Sullivan recorded, "Camp rations are rather scarce. Only one pound of meal and beef a day." Later in the week he learned that Selma, Alabama, had been taken by the enemy, and recorded his thoughts: "Well, let them have every town in the South. It will only put more men in the field and we will begin to whip the Yanks when they get all the cities we have. I dislike very much to be cut off from home but hope we will soon be where we can hear from them again."[43]

Johnston had troops from many Departments and various detachments, which resulted in an unwieldy and confused command. Combining these forces allowed for more streamlined, and hopefully more effective, leadership. Under his command there were soldiers from the Department of the Carolinas, Georgia, and Florida; the Department of North Carolina; detachments from the Army of Northern Virginia; and lastly the Army of Tennessee.[44] Consolidation was unpopular in the ranks, as it removed many qualified officers from command. With units combined, excess regimental officers were sent home, ostensibly to await further orders and reassignment. Apparently many soldiers did not even know about the consolidations and never fully understood how they had been reorganized.[45]

Consolidation was nothing new to the Army of Tennessee, which had been combining understrength regiments since early in the war (after Shiloh, its first major battle, in fact) and after other major battles like Stones River/Murfreesboro and Chattanooga, but it had never been done on such a massive scale.[46] The army reduced thirty batteries of artillery to ten. Eleven Arkansas regiments were consolidated into one; seven from Florida became one unit; eight Texas regiments merged into one; and thirty-nine Tennessee regiments were consolidated into four (each having nine or twelve of the old commands).[47] This swift and sweeping action immediately erased unit histories and unit pride. Morale plummeted, as commands that had fought numerous battles, marched hundreds of miles, and endured extended hardships suddenly ceased to exist.

Private John Croxton of the 2nd South Carolina Regiment simply noted in his writings, "About April 9th, 1865, the 2d (Palmetto) Regiment South Carolina Infantry was consolidated with the 20th Regiment South Carolina Infantry and a part of Blanchard's South Carolina Reserves and formed the (New) 2nd South Carolina Infantry...."[48] George Guild of the 4th Tennessee Cavalry summarized the mood following the massive consolidation: "I remember after the reorganization to have met a soldier in the old Second Tennessee Infantry and I asked him what was the number of his regiment since the reorganization. He replied that he did not know, as it was one of the questions that was past finding out...."[49] Colonel Charles Olmstead of the 1st Georgia wrote "So many of the Regiments Brigades and Divisions had been depleted by the exigencies of service that a thorough reorganization took place here and in this what remained of the 57th and 63rd Georgia Regiments were consolidated with the 1st and under its Regimental name. There were something over 800 of the rank and file, men who had borne the heat and burden of the day, tough, wiry, and hardened by service and experienced.

They made a Regiment that any man might be proud of and I *was* proud, but it never fired another shot, for the war was practically at its end."[50] Captain William D. Dixon of the 1st Georgia recorded a journal over these days:

> Sunday 9th There has been considerable excitement in Camp today caused by the proposed consolidation. Regimental commanders were consulted this morning as to officers to be appointed. I have heard the result, but will await its announcement. The men are very much opposed to it but I think their opposition will only be temporary, as they must have something to talk about....
>
> Monday 10th The command was formed in line at 9 oclock this morning when the consolidation took place. One Regiment and a Battalion was made out of the Brigade. Our Regiment formed two companies, Companies A.B.C.D & E. making the first company and F.G.H.I &K making the second.... I have not heard as yet what the regiment will be called.... It rained all last night and today making it very disagreeable.[51]

Sumner A. Cunningham of the 41st Tennessee wrote that his unit had only about forty-five men and became a company of the new 3rd Tennessee Consolidated Regiment.[52]

During the consolidation a regiment's under-strength companies were combined into new companies, the first five (A–E) often becoming new company A, with the second five (F–K) becoming company B, as Dixon noted in the 1st Georgia. Then regiments were combined to form new regiments, state by state. A regiment normally had ten companies, lettered A–M, with no I. Captain Charles F. Bahnson of Manly's Battalion of Light Artillery wrote, "The army has been completely 'transmogrified' several times, and great and numerous have been the changes." He went on to say, "The men all feel safe in the hands of the leaders who now command us, and should we ever join the gallant band under the noble Lee, the feeling of confidence will be greatly strengthened."[53]

Not all units merged together into new regiments. The 6th Mississippi had seven companies go into the remnants of the 14th and 43rd Mississippi, while its three other companies joined the residue of the 15th, 20th, and 23rd regiments. It was extremely depressing. Private John Edwards wrote, "We were very much Demoralized by being consolidated with other Commands." An officer took the battle flag of the 6th and hid it under his shirt for the remainder of the campaign, eventually taking it home with him. Battle flags were important symbols of pride for the units.[54]

Sometimes the consolidation was met with opposition. Sergeant William Andrews of the 1st Georgia Regulars (not to be confused with the 1st Georgia) wrote, "April 9, Gen. Johnston's Army was reorganized and consolidated. The 1st Ga. Regulars, 47th Regiment, and Bonaud's 28th Ga. Battalion was placed in one regiment. The 1st Regiment of Georgia Regulars formed five companies of the 1st, three of the 47th, and two of the 28th, with R.A. Wayne colonel.... The 47th and 28th kicked like anything on being assigned to the Regulars, but was of no use."[55]

The Army of Tennessee's only two regular North Carolina infantry regiments, the 58th and 60th, were combined into a new Consolidated 58th Regiment. The old 58th became Companies A, B, D, and G, while the men of the old 60th formed Companies C, E, and H.[56] South Carolina General Johnson Hagood wrote, "There was but one course left to put the armies of the Confederacy upon a footing of efficiency sufficient to continue the contest, and that was to consolidate and reorganize the good men ... into new regiments and brigades of proper strength...."[57] Describing his experience, he noted, "This consolidation was a matter of much interest to both officers and men. In our particular case, a strong feeling was manifested to unite the volunteer South Carolina troops...."[58] Another Palmetto State soldier felt that "the only effect these changes had was the throwing out of some our best and bravest officers."[59] Excess officers were given furloughs and sent to their home regions to recruit for the regiments in the field. Most were probably still on their way home when the surrender occurred.[60]

While the extensive consolidation went into effect, the flags of the regiments met various fates. Some consolidated units kept both flags actively in use, while others hid them, eventually taking them home after the surrender. Col. J.M. Dedham, for example, preserved the flag of the 20th Alabama when that regiment was consolidated with other regiments.[61] Cornelius Walker of the 10th South Carolina was upset that he could find no trace of his unit's flag when his regiment was combined with the 19th Regiment. As the senior unit, the 10th's flag should have become the consolidated unit's new battle flag.[62] A few days later he learned the reason. During the battle of Bentonville the color guard of the 10th had been cut off, and they hid in the woods for several days, taking the flag off the staff to hide it. When they rejoined the regiment, the flag had no staff, so the 19th's flag was used as the regiment's banner.[63]

Straggling and desertion were becoming serious problems during encampment around Smithfield. General Lafayette McLaws wrote that he had to send out patrols to arrest deserters and eventually resorted to holding roll call five times a day.[64] Artilleryman Charles W. Hutson recorded his experiences over these days. He wrote, "We had some tent-flies to protect us at this time, but much of our marching was done in the rain and we were often drenched to the skin. The men had many of them become despondent about our cause, and I did a good deal of talk to hearten them, believing strongly as I did I our final triumph."[65]

In the meantime, General P.G.T. Beauregard had arrived in Greensboro on April 3. Upon inspecting the city, he ordered fortifications built on the eastern side of the town, today likely covered by development. Beauregard had three railroad cars for his traveling headquarters: one with his office, bedroom, and dining room, another for his staff, and one for their weary horses.[66]

On April 10 the streamlined Army of Tennessee left the Smithfield area for Raleigh, arriving two days later. From Union prisoners and deserters, Johnston learned that Sherman was preparing to move after him.[67] As before, rail transport was problematic. Not enough rolling stock existed to move all the army's supplies, and much was destroyed, as it could not be transported.[68]

Johnston noted the routes taken by the various units of his army: "Hardee's corps, with Butler's division as rearguard, by the Goldsboro' Road, which the Federal army was following; and Stewart's and Lee's, with Wheeler's division as rear-guard, by that crossing the Neuse at Battle's Bridge." The army reached the capital city early in the afternoon. A soldier in the 2nd South Carolina Consolidated noted simply, "roads horrible."[69]

For some in the ranks, the movement was in the wrong direction. Sumner Cunningham of the 4th Tennessee Consolidated noted that he and his comrades were anxious to engage Sherman. He said, "So confident were we that we were to march upon him, that we were not a little chagrinned to find that we were moving in the opposite direction."[70] Alfred Tyler Fielder of the 12th Tennessee recorded in his diary the march through the capital city:

[W]e entered the city on the East side marched directly up to the State Capitol filed left with the Capitol grounds at the corner of which we filed right passing immediately along the Iron railing enclosing the Capitol and near where was a Statue of George Washington standing about midway from the railing to the Capitol the Statue was facing the south at the end of the railing or enclosure on that side we again filed right until we arrived opposite the center of the Capitol when we filed left taking the street running West. The Capitol is a rock build-ing....[71]

Conceding that Raleigh was to be "left uncovered to the enemy," Tyler noted "there is no waving of handkerchiefs or any other demonstration by the ladies or citizens but ... front doors were shut and the inmates were only to be seen through the windows and generally then up stairs. There were but very few citizens about the streets or else where to be seen."[72]

Colonel John Logan Black of the 1st South Carolina Cavalry wrote, "[W]e commenced our retreat, having camped some 5 miles above Smithfield, and fell back before the enemy who had crossed the Neuse at perhaps Smithfield & perhaps at the Railroad crossing higher up the river."[73] He continues: "We moved slowly & could hear some firing in our rear — light skirmishing. About

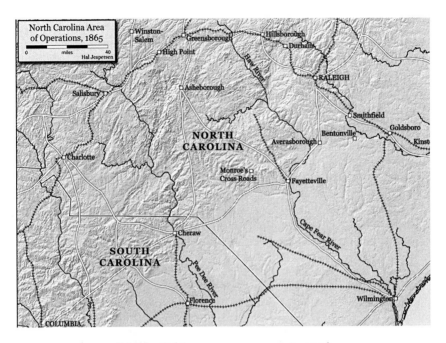

(Map by Hal Jesperson, *www.cwmaps.com.*)

11 A.M. I got an order from Maj. Gen'l. Law in person to halt until the ... rear guard came up & to support it. My orders were to keep 200 to 300 paces in its rear and to prevent its being "gobbled up."[74] Private George W. Bussey of the 7th South Carolina carefully recorded his thoughts during these weeks. The unit was moving with some Union prisoners in tow. During one of the few lighter moments of the retreat, he wrote, "As we marched through Raleigh, N.C., a young lady made fun of the Yankees we had in charge. The Major eyed her closely and said: 'I will remember this, young lady.'"[75]

Everyone had a different experience, and some had more luck than others. As the army passed through Hillsborough another South Carolinian noted, "It is a pretty place." The ladies turned out to greet and assist the soldiers; as he noted, "The ladies did all they could for us." These veterans had not seen local civilians coming out to support them in some time. And no doubt it was a comforting feeling.[76]

While in Hillsborough artilleryman Charles W. Hutson of South Carolina noted, "We ate a nice lunch at the Ferndale Seminary, the girls depriving themselves of their lunch that day for the soldiers—, heard music, and talked to the young ladies. Then we went to a private house and had some old French brandy and a taste of wine."[77] Charles Jones of the Chatham Artillery (GA) wrote of the movement: "On the retreat some ten battery animals had perished for lack of forage, and here great difficulty was experienced in procuring even a limited amount of corn, fodder, and peas. The country was scoured for twenty-five miles around for forage."[78]

During the retreat rain dampened the spirits of the Army of Tennessee. Yet some of the men retained their sense of humor. A Georgia soldier recalled one incident that occurred while they were crossing a creek:

> A division of cavalry was passing in the column of infantry on the march and on reaching a creek that we had to cross, the cavalry forded the stream and the infantry crossed on some rails just above the ford. Some of the cavalry asked the boys if they did not wish to ride over. At least a half dozen would make for the horsemen to ride. He would tell them to get on behind him. The cut in the road was about level with the horse's back, and by riding up close the foot soldier could get on. The cavalryman was very kind and seemed anxious to carry the poor fellow over the creek. But just as the soldier made a movement to put his foot over the horse's back to sit down on him, the horseman would stick spurs to his horse and jump from under him, leaving him sitting in the creek and horseman dashing up the hill on the other side. The boys would have to lie down and roll over and yelled themselves hoarse. I saw while standing there at least three ducked in the same way.[79]

Artilleryman Charles W. Hutson wrote of "waiting impatiently in the rain for orders to move. We got drenched to the skin, but did not march until about 3 in the evening."[80] William Worsham of the 3rd Tennessee Consolidated Regiment (formerly of the 19th) wrote of the miserable conditions:

> There had fallen and was still falling a great deal of rain, and all the streams were full, there being no bridges we had to wade and swim them all. When we came to Cape Fear river it was much swollen and rising rapidly. There was no way to crossing but to swim. The men tried to form the Monkey's chain by holding each others hands, but the current was too strong and broke their hold. When it came our time to try the water we gave our watch to Col. Heiskell to keep it from getting wet. We went in and halted and debated in our minds whether to go on or return as the water then was under our arms and deeper further on. Just then Gen. Cheatham came riding in and as he passed us we caught hold of his horse's tail and landed safely on the other side. Finally all were over and midnight found us standing around our camp fires drying ourselves. The next morning we moved out and camped within thirteen miles of Greensborough....[81]

Artilleryman D.E. Huger Smith of Parker's Battery (SC) noted that his shoes had come apart, and he was forced to do away with the remnants as he could no longer walk in them. He stopped at a cobbler's shop along the line of march and purchased a pair of cow-belly shoes for $125. Made of cowhide, not leather, they reflected the conditions in the Confederacy by that point.[82] A fellow gunner in the battery got new shoes as well. A column of cavalry was passing the artillerymen, and they noticed Smith's friend Bill had no shoes. "Give that fellow a pair of shoes!" cried out one trooper. The call rang out among all the cavalrymen, until one passed by and slung a pair of shoes at him, yelling, "Catch!" "Oh don't do that," said the startled gunner. "Why not?" replied the horseman. "I'll steal another pair at the next town we reach."[83]

Colonel Olmstead of the 1st Georgia Consolidated Regiment described his point of view from the ranks, one that was probably shared by many weary foot soldiers: "We did a lot of marching about ... though exactly to what purpose I never knew. Probably our movements had relation to those of the enemy, but the armies were not in very close contact."[84] Captain Dixon of the same unit recorded incidents of the march in his journal:

> Wednesday 12th We left bivouac at 6 oclock marching through Raleigh with music and in order. We saw very few people. It does not look like much of a place. We took the rail road on foot after leaving Raleigh and was in hopes of taking the train at some point but was mistaken. Marching 10 miles we bivouacked at 1 oclock pretty well used up. The march yesterday was hard and then on the rail road today which is the hardest kind of marching used all hands up....
>
> Thursday 13th We left bivouac at 6 oclock on the NC rail road, marching 4 miles, then taking the Chapel Hill road which was in very good condition. We passed through Chapel Hill which is a very pretty place and quite large. Quite a crowd of ladies were out to see us, many of whom were crying — I suppose at being left to the Yanks. We bivouacked about a mile from the hill at 4 oclock, having marched 20 miles. I am used up tonight....[85]

As they passed through Chapel Hill, the men of the North Carolina Junior Reserves noted that the town was nearly deserted. Those civilians remaining were observed preparing to leave. A keen observer noted that they were treading the same roads used by the British army in the Revolution eighty years earlier.[86]

Colonel John Hinsdale of the 3rd North Carolina Junior Reserves noted, "our line of march was on the Salisbury and Hillsboro Road, over which two hundred years before the Catawba Indians passed in their visits to the Tuscarora in the East. Governor Tryon and later Lord Cornwallis had led their troops over this historic way in the vain endeavor to subdue the men whose sons now trod footsore and weary over the same red hills, engaged in a like struggle for local self government."[87]

The 3rd North Carolina Junior Reserves included many local soldiers. Company C had been raised in Forsyth and Alamance counties. These sixteen — and seventeen-year — olds no doubt wondered about the fate of their homes and communities as they marched through, headed west.[88] That same day, Lieutenant Colonel James W. Brown recorded, "Started at 7 A.M. and the rain pouring down. Stopped almost 3 hours by the wagons, and marched 22 miles reaching camp at 8 P.M. and everyone broken down. We are now 3 miles from Hillsboro."[89] In his diary, Henry M. Holmes of the 6th Florida noted "had to wade the river hip deep, also to wade Alamance Creek, arm pit deep, raining."[90]

William Andrews of the 1st Georgia Regulars recalled the rumors floating around the army while on the march. He wrote, "Officers rode along the line of march telling the men that Gen. Lee was holding his own along the banks of the Appomattox, after causing the enemy the loss of 30,000 men. 'So cheer up boys, don't let your spirits go down, for there are many a girl that I know well, waiting for you in town.'"[91]

Dixon of the 1st Georgia Consolidated noted, "[W]e had a terrible time of it, the road being in such a bad condition. It rained all day and I think the march as hard as any we have had being ankle deep in mud the whole way.... Reports from Lee's Army are getting alarming but as yet I cannot believe them."[92] The rumors Dixon and others heard were as varied as can be imagined: "Some have the entire army [Lee's army] captured, others half of it, while others still say three thousand and the army falling back on Greensboro. It has caused a great many to wear long faces."[93]

William A. Johnson of the 2nd South Carolina Consolidated noted during the movement, "Marched slowly. Road not good. All sorts of rumor afloat on camp about General lee's army."[94] Lieutenant Colonel Joseph Frederick Waring of the Jeff Davis Legion (MS) wrote on April 14 that as his command moved from Raleigh that they also encountered the rumors. "All bosh," he wrote in his diary.[95] Sidney Wilkinson of the 72nd North Carolina (3rd NC Junior Reserves) recalled that "when the news got thoroughly spread in the evening and was confirmed by some parolled [sic] soldiers passing, just such a scene I never have witnessed, some were sad, some joyful, some crying, some shouting at the top of their voices and here and there you could find a squad dancing, and every little distance an officer would have a stand making a speech, trying to quiet the uproar."[96]

W.W. Gordon, a Georgia cavalryman, noted that he met some civilians who "told me the dreadful news of Lee's surrender, but I could not credit it. My mind couldn't grasp or comprehend so vast a misfortune." The ladies who told him certainly believed it, for they "were all in tears and almost in despair at the news from Va."[97] J.W. Evans, riding with Hampton's Cavalry, recalled the moment when he heard the news of Lee's surrender: "What a shock. I was nineteen years of age, color bearer for Phillips Legion. I dropped down by my flag, and for two days and nights I rolled in the dust, kicked, and cussed and vowed, neither ate nor slept much. Lee's veterans continued to pass by."[98]

Captain William E. Stoney of Hagood's South Carolina Brigade kept a journal of the march. On April 11 he noted, "Troops out of marching condition from even the short rest at Smithfield, straggled badly." The next day he recorded, "Rumors in regard to General Lee assuming an unpleasant air of probability." Heavy rains made the march miserable.[99] Captain Samuel T. Foster of the 1st Texas Consolidated Regiment (formerly in the 24th Texas Cavalry Dismounted) wrote, "Various rumors afloat about Lee's surrender. One is that he surrendered 42,000 men, and himself with them." He later added, "The whole army (or at least as far as I know) are badly demoralized."[100] Jacob H. Smith, pastor of First Presbyterian Church in Greensboro, wrote in his diary, "Saddest of days! It is rumored that General Lee and his whole army have surrendered. It is impossible to record my feelings."[101]

In Parker's Battery (SC), D.E. Huger Smith recalled that "an infantryman walked alongside of me a little distance and passed to me the last news. 'General Lee has surrendered!'" I stopped short and faced him and answered with the most suitable words I could find on such short notice, 'You are a damned liar!' he smiled like one who understands and answered, 'I only wish it was a lie, but General _____ has just told me about it.'"[102] A South Carolina officer in General Robert F. Hoke's Division reported, "Major Celand Hager of the artillery, upon today's march, intimated to me that General Lee had met a disaster, a few hours after the army was filled with vague rumors upon the subject."[103] Charles Beatty Mallett, living in Chapel Hill, recorded events in his diary. He wrote, "Monday 10th we had the first intimation of the surrender of Gen. Lee, which altho coming very strait we could not believe — All day troops wagons &c were passing."[104]

Rumors made their way through Union lines as well. Corporal Joseph Crowther of the 128th New York wrote from Kinston: "We received the news from Grant's army that after 3 days hard fighting before Petersburg and Richmond Gen. Grant occupied the 2 rebel strong holds. Also that he had captured 25,000 prisoners and 500 pieces of artillery. Also that rebel Gen. Lee with his army was in full retreat towards Harrison's Farms in the direction of Lynchburg."[105] After taking Smithfield on April 11, Union troops officially received the news of Lee's surrender at Appomattox the next day. Sherman had received a telegraph message from Grant on the previous evening.[106]

Back with the Confederates, Captain Stoney described crossing the Haw River, "swollen with a freshet." They soon met other obstacles:

> On this road a mill stream was encountered, about twenty feet wide, but so rapid and deep that the wagons were gotten over with difficulty. The Allemance, out of its banks, next crossed our path. A few men had succeeded in crossing by chaining their hands or by holding on to horses' tails of the mounted men, who half waded, half swam over, but the wagons were at a hopeless standstill. General

Hardee was on the further bank, evidently anxious for rapid movement and non-plussed by the obstacle. At length the leading teamster was ordered to attempt the passage. With a crack of the whip, and a shout to his mules he is in and under, rises, struggles, and is swept away. Everything was again at a standstill; the rain was falling in torrents, the river was rapidly rising, something had to be done, and our lieutenant-general determined to try to send another wagon and team across. The order was given, and followed by the same result. Mules, wagon and teamster were swept down the stream; and it was hard to tell which was uppermost in the struggle with the flood. The general's resources seemed now exhausted and he ordered the destruction of the train. General Hoke suggested that a more practicable crossing might be found, and he was permitted to seek it. Four miles higher up were crossed without difficulty at Holt's mill, and the train was saved. Encamped half a mile beyond the river after a most fatiguing day's march. Tonight, Colonel Olmstead, of the First Georgia regiment, tells me positively that General Lee has surrendered. Great God! Can it be true? I have never for a moment doubted the ultimate success of our cause. I cannot believe it.[107]

Daniel Dantzler of the 2nd South Carolina Artillery, now armed as infantry, wrote of the march: "Portions of the road were bad, bad, and we were required to plunge right through mud and slush like cattle. This march has been very trying. A lot of men straggled. They could not keep up. A.W. Bull, of our company, and of my mess, dropped out on roadside completely exhausted. I knelt down by him and poured some water out of my canteen into his, bade him good by and hurried on. I never saw him again. Suppose he died there."[108] That night Dantlzer and comrade Ed Staley, falling behind and separated from their unit, slept in the corridor of the statehouse in Raleigh. He wrote of this day: "We are enduring hardships now, which try our souls, and test all our physical powers of endurance." It was no understatement.[109]

Robert Alexander Jenkins and a detachment of the 12th North Carolina had been sent from Virginia to the Army of Tennessee, and found themselves caught up in the retreat. Before reaching Raleigh, he and the 200 men were assigned to find, prepare, and distribute rations for his division. With the typical ingenuity of veteran soldiers, they managed to perform their mission admirably. He wrote of it:

I found nothing at the Confederate Department in Raleigh, but got an order to the State Department for wagons and provisions, obtaining only cornmeal and fat meat. These we carried out near to the location where the fair grounds are now, two miles west of Raleigh. Finding piles of wood near the track, we set fire to them. Finding some plan, also, we made a large trough, made up the meal into dough, baked it in the hot ashes, sliced the meat and broiled it the best we could on the coals. Brushing off the ashes from the cakes, we put one piece of meat on each cake, and secured it there with small wooden pins. Then we piled them up in rows, and as the army passed, the two hundred and fifty men detailed handed a cake of bread with the meat pinned on it, to each soldier, the army not stopping for the meal. When all had passed, there were yet eighteen cakes of bread. I took two, and galloped ahead, presenting one to Gen. Beauregard, which he took, saying it was the best meal he had had for several days.

Coming on as far as Greensboro, we were then stopped and received the first news of Gen. Lee's surrender. Then, provisions being short, the General gave me another detail of men and two trains, that we carried to Salisbury to get a quantity of supplies that had been stored there, which supplies we obtained. Before starting back, we received a message stating that the enemy were raiding between Salisbury and Greensboro, and to run with all possible speed, regardless of obstacles. Coming to High Point, and running a very rapid rate, we saw a troop of obstacles. Coming to High Point, and running at a very rapid rate, we saw a building not very far from the track, in which cotton was stored, and set fire to the building. This act of vandalism was being done just as our train flew past the station. I jerked a gun from one of the guards, and fired at the officer, but never knew whether the ball took effect or was burning, but as he had previous orders to ignore all obstructions, he dashed along and ran through the burning bridge safely.

Arriving at Greensboro with the provisions, which were greatly needed, we found that a large part of the Confederate army had arrived, together with a special train from Richmond bearing president Davis and a part of his cabinet.[110]

Ever since fleeing Richmond on April 2, President Jefferson Davis and the Confederate Cabinet had been moving southwest on a rickety rail line towards North Carolina. While Lee and Grant met at Appomattox, the refugee government was in Danville, Virginia, near the border with North Carolina. The group included the secretary of the navy, Stephen Mallory; the secretary of state, Judah P. Benjamin; the secretary of the treasury, George Trenholm; the postmaster, General John H. Reagan; Adjutant General Samuel Cooper; the attorney general, George Davis; President Davis; some aides and clerks, and a detachment of guards. The secretary of war, Major General John C. Breckinridge, was following a few days behind.

One soldier passing through Danville gives a glimpse of the chaos unfolding there. Curtis R. Burke, a Kentuckian captured and held in a Union prison, had been released and was on his way home. He passed through Virginia just as the climactic events of early April were unfolding. He observed:

We got to Danville, Va. late in the evening and found the place crowded with cars and wagons and soldiers. We got off after looking around for awhile we took possession of an empty ambulance and spread our supper out of our haversacks. After which I sat for about an hour and saw a gang of darkies carrying kegs of money and bullion from a car to another train between a line of guards and as soon as it was all aboard I saw Present Jeff Davis and company get aboard and the train moved off under a strong guard that would not let us ride so we slept in the ambulance all night.

The money he observed being moved was the Confederate treasury, which would surface again in Greensboro.[111]

The presidential party prepared to move on to Greensboro. The naval secretary, Stephen Mallory, captured the chaos of the moment while they waited in Danville:

> Nothing seemed to be ready or in order.... [M]uch rain had fallen and the depot could only be reached through mud knee deep; and with the utter darkness, the crowding of QrMaster's wagons, the yells of their contending drivers, the curses, loud and deep, of soldiers, organized and disorganized, determined to get upon the train in defiance of the guard, the mutual shouts of inquiry and response as to the missing individuals or luggage, the want of baggage arrangements, and the insufficient and dangerous provision made for getting horses into their cars, the crushing of the crowd and the determination to get transportation at any hazard, together with the absence of any recognized authority, all seasoned by sub rosa rumors, that the enemy had already cut the Greensboro road, crated a confusion such as it was never before in the fortune of old Danville to witness— At ten o'clock the Cabinet officers and other chiefs of the government, each seated upon, or jealously guarding his baggage, formed near the cars, a little silent group by themselves, in the darkness lighted only by Mr. [Judah P.] Benjamin's inextinguishable segar. It was nearly eleven o'clock when the President took his seat and the train moved off.[112]

About noon on the 11th President Davis and his entourage arrived in a very tense and chaotic Greensboro. Over the next few days Johnston's troops began arriving and setting up camp around the town.[113]

Upon arriving in the Gate City, Davis greeted residents with a patriotic speech. Mary Smith was at the station and wrote of it: "I am just from the depot where I had the pleasure of seeing President Davis and hearing his little address, and had the distinguished honor of serving him a cup of coffee which he very graciously drank out of my silver cup. Long will this day be remembered!"[114] Davis and his party were given shelter by Colonel John T. Wood, an aide to Davis and nephew to his first wife, Sarah Taylor. The home, rented by Wood, apparently stood on South Elm Street. The Wood family had arrived in the city several months earlier.[115] Wood himself wrote: "Fitted up an empty room for him in our quarters. Houses all closed. The people are afraid to take any one in; the Cabinet, Genl. Cooper & others are sleeping in the cars."[116]

Davis spent some time at Wood's rented home near the railroad station, and the rest of his stay he returned to his railroad car at the station. Other residents of the city offered Davis shelter, including former governor John Morehead, and the owner of the Britton Hotel, but he politely declined.[117] Historians have debated the reception city residents gave Davis. It seems that he was not warmly welcomed, but some citizens did greet him and offer support. It was probably the typical reaction that residents of any city would have given Davis in mid–April of 1865 with their world caving in around them.[118]

Mallory's diary provides the best description of conditions for the Confederate government. He noted that they received "bread & bacon & by the active foraging of Paymaster Semple & others of the party, biscuits, eggs & coffee were added; & with a few tin cups, spoons & pocket knives, & a liberal use of fingers, & capital appetites, they managed to get enough to eat, and to sleep as best they could."[119] Davis communicated with Governor Vance, and the message indicates the president's mindset: "We must redouble our efforts to meet [the] present disaster. An army holding its position with determination to fight on, and manifest ability to maintain the struggle, will attract all the scattered soldiers and daily rapidly gather strength. Moral influence is wanting, and I am sure you can do much now to revive the sprit and hope of the people."[120]

City residents Charles Eugene Eckel and his sister Matilda recalled after the war how their father, Alexander Perry Eckel, allowed some money from the Confederate treasury to be hidden on their property. Mr. Eckel was the mayor of Greensboro and their residence was one of its showpieces. The home, Rose Villa, stood at the corner of South Davie and East Washington streets. The property had many trees and shrubberies, but Mr. Eckel directed that a wooden post be lifted up, the money hidden under it, and the post replaced in the ground.[121]

The governor, after learning of Appomattox, ordered state records and supplies moved out of harm's way. Directions went out to move 40,000 blankets, 100,000 uniforms, 10,000 pairs of shoes, 150,000 pounds of bacon, and 40,000 bushels of corn from Raleigh and nearby warehouse locations further to the west. Cotton, yarn, and medicine were also collected as the process to move the supplies went into motion.[122]

In the meantime, the Army of Tennessee continued its withdraw to the west. From Smithfield, General Hardee's Corps marched through Gulley's Store and Auburn, with Butler's Cavalry Division as its rear guard. The forces of Generals Stewart and S.D. Lee moved toward Pineville and Battle's Bridge on the Neuse River, with Wheeler's cavalry protecting them. Modern U.S. 70 roughly parallels, and snakes in between, their lines of march between Smithfield and Raleigh.[123] Gradually the troops left the flat, sandy soil and pine trees and encountered rolling hills, hardwoods, and small farm fields. Most of the time they were up at 4:30 or 5:30 A.M. and marching within an hour.[124]

At around 1 o'clock in the morning of the 12th, Lieutenant Archer Anderson, one of Johnston's staff officers, received a note from President Davis

The Eckel house. Alexander Eckel was the mayor of Greensboro in 1865. Confederate money was hidden on his property during the Union occupation (Greensboro Historical Museum Archives).

while on the road between Smithfield and Raleigh. It was in code and he quickly translated the ciphered message. It read: "A scout reports that General Lee surrendered the remnant of his army near to Appomattox Court-House yesterday. No official intelligence of the event but there is little room for doubt as to result. Gen. H.H. Walker is ordered with forces here to join you at Greensborough, let me hear from you there. I will have need to see you to confer as to future action." Staff officer Joseph B. Cumming of Georgia recalled the night when the news arrived. He wrote the following:

> In the course of the afternoon Gen. Johnston and his staff followed on after the troops. We bivouacked some little time after dark, the General establishing himself under a tent fly, and the members of his staff, orderlies, couriers, etc., scattering about in different places in the immediate neighborhood. Col. Archer Anderson, his chief of staff, myself, and two or three others took shelter in a little house in the neighborhood. I lay down on the floor and fell asleep. I was very weary, though later in the night and several times during the night, when the hardness of the floor induced me to change my position and I awoke for a few moments, I noticed that Col. Anderson, seated at a table with a dim light, was hard at work over a paper. I thought at the time it was a long cipher dispatch that he was deciphering, and in the state of expectation that I shared with all at that time, I jumped to the conclusion that it conveyed confirmation of the rumor that we had been hearing during the day, that Lee had surrendered.[125]

Cumming, was in fact, correct, for while he slept on the floor Archer was translating the message from Jefferson Davis. General Johnston was at Battle's Bridge when he learned of Lee's surrender. Its effect on his mind cannot be imagined; his last hope for continuing the war was now gone.[126] Major Cumming also noted that he was to carry out the execution of a deserter from a South Carolina regiment in General John Kennedy's Brigade. Cumming had appealed the decision to Johnston, but to no avail. The morning following confirmation of Lee's surrender, however, the commanding general sent an urgent note to Cumming to suspend the sentence.[127]

The army trudged along, reaching the state capital and marching through it. Stewart's and Lee's corps camped west of town on the Hillsboro and Chapel Hill roads, while Hardee's troops bivouacked three miles east of Raleigh.[128] Albert Q. Porter, a musician with the 33rd Mississippi wrote "all wagons were passing [through] town.... Rawley is quite a large ... beautiful city...."[129]

When the news of Appomattox reached Sherman's army, it touched off huge celebrations among the pursuing Union troops. One sergeant wrote, "For the three nights past the men have been so jubilant over the recent achievements to our armies that it has been difficult to restrain their enthusiasm." A Minnesota soldier recalled, "I never heard such cheering in my life. It was one continuous roar for three hours."[130] In the 9th New Jersey, Hermann Everts observed,

> Newspapers may write about and the people of large cities may make large processions ... at such a joyful event, but it cannot be compared with the pleasure — the deep-felt pleasure of an army receiving such great news. Hear the cheer of about 100,000 veteran soldiers, who have withstood the enemy's steel, and faced the canon's mouth in many battles; hear the music of thirty-five bands, who have played their martial music in numberless attacks, joined by drums and fifes innumerable; see old, hard-looking warriors, who would not falter when their comrade fell at their site; see these brave men, young and old, weep for joy, embrace and kiss each other; see how they carry regimental or Brigade officers on their shoulders, to have the news read again and again; see battle-worn and bullet-riddled flags waved and raised on highest poles; see all that ... it would be impossible to describe.[131]

Corporal Joseph Crowther of the 128th New York wrote that "the news made the men wild with joy" and noted that troops marched "with pace quickened by enthusiasm."[132] Sergeant Rice Bull with the 123rd New York recalled that the regiment was assembled for an announcement. His colonel read from a telegram and before he had finished, Bull noted, "it would be impossible for me to describe the scene that followed. The men went wild, ranks were broken, and shouting and crying...."[133]

Although troops displayed the full range of emotions, when writing about the ragged and worn out Confederates an Indiana soldier felt "although I have met them on the battlefields and helped lay waste their country my heart goes out to them in sympathy. They have shown themselves to be worthy Americans and brave men." It was a sentiment shared by many Union soldiers that spring.[134] Yet many Confederates were still willing to fight. Samuel Foster of General Brown's division wrote, "I do hope and I do believe that we shall whip this fight yet." Such optimism among the ranks did not last long.[135]

The number of rumors was as varied as can possibly be imagined. One tale related that the Confederates would join with Union forces to fight in Mexico (which the French had invaded, drawing the hostility of the Lincoln administration). Another had the governments of Austria, France, and Mexico sending troops to bolster the Confederacy against Sherman.[136] Captain Samuel Foster of the 1st Texas Consolidated noted, "It is also reported that the United States has recognized the Confederacy, and agrees to give us all our rights (and slavery) if we will help them to fight all their enemies whatsoever."[137]

Sumner Cunningham of the 4th Tennessee Consolidated said that word of Appomattox was "crushing news" to the men. He went on to say that the "last news we had was that Lee was repulsing Grant." Disbelief and shock followed.[138] He went on to say, "Strange to say, this news, after the first shock, did not depress our army. They seemed to think that now all depends upon them, and we will yet save the Confederacy. If we can't contend against the forces here, Kirby Smith has a splendid army, and plenty of supplies of every kind. We will cut across the Mississippi, and continue the war over there." This optimism would not last long, as it became evident that such hopes were unrealistic.[139]

On the afternoon of April 11 the Confederate forces marched through Raleigh. After midnight, while at Battle's Bridge, Johnston received a telegram from President Davis in Greensboro, instructing him to meet Davis there for a conference. With General Hardee in temporary charge of the army, Johnston hastened to Greensboro, arriving around 8 o'clock on the morning of the 12th.[140] Johnston first went to General Beauregard's headquarters, a railroad car near the one occupied by the president at the railroad station. An hour later both officers were standing in front of Davis and the cabinet in Wood's rented house.[141]

Johnston was expecting to be consulted as to the situation regarding the Army of Tennessee; instead Davis gave his opinion of the war's status, indicating that he hoped to raise another army through rounding up deserters and another round of conscription. In Johnston's words, the goal of Davis's meeting seemed to be "to give, not to obtain information," adding that "neither opinions nor information was asked."[142] Such wild fantasies were simply beyond the realm of possibility, as the Confederacy no longer had any means to wage war: its industry was in a shambles, its transportation network wrecked, and its armies were on the run on all fronts. Nearly every eligible white male in the Confederacy who could be enlisted was already under arms. The meeting ended when the group decided to meet again after the secretary of war, Major General John C. Breckinridge, arrived from Virginia with definite news of the situation there.[143]

Learning of Lee's surrender from

Coded Message from Davis to Johnston. It reads, "A scout reports that Genl. Lee surrendered the remnant of his army near to Appomattox C.H. yesterday. No official intelligence of the event, but there is little room for doubt, as to result. Genl. H.H. Walker is ordered with forces here to join you at Greensboro. Let me hear from you there. I will/have need/to see you to confer as to future action" (Museum of the Confederacy, Richmond, Virginia).

Breckinridge, Generals Beauregard and Johnston decided that the war simply could not go on. They also met privately with cabinet member Stephen Mallory and reviewed the situation of the other armies throughout the South. All were in agreement that Davis should try to end the war.[144] Beauregard and Johnston returned to Davis's railroad car the next morning. Johnston carefully outlined the estimated numbers of his own forces and those of Grant and Sherman. He went on to note that the Confederacy's economy was wrecked and that it had no ability to wage war. He followed by urging Davis to open negotiations with Federal forces.[145]

No doubt adding tension to the crowded room was the fact that Johnston and Jefferson Davis were not on the best terms. From the start of the war Johnston felt that Davis had disregarded his rank in the United States Army and that he should have held a higher command. Through the course of the war their relationship only worsened. Johnston felt betrayed by Davis and refused to share his plans or communicate frequently. Davis mistrusted Johnston and blamed him for defeats at Vicksburg and Atlanta. Having commanded both of the South's major armies at one time or another, and been shuffled all across the South, Johnston now found himself trying to work with the one man whom he disliked most.

Davis then asked Johnston's assessment of the situation. Stephen Mallory recorded the general's words:

> Upon this the General, without preface or introduction, — his words translating the expression which his face had worn since he entered the room — said, in his terse, concise, demonstrative way, as if seeking to condense thoughts that were crowding for utterance.—"My views are Sir, that our people are tired of the war, feel themselves whipped, and will not fight. Our country is overrun, its military resources greatly diminished, while the enemy's military power and resources were never greater, and may be increased to any desired extent. We cannot place another large army in the field; and, cut off as we are from foreign intercourse, I do not see how we could maintain it in fighting condition if we had it. My men are daily deserting in large numbers, and are taking my artillery teams to aid their escape to their homes. Since Lee's defeat they regard the war at an end. If I march out of North Carolina her people will all leave my ranks. It will be the same as I proceed south through South Carolina and Georgia, and I shall expect to retain no man beyond the by-road or cow path that leads to his house. My small force is melting away like snow before the sun and I am hopeless of recruiting it. We may, perhaps, obtain terms which we ought to accept.[146]

This is clearly not what President Davies wanted to hear. A poll of the cabinet members present revealed that John C. Breckenridge, Stephen Mallory, and John H. Reagan all agreed the war was lost, while only Judah P. Benjamin disagreed. According to Johnston, Davis seemed "annoyed" at the results. Davis reluctantly agreed to open communications with General Sherman to discuss negotiations for peace.[147] Davis dictated a letter for Johnston to sign:

> Maj. Gen. W.T. Sherman, Commanding U.S. Forces:
> General: The results of the recent campaign in Virginia have changed the relative military condition of the belligerents. I am therefore induced to address you in this form of inquiry, whether, in order to stop the further effusion of blood and devastation of property, you are willing to make a temporary suspension of active operations, and to communicate to Lieutenant-General Grant, commanding the armies of the United States, the request that he will take like action in regard to other armies; the object being to permit the civil authorities to enter into the needful arrangements to terminate the existing war.
> I have the honor to be, very respectfully, your obedient servant,
> J.E. Johnston General[148]

Davis also wrote to his wife, Varina, in Chester, South Carolina: "I will come to you if I can—Everything is dark—you should prepare for the worst by dividing your baggage so as to move in wagons.... I have lingered on the road and labored to little purpose."[149] Not even the commanding general could escape the turmoil growing around him; during his meeting with Davis, Johnston's horse, as well as those of his staff, was stolen. On the evening of April 13, Johnston departed for Hillsboro, where he rejoined elements of the army under General Stewart.[150] The news of Lee's surrender at Appomattox was spreading rapidly through the streets of Greensboro that day. General Samuel W. Ferguson wrote, "I arrived there quite early on the morning of April 12th and an hour or two afterwards, came the sad news of Lees surrender. Old soldiers could be seen by the hundreds, weeping as though their hearts would break, my feeling I cannot attempt to describe."[151]

In the meantime, the Army of Tennessee continued its slow movement westward. On the afternoon of the 12th Stewart's corps reached Durham. One soldier noted that they set up camp at 2:30 P.M. Further to the south, Hardee's men marched through Raleigh and out to the west of the city. Soldiers noted that mountains of supplies—clothing, shoes, uniforms, leather, blankets, and food—were hastily being loaded onto trains to ship them west. Not only did Johnston have to keep his army moving, but he also had to ensure that his stockpiled supplies were kept out of Sherman's reach.[152]

Next the troops passed through Burlington, Alamance, and Hillsborough in the rain. That night S.D. Lee's troops camped at Haw River Bridge east of Graham while Hardee's men forded at Ruffin's Mill, two miles south of the bridge (near modern-day Swepsonville). General Wade Hampton ensured that his cavalry screened the roads leading to the southwest to prevent Union forces from getting between the army and Charlotte. The capital of Raleigh was thus abandoned without a fight, one of the last Confederate state capitals to fall to Union forces.[153]

Governor Vance resisted surrendering the capital without a fight, but he soon realized that the army was leaving and it would not be defended. He met with former governor and president of the University of North Carolina, David L. Swain. His predecessor suggested sending a commission to meet with Sherman to suspend hostilities and end the war.[154] General Robert F. Hoke, who had plenty of fight left in him, heard the rumor and sped to meet Vance at the capitol. The two spoke in private, and Vance assured him that he was resisting pressure to surrender the state and "all hell cannot make me do it." It was what the impatient general wanted to hear, for if Vance was in fact going to do so, Hoke intended "to arrest him and take him along with me and in that way prevent it."[155]

At nine o'clock that evening the last trainload of state records left the city. Raleigh's streets were deserted except for refugees and stragglers. Near midnight, Vance left, having authorized the mayor to meet Sherman and ask that the city be spared the fate of Columbia. He wrote, "I rode out of Raleigh at midnight without a single officer of all my staff with me! Not one. I shall hit the deserters some day, hard."[156]

Vance caught up with Hoke's division and spent the night with him. The two Tar Heels, the general and the governor, discussed affairs long into the night. Hoke later wrote, "I was very much trouble in securing a place for him to sleep, but after awhile secured a cot, as I was afraid for him to sleep upon the ground as we were; that it might make him sick, give him pneumonia."[157] The next day Hoke's division marched towards Chapel Hill. Men of the 8th North Carolina saw Vance and yelled to him, "Hello, Governor, where are you going?" He answered, "To the western part of the state to prepare a spout for you all to go up."[158]

Massive amounts of supplies had been evacuated from the capital. Among them were 40,000 blankets, overcoats, and uniforms, cloth for 200,000 uniforms, leather for 10,000 shoes, 150,000 pounds of bacon, and 40,000 bushels of corn, along with tools, yarn, cotton, and medicines.[159]

Hardee's Corps moved into Chapel Hill on the 13th. Cavalry consisting of the 3rd Arkansas, 4th Tennessee, and 8th and 11th Texas arrived in the area as well. George Guild of the 4th Tennessee wrote, "Our headquarters being at a line of fence incircling the college campus, and picketed the roads leading toward Raleigh...."[160] Bromfield Ridley of General Alexander Stewart's staff wrote of his march from the capital:

> Started about 7 o'clock this morning and pitched tents three miles west of Raleigh on the Hillsboro road. Have heard nothing of enemy's progress. As we passed the female seminary in Raleigh the beautiful school girls greeted us warmly. Each one had a pitcher of water and goblet. We drank, took their addresses, and had a big time. It was a terrible task to get Terry, Cahil, Caruthers, Stewart, and the others of the staff away from them. On this march my faithful boy, Hannibal, gladdened us with a rich box of edibles from my old grandmother at Oxford.[161]

When news of Lee's surrender at Appomattox reached the troops, its effect was telling. For men who whose military organizations had been undone and scrapped, who had learned of the fall of Richmond, and who were retreating, it seemed as if things could not get any worse. Yet, worse was about to come. William Dixon of the 1st Georgia Consolidated Regiment noted that after hearing of Appomattox, rumors began circulating regarding their own army. He wrote:

> I heard today that the surrender of the whole army had been confirmed, all the men being paroled and allowed to go to their homes. Things are indeed looking dark.... I have been told today for a fact that Gen Johnston is engaged in arranging terms for the Surrender of his army. It seems to be generally known and

believed. If true we are a whipped people, caused by our own actions, as we can safely say one half of the army are deserters from the Cause and like a set of cowards have taken to the woods.[162]

Captain William Calhoun of the 42nd Georgia wrote, "[W]e met an old Confederate veteran [who said] our army in Virginia had now surrendered. This statement was disbelieved, and our general commanding ordered his arrest.... [O]ther reports ... seemed to confirm it. He was released in the morning with apology."[163]

There were plenty of other instances of disbelief. George Guild of the 4th Tennessee Cavalry recalled:

> One morning our chaplain came into camp after a visit to the town of Chapel Hill, and told among the soldiers that General Lee had surrendered his army to General Grant at Appomattox. Of course a matter of such importance was circulated through the camp. When Colonel Smith heard it, he sent a guard down and had the chaplain arrested and brought to his quarters. Upon being asked why he was telling so improbable a tale among the soldiers, he replied he was only telling what he had heard fully discussed and told by the citizens he had met. The Colonel told him to consider himself under arrest and to take a seat.
>
> Hardly had fifteen minutes elapsed before one of the pickets brought in a man, saying he had been arrested while trying to get through the picket stand to go home, saying he had been surrendered. Telling pretty much the same tale that the chaplain had, he drew from his pocket a paper, which he handed to Colonel Smith, reciting the fact of his surrender under General Lee.

The paper was a parole pass, printed for the Army of Northern Virginia. The chaplain was let go, as was the ex-soldier, and Smith's Cavalry Brigade now had confirmation of the demise of Lee's command.[164]

Lieutenant Colonel James Lewis of the 1st Tennessee Cavalry wrote of his reactions to Appomattox: "There was little sleep in our camp that night.... Gloom and despondency settled down over the camp."[165] The Jeff Davis Cavalry, a Mississippi unit, camped at the fairground at Hillsboro. The men encountered paroled prisoners from Lee's army headed for home, and some decided to join them and desert.[166] A Texan writing to his sister noted, "There are quite a number of the Houston boys, captured in Va, now passing through here on their way home." These men were veterans of the famed Texas Brigade of Lee's army.[167]

Weather soon became a factor in the march of the army. Captain C.A. DeSaussure of Stuart's Battery (SC) reported: "After leaving Raleigh wet weather set in. We followed the line of the railroad and when we reached Haw River, it was a roaring, raging torrent between its high banks. There was no wagon bridge and fording was impossible. To wait was equally impossible."[168] He continues: "The railroad bridge, a single track deck structure, no trusses of anything to even suggest protection from a fall into the rushing waters (it seems to me now 100 feet below. But the ten or twelve foot width of this 250-foot length was covered with planks and our battery, four guns, four caissons, ammunition, commissary and baggage wagons and forge, went across this narrow path. It looked like a mile. We got across in safety, but I recollect seeing a wagon and team go over the side onto the rocks and into the water below." One of the mules survived the fall and was swept downstream. It was rescued by a local family who put it to use in working their crops that summer.[169]

Colonel John W. Hinsdale of the 3rd North Carolina Junior Reserves wrote of "a bacon wagon and two wagons carrying guns" being lost in the crossing, along with several mules and even a few men. Another soldier wrote of "water up to their cartridge boxes." Colonel Charles W. Broadfoot of the 1st North Carolina Junior Reserves wrote "many narrow escapes from drowning occurred, especially among the boys." The unit had boys, from fifteen to eighteen years old, and they were marching through or near their home counties, abandoning them to the enemy.[170]

Several wagons and artillery guns with the Junior Reserves were swept away in the current. At one point a young soldier went under, and a comrade pulled him out of the raging water. The youth dove in again and was again rescued. After a third time, the irritated and drenched man asked the soldier why he was going down into the water. "My gun's down thar and I'm trying to git hit," came the honest reply.[171] Colonel John Hinsdale of the 3rd North Carolina Junior Reserves observed an incident during the crossing, writing: "In the midst of the peril of the crossing of the river, Lieutenant Colonel French, realizing the danger to which the smaller boys were exposed, jumped from his horse, and stationing himself in mid-stream just below the line of march, rescued several brave lads from inevitable death. Standing there, watching his chance to save life, he was every inch the faithful officer and brave soldier, and no wonder the boys loved him."[172]

An officer with General Robert Hoke's Division recalled the raging water of the Haw River: "The water was generally waist-deep, sometimes when on a rock not so deep, then deeper as the rock was stepped off. It was rough wading."[173] Hoke's Division ended up crossing near Holt's Mill. Lieutenant Janius C. Ellington of the 15th North Carolina wrote of the general's actions: "He moved the head of his column to this point, directed one man to seize his horse's tail, and another to grasp this man's shoulder, and another and another until he had a long line, swam his horse across the narrow stream and discharging his cargo safely on the opposite bank, would quickly return for another. The rapidity with which the men were carried over was astonishing."[174]

Another general also tried to motivate his men, with less success. General Benjamin F. Cheatham, frustrated with the delay in crossing, expressed his displeasure to the soldiers standing along the flooded banks. They refused to cross, and "emphasized their determination with some pretty lively swearing." Cheatham tried to force one man into the water, and the two ended up wrestling, falling to the ground, and rolling into the cold water. The regiment agreed to cross, but stopped when three wagons attempting the ford were swept away.[175]

Moving with the army was an unusual contingent: sailors from the Confederate navy under Admiral (and Brigadier General) Raphael Semmes. He was the only person to hold both of these ranks for the Confederacy. After daring exploits on the high seas, Semmes was back on solid ground and had joined the army in North Carolina. He wrote in his diary of the confusion he encountered: "Country people carrying off cotton & general disorder prevalent." He also recorded, "My sailors are dropping off from me at every camp having caught the universal contagion of desertion which has descended upon this army. They run as they reach the neighborhood of their homes."[176] In one town near Greensboro he reported "a scene of desolation. All the public stores having been plundered the day before. The vultures scouting their prey for ten miles around. Public papers scattered among a few blankets (new) and muskets & a small lot of harness stored in a neighboring warehouse remaining. Eight pieces of artillery in the cart, but the fixed ammunition broken wide & wasted. Placed a guard."[177]

Private M.M. Buford with the 5th South Carolina Cavalry recalled an incident during the retreat:

> After leaving Raleigh my command fell back toward Greensboro, tired and hungry and depending on their own exertions to get something to eat. As an illustration of the straits to which we were put for food, I will relate this little incident: While out foraging a great big husky fellow and I were chasing the same chicken, and we caught it at the same time. I weighed only about a hundred and twenty, but was holding on to the chicken with all my might, when he said, and he meant it too, 'Damn you, if you don't get go, I'll kill you,' and I let go and went hungry.[178]

Another cavalryman, W.W. Gordon of Georgia, simply wrote in his diary, "Rain, rain, rain." More depressing was the news the army was to get of developments to the west.[179]

Word reached the Confederates of Union General George Stoneman's raid, and Johnston ordered three brigades to Greensboro to protect the city from this threat. This force of Union cavalry entered the state from the west, intent on destroying railroads and industrial facilities. Troops of Shelley's, Govan's, and Featherston's command arrived in the city, along with Abel's and Bachman's batteries.[180] Rather than move directly on Greensboro or Salisbury, Stonemans' cavalry turned unexpectedly north and rode to the very outskirts of Lynchburg, Virginia. Unsure of Union intentions, troops from Greensboro moved up to Danville, Virginia.[181]

On April 12 the Army of Tennessee's artillery batteries arrived at Salisbury. Commanding here was General John C. Pemberton, the Philadelphia-born officer who had defended Vicksburg in 1863. Artillerymen deployed the guns around the town in anticipation of defending it from the Union cavalry of General George Stoneman. This new threat, a 5,000 man cavalry division that launched a raid from eastern Tennessee, became a major distraction and wreaked havoc in an already unstable area.[182] Stoneman took most of the guns, eighteen, and about 1,200 prisoners. It was ironic, having come so far only to lose the cannons in a small, obscure battle. Much of this artillery had come all the way from Tupelo, Mississippi, passing through devastated areas and avoiding Union forces along the way.[183]

Early that morning Stoneman's troopers closed in on Salisbury from the north. Confederate defenders skirmished with them above Grant's Creek, which flows above the town, but made their main stand below the creek.[184] One Federal officer wrote that as they neared the town "the trains could be distinctly heard leaving Salisbury on both the South Carolina and Morganton Railroads." The Union cavalry, troopers from the 11th Kentucky, 8th Tennessee, and 13th Tennessee, moved out in three groups to strike the Confederates head on and from both flanks. "Their retreat soon became a rout," and the Union troopers pushed them back into the town.[185] Union troopers noted that one of the batteries was manned by "Galvanized Yanks," Union prisoners who agreed to join the Confederate army to get out of Salisbury Prison. They intentionally fired too high during the battle, and when the Federal cavalry closed in, they stopped firing altogether. After securing the area, they moved into town and destroyed the railroad depot in Salisbury.[186] Mary Elizabeth Ramsay wrote in her diary of the event:

> Have just heard a few minutes ago, finished (6½ o'clock) dressing, and after having asked the protection of my heavenly Father, I sit down to write all in my little journal. Oh! Could I write all my thoughts, I would soon have this volume full. Aunt Nellie came in about daylight and said that they were fighting about two miles from here. By the time I got dressed the firing had cased.
>
> 10 o'clock: The Yankees have come! Alex Helper came round here about 9 o'clock and after standing in the front porch 1½ hours, the Yankees came dashing in shouting and firing. They came in all directions.
>
> 12 o'clock: They are breaking open the commissary stores, and throwing them out in the street. It is not very far from here only one square, and if they blow it up, I am afraid some of the pieces will fly over here. The Negroes and the poor

are gathering it up and carrying it off as fast as possible. I think they are right in doing so for it will be destroyed. I was frightened this morning.[187]

Salisbury was an important supply station for the Confederate war effort. General Stoneman reported that here his forces destroyed four cotton factories, 7,000 bales of cotton, 70,000 pounds of gunpowder, 35,000 bushels of corn, 50,000 bushels of wheat, 160,000 pounds of bacon, 100,000 uniforms, 25,000 blankets, 2,0000 pounds of harness leather, and 10,000 pounds of saltpeter. Two days later they received news of Lee's surrender at Appomattox.[188]

Stoneman's force had destroyed bridges, factories, and warehouses throughout the region just as the Army of Tennessee, and President Davis's party approached Greensboro. Union cavalry struck High Point, Jamestown, and points just west and north of Greensboro itself before turning south toward Salisbury.[189] Arriving in the towns of Winston and Salem, Captain Harry K. Weand of the 15th Pennsylvania Cavalry noted, "Here we met with a most cordial reception, very different from the usual greetings we receive. The ladies cheered us, and brought out bread pies and cakes. The people showed much enthusiasm at the sight of the flag we carried, and many were the touching remarks made about it. Old men wept like children and prominent citizens took off their hats and bowed to it. There are plenty of stores here, and in the center of the town one of the finest seminaries we have seen in the South."[190]

From Salem on April 11 the cavalry split up and struck several points simultaneously. Their movements kept the Confederates guessing and spread chaos among already overtaxed and disorganized Confederate military forces. The raid was equally chaotic for civilians, who had yet to feel the presence of the enemy in piedmont North Carolina.[191] It further eroded confidence in the Confederate cause and increased the chaos in an area that was supposedly secure behind Confederate lines. Captain Nicholas Schenck wrote of carrying out his duties between Greensboro and Charlotte: "At James town — found the tracks torn-up and bridges burnt — being only a few miles from High Point — I footed it [but] could find no accommodations — so I slept on someone's piazza.... I had occasion to visit Salisbury — under orders — and went to a hotel...." When he tried to pay with Confederate money it was refused. "Only specie taken — I told him I had no money but Confederate." The hotel manager told him to "send it to me later."[192]

One group of Union troopers missed Davis's train at the bridge over Reedy Fork Creek, north of Greensboro, by just an hour. They did manage, however, to capture a large number of the 3rd South Carolina Cavalry on the western edge of Greensboro.[193]

A detachment of ninety men of the 15th Pennsylvania Cavalry, led by

Colonel Charles Betts, happened upon a slave belonging to Colonel Thomas Johnson of the 3rd South Carolina Cavalry. He quickly agreed to show the Union horsemen the way to the camp. Feeling they were secure in the area, the southern troopers had no pickets out and were cooking breakfast.[194] Betts's men approached the camp and noticed that they were outnumbered. With the element of surprise, they charged in, making as much noise as they could. The South Carolinians scattered, some escaping, but many surrendering. The victorious troopers ate their food, destroyed the supply wagons, and left with their prisoners.[195] While riding back under guard, Colonel Johnson asked, "Why, Colonel Betts, where are your men?" Not wanting to give away his true numbers Betts answered, "There are others within supporting distance."[196]

Next at Jamestown, Captain Frank Renont with twelve cavalrymen took thirty-five prisoners, along with sixty horses and mules, two railroad cars of cotton, 1,000 weapons, fifty barrels of flour, five bales of cotton cloth, twelve sacks of salt, and several barrels of molasses. The Florence Armory weapons factory was destroyed here, with 800 newly made weapons and 2,500 unfinished ones going up in flames.[197] Another group of the 15th Pennsylvania under Captain Adam Kramer burned the railroad bridge over the Deep River at Jamestown. The scattered commands reunited at Salem for their next move.[198]

High Point had been a hospital center due to its location along the railroad line. The Bellview Hotel (later known as the Barbee Hotel), located on the corner of High and Willowbrook streets, as well as the High Point Female Academy and the Methodist and Presbyterian churches, held over 5,700 wounded.[199] From here the wounded were sent to larger hospitals in Goldsboro, Richmond, and Petersburg. In late March the battle of Bentonville resulted in a flood of new wounded. Local women like Mrs. Manliff Jarrell, Mary Jarrell Perry, and others nursed the soldiers.[200]

Twenty-year-old Laura Wesson of Virginia assisted them. She was traveling with her father to join her fiancé in Charleston. Their train could not proceed past High Point due to Stoneman's raiders, and she was stranded there for three months. Laura joined in nursing the wounded and died of smallpox exposure. Wesson, and the wounded who succumbed to disease and wounds, were buried in Oakwood Cemetery.[201]

Among those at one of the hospitals was Henry C. Baldwin of the 15th Connecticut, who had been captured at Kinston in March. He was severely wounded, and wrote later of his experiences:

> The weather had become cold and there was not covering enough for one-half the men, and one of the wounded pulled off the blanket I had spread over poor Burke's body and wrapped it around himself. Teams came suddenly with orders to load in the officers and al privates able to be moved. I found the surgeon and

implored him to have the order delayed, but it was of no avail. I felt sure Gen. Schofield's force would free us in twenty-four hours or more if we remained where we were. Maj. Osborn, Lieut. Bishop and many others were loaded into the wagons and it was my last farewell to them, for they were all carried away to the Salisbury prison-pen. Two days later I found myself in the little Masonic hall at High Point, N.C.

A Confederate surgeon informed me that I was expected to take care of all these, and that he would come now and then and see how we got along. Some of the wounded required attention every hour, and bandages were so scarce I had to wash them out and use them over and over again. I worked night and day at my task until March 25, and never once undressed or lay down to sleep; all the rest I took from March 8th to the 25th was sitting with my head against the wall and never over an hour at a time.

About ten o'clock I tried to rise and get the dish of water to wet the bandages, but was unable to do so. I crawled to the fire-place, lit my rag, and worked round the room on my hands and knees and attended to each wound ... and then the room spun with me like a top and I was lost in darkness.

On the morning of April 11th I woke hearing some pounding. I tried to think where I was and how I came there. I made an effort to raise my head, it would not move. Then I hear a kindly voice say: "Give him a spoonful of this every half hour. He will live or die to-day." I had come back to life and knew where I was. I was in the anteroom of the hall on a straw bed. I spoke and Dr. B.F. Smallwood, Confederate that he was, came to me and said in a gentle tone, "Keep quiet you have been very sick." No man ever more tenderly nursed a brother back to life than he did me. He sat by me for hours the next few days, and his wife would frequently take his place in watching and tenderly administering medicine and nourishment....[202]

In High Point the raiders burned the gun factory of Seborn Perry and Manlief Jarrell on West Green Street. Hundreds of cotton bales stacked alongside the tracks fell victim to the torch as well.[203] With smoke rising behind them from the railroad tracks and factories, Stoneman's cavalry moved south, destroying the important railroad bridges over the Catawba between Charlotte and Chester, and Charlotte and Lincolnton.[204] In riding on to Statesville, Stoneman's Division encountered soldiers from Lee's army returning home — confirmation of rumors of the fall of Richmond and the surrender at Appomattox.[205]

At Hickory the Union cavalry rode into town to find that the Confederates had destroyed military supplies and cotton. Captain Harry Weand of the15th Pennsylvania Cavalry noted, "In a military sense it was wise to destroy the stores that might be of use to us, but to burn their cotton was rank foolishness. We cannot use it and have no way to transport it North.... Everyone recognized that the rebellion is on its last legs, and that in a short time they could realize from a waiting market an amount of money which would go far to make up for their losses."[206]

As the column entered Lincolnton, a shot rang out and nearly hit General William Palmer, commanding the division. Several men then rode forward, chasing a bushwhacker who fled across a field. The guerilla turned out to be a fifteen-year-old boy, who was taken to General Stoneman. His mother then arrived and pleaded for his release. As Weand observed, the "General told her to take the boy home and keep a better watch over his actions." It was also here that Stoneman received news of the truce between Johnston and Sherman.[207]

One civilian living near Lincolnton, Margaret Stanly Beckwith, expressed her faith in ultimate victory, despite the growing signs of defeat all around her. She wrote of the "anxious longing for news" and "no relief from suspense." She also wrote, "As bitter a pill it is to swallow, we are over-run by the enemy, out numbered ... but not conquered — Our liberty will yet be gained...."[208]

In the meantime, the Army of Tennessee continued its movement from Raleigh towards Greensboro. On April 15 Stewart moved his corps west on a lower road, while Lee directed his men west on an upper road. They marched parallel to the railroad tracks. General Robert Hoke's Division, after crossing the raging Haw River, camped on both sides of the road about two miles southwest of the Alamance Battlefield. This was the site of a colonial uprising in 1774, in which frontier settlers lashed out against a corrupt and uncompassionate royal governor.[209] Cavalry under General Wheeler set up barricades on Piney Prospect Hill near Chapel Hill. The Confederate cavalry acted as a rear guard, staying between the main army and the advancing Union troops.[210]

Major George Washington Harper of the 58th North Carolina Consolidated wrote, "Marched, 6 AM — Graham, Company Shops, etc. Good dinner near the road — Troops marching on railroad. Trains and mounted officers on dirt road.... Camped fifteen miles from Greensboro at 1 PM having made 8 or 9 miles.... Reports of Lee's surrender confirmed."[211]

3

Arrival in the Gate City

Guilford County had a long history of arms manufacturing dating back to its early German settlers in the colonial period. Jamestown, Whitesett, and High Point were centers of gunsmithing. Arms manufacturing had sprung up in the region by the time of the Civil War.[1] It was also well known as the site of a tenacious 1781 battle during the American Revolution. American forces under General Nathanael Greene fought those of General Lord Charles Cornwallis. The battle at Guilford Courthouse was in many ways the high tide of the British invasion of the southern colonies. Cornwallis surrendered later that year at Yorktown, Virginia.

The Guilford battlefield was a well known local landmark in the nineteenth century. The small community that stood at the courthouse had fallen into decline, and in the early 1800s the town of Greensboro sprang up a few miles to the southeast. The town grew rapidly in the following decades. Greensboro itself had been a major weapons producing center for the Confederacy and was also a key railroad stop and crossroads. The city first fully felt the impact of the war after Bentonville, when large numbers of casualties arrived there for treatment in late March of 1865. Wounded men overflowed makeshift hospitals in the city of 2,000 residents. Wounded soldiers lined the streets, stragglers began arriving. Old carpets, bedding, and blankets were cut up for bandages, and the civilians donated blankets, food and other supplies for the men.[2]

There was a sense of uneasiness among the city's inhabitants that spring, even before the Confederate army arrived. In February, over 4,000 Union prisoners were marched into Greensboro. They came from the large prisons at Andersonville, Georgia; Florence, South Carolina; and nearby Salisbury. From the railroad station downtown, some were sent to Richmond and others to Wilmington, where they were destined for exchange. The operation was under the direction of General Robert Hoke. Lax security and too few guards resulted in many prisoners wandering the streets unsupervised.[3]

Apprehension grew among the residents as the Army of Tennessee arrived in mid–April. Jesse H. Lindsay, president of the Bank of the Cape Fear, enlisted the help of a friend, John C. Wharton, in hiding the institution's funds. They removed the money, and buried it in a hole. To complete the deception, a pigpen was built over the top of the site. The buried money remained safe through the chaotic days of April and May, and was recovered after Union troops left that summer.[4] Robert Herriot of Bachman's Battery (SC) wrote that "Greensboro ... was practically the capital of the Confederacy, and for one to see the large number of general officers in fine uniforms, together with many orderlies riding hurriedly to and fro, was an inspiring sight."[5] Among the recuperating soldiers was Daniel Dantlzer of South Carolina. He wrote that he was "hungry and weak." While in the city, he "tramped around, and begged something to eat at homes of people."[6]

Greensboro, according to one observer, "is notable for extreme length and extreme absence of width. There is a Main street, broad and dirty, about a mile in length, with a deep well and great pump in the middle of the carriage-way toward each end, and another about half-way between; one narrow and dirty street on each side of the broad avenue; about a dozen dirty cross-streets.... [T]he business is mainly done on the principal street, and ... the best private residences are at either end of this principal street."[7] A traveler, a reporter, wrote of the city as follows:

This rural town is one of the principal places in Western North Carolina. In size and population it is about equal to Danville, Virginia.... In advantages for trade and manufactures, the Virginia town is the better off of the two, being the centre of a rather agricultural region, and possessing abundant water power, of which this place is entirely destitute. But in the elements of oppidan beauty, Greensboro is the more favored locality ... owing to the superior taste with which it has been laid out. At the intersection of the two principal streets, one corner is occupied by the court-house, the temple of justice in Guilford county, a very respectable structure of yellowish brown sandstone, and the other corners, with the adjacent portions of each street, are occupied by principal stores, hotels, and other business places of the city.

Near this central point the buildings are congruous; but before you advance half a square in any direction the aspect of the place becomes decidedly rural, the houses standing apart in shade gardens, and small patches of tall tasseled fern filling up the intervening spaces. Near the outskirts of the town, especially on the north and west, are a number of quite handsome private residences, several of them so deeply embowered in groves of tall, shadowy oaks as to give the idea of a retired forest mansion, or suggest the lodge in some vast wilderness.... Indeed the abundance of shade trees is the most commendable feature in the general appearance of the place. The streets are lined throughout with rows of mingled oak, elm, locust and various other trees, which, combined with the fine groves above mentioned and the patches of shady woodland that environ and almost creep up into the city, give the visitor a very agreeable sylvan aspect. Aside from the beautifying features just mentioned, shabbiness is the prevailing characteristic. Little frame huts, fallen out of shape for the lack of power to stand upright, their paint washed out of remembrance by long exposure, and their weather-boarding worm-eaten through age, thrust themselves into offensive contiguity with the sidewalk and shame their more respectable neighbors which modestly stand further back; dilapidated fences inclose waste lots, cumbered with brush, sticks of cord wood and miscellaneous rubbish; and even the yards around many respectable dwellings show lawns trampled bare of grass unintended shrubbery growing into a wilderness of tangled thicket.[8]

In 1865 Greensboro had two churches, five hotels, and three schools. It also had the county courthouse and was a major transportation hub, with several major roads and railroads. Two main streets, Elm and Market, intersected at the center of town where the courthouse stood. The city was built in a grid pattern with several blocks radiating out from the courthouse.[9]

The city's civilians, like most across the South, had endured years of high prices, declining wages, rampant inflation, and food and supply shortages. Now the threat of violence arrived. Wartime shortages and the demands of the military prevented the South's industry from producing goods for civilian consumption. Supplies were substituted and most people "made do." A factory in Raleigh produced wooden-sole shoes with leather tops. Shoe leather was scarce and this adaptation allowed for the continued production of new shoes. Yet this makeshift footwear was hard on carpets and forced civilians to stop wearing shoes at home, in just one of the many personal adjustments made in daily life as the war ground on.[10]

Wartime shortages had forced some women to revert to obsolete skills like carding and spinning wool on spinning wheels. Cards, which straightened and cleaned the wool, were rare, and thus in high demand. Over the course of the war, prices for a set of cards jumped from 40 cents to thirty dollars by 1863.[11] Greensboro women, like others across the South, attempted to produce substitutes for goods they could no longer afford or find. Local women experimented with sweet potatoes and parched rye to produce coffee.[12]

William C. McLean, a boy at the time of the army's arrival, wrote later in life of his experiences: "I had six brothers in the Civil War; the oldest of these had left home, when very young, and I had never seen him until he came back to Greensboro as one of General Johnston's soldiers. I visited him several times at their place of encampment, which was about the present location of the A. & T. College on East Market Street, but then known as the Hillsborough Road. Johnston's main army encamped in a body of woods, on the left-hand side of the road, across from the Landreth place." McLean continues,

"I also saw General Johnston several times while he was in Greensboro ... once on East Market Street, and each time he wore the full uniform (gray) of a Confederate officer, epaulets, etc. He was not a large man, but his bearing was that of a dignified Confederate officer. I also saw President Jefferson Davis several times while he was in Greensboro; he wore a black frock coat...."[13]

James Reid Cole, a soldier in the North Carolina Home Guard, wrote of the city: "Greensboro was a central Rail Road thoroughfare and of great importance to the Confederacy. Huge trains of cars swept through almost hourly, bearing the great loads from the Southern State and mountain regions to the great consumer and fighter — the Army of Northern Virginia. Now and then an army of 'Gray-Backs' would roll by yelling and reckless, headed by one of those giants of war who shook the panes with their martial tread."[14] Greensboro's women also noted the heavy rail traffic. As in other southern towns, the women organized a Ladies Soldiers Aid Society to assist wounded men and gather supplies for soldiers at the front. One member, Mary Kelly Watson Smith (wife of First Presbyterian Church pastor Jacob Henry), recalled this after the war:

> An amateur band of canteen-workers met the trains ... often in the darkness of night, with such refreshment as they could provide for the weary men; and in those fleeting moments of loving ministry, precious items of news from home and camp and friend were eagerly sought and given, ere the train sped onward.... [W]henever the train came in with gray-coats on board, it was a signal to broil bacon, bake corn bread, and set out all the milk, buttermilk and sorghum one could lay hands on, the only delicacies one could then afford.[15]

Mary also noted other activities of the city's women: "A central room was established where quilting and sewing were daily and diligently done. Every piece of old linen was cherished and scraped, bandages made, carpets taken up, and all the bedding, blankets, clothing, food, and whatever could be relinquished for the comfort of the soldiers, was sent to the camps. Even [the Presbyterian] church bell, which for a generation had called the people to prayer, was lowered from its belfry" [for scrap metal].[16]

Although piedmont North Carolina had been spared the movement of armies and devastation of battle, the war was brought to the citizens in late March with the arrival of casualties from Bentonville. Mary Smith noted the following:

> On that memorable night, without warning or preparation, the wounded were brought to Greensboro, in such numbers as to fill the churches, the court house, and every available space in the town. To that clarion call the women of Greensboro responded nobly and with one accord. All else was forgotten as with eager

hands and tender hearts they sought to make the poor fellows comfortable in their hastily improvised beds and comfortless quarters.

That night in the old Presbyterian church and lecture room I saw the first wounded and dying men and witnessed the grief of their comrades.[17]

Her husband wrote that authorities in the city "have impressed the Methodist church, Odd Fellows Hall, Brittain's Hotel, Garrett's building...." His own church, the First Presbyterian, was also soon used.[18] His five-year-old son, O. Norris Smith observed as follows:

[E]ach soldier was placed on what might be called a table, several planks joined together into a platform about 4 × 7 feet. The patient lay on a blanket and was covered by another. These boards were laid across the pews and the nurse standing between the pews found her patient easily reached and at the right level for feeding and other attendance. Mother took me each morning to help carry the water, towels, food, etc. My first trip on entering the church was to go to the pulpit and see how many had died during the night. Each dead soldier was wrapped in a blanket and laid in front of the pulpit, the number ranging from none to four or five. I do not remember seeing anyone buried, but I think most of them were buried close together in the back part of our graveyard behind the church.[19]

Arthur P. Ford of Maingault's Battery (SC), was one of those wounded men. He described his experiences in makeshift hospital:

We reached Greensboro at dark, making about 90 miles run in ten hours, very good for the speed of railway trains at that time. At Greensboro the court-house was used as a hospital, all the benches, desks, etc., being removed. We had no mattresses nor bedding of any kind, and about 200 of us were laid off in rows on the floor, with only our own blankets that we brought with us. After looking over the accommodations I selected the platform inside of the rail, where the judge's desk used to be, for my place, and went out into the street and begged an armful of hay from a wagon and with two bricks for a pillow made my bed. Here I lay for about three weeks with fever, and at times really very ill. Three times a day the ladies of the town came and brought us food, and were devoted in their attentions.[20]

The city's civilian population of 2,000 was swollen by soldiers, war industries, refugees, wounded, and others. The strain on Greensboro's resources would bring the city to the breaking point.[21] James Cole noted the changes in the city, describing it in detail:

As April 1865 dawned upon the world Greensboro was no longer the beautiful, quiet, delightful place of yore. The streets wee swimming in mud, and the houses looked as if they sympathized with their deplorable condition. "Tramp, tramp, tramp" was heard at all hours, day and night, as our infantry marched to their lines of battle. Horses and horsemen were dashing through the mud from street to street. The drum and fife and bugle were heard giving out their discordant sounds whenever a group of Confederate could be seen; and the nightly camp fires sparked and blazed from every hill-top and on every street in and around the town. The rumbling of passing cannons, the neighing of frightened horses, the jingling of spurs and clashing sabers, the shrill whistle of the coming engines, the tramp of the soldiery, the movement of wagons, the preparations for battle, the excitement of war and fear, the rushing to and fro of citizens and soldiers, the insubordination of desperate men, the stern men of our veteran soldiers, the calm defiant air of our noble commanders and rulers, all presented a scene of sound and aspect never before witnessed or heard in the wild woods of the inland town , and nothing resembling it since the clash of the patriot and tory, and the stern onset of the struggle of Cornwallis and Greene in the days of the Revolution which "tried men's souls."[22]

Like many residents of Greensboro, Cole was well aware of the area's role in the Revolution. There was no town of Greensboro in 1781 when British and American forces clashed at the Battle of Guilford Courthouse. It was an incredibly hard-fought and bloody engagement, one that shattered the British army. From here the British army led by General Lord Charles Cornwallis fell back all the way to Wilmington. Resting there for two weeks, they continued north to Virginia, ending their march at Yorktown. The battle of Guilford Courthouse was seen as a turning point of the campaign. Throughout the Civil War both sides drew inspiration from memories of the Revolution, and now that the war had brutally come to Greensboro, no doubt many citizens made the connection between 1781 and 1865.

Mary K. Smith, wife of Presbyterian minister Jacob H. Smith. Her writings provide detailed observations of the events from the point of view of a Greensboro civilian (Greensboro Historical Museum Archives).

Of more immediate concern to most of the soldiers that April, however, was eating. George Bussey of the 7th South Carolina wrote of their arrival in Greensboro: "While here some of us learned that by walking a few miles down this railroad, we could get into some box cars, filled with peas and bacon, so we went and lugged back as many peas as we could walk under, and sold them out by the pint at an enormous price, about $1.00 per pint." Of course, the money that he and his comrades had made would soon be worthless.[23] He also recorded that "some of the men found some barrels of whiskey buried under some brush, and you could see men going from every direction with canteens and with water buckets for it. Before I could reach the spot, it was reported that it was all gone. There were a great many drunken men in camp that day."[24]

Robert Herriot of Bachman's Battery (SC) recalled their experience after the retreat through Raleigh with Hampton's Cavalry: "We lay encamped at Hillsboro for a week or ten days ... and thoroughly enjoyed the rest after the long hike from the South Carolina coast. Also we were fortunate in drawing liberal rations while at Hillsboro."[25] After transferring to Greensboro, he recorded his impressions of the city:

> What attracted our attention mostly on our arrival at Greensboro was the great number of general officers, mounted and riding around, and the quantity of whisky and tobacco in sight. The main street was lined with empty whisky barrels with the heads knocked in and near-by vacant lots were covered with tobacco hogsheads. Any one who wished could help himself to the tobacco, the latter being the property of the Confederacy. Quite a lot of it was appropriated by the writer, who, with the assistance of one of his mess, who was in the tobacco-growing region of South Carolina, manufactured a lot of it into twists and on the march home used it as currency. As the heads of the barrels were knocked in the whisky ran down, making a lake a foot deep in a low place near the track. The boys were dipping so much of the stuff that the army officer in charge of the operation ordered the conductor of the train to run forward and then back up, and continue to keep the cars moving, so the liquor could not be secured by the soldiers. I dipped up a camp kettle full and took it to camp, where my mess and others of the boys drank hot toddies all night, having plenty of hot water and Confederate brown sugar. Being a kid at the time, this was the first liquor I had ever tasted.

Throughout the region, Confederate soldiers were trying to get food, shelter, and better clothing. Artilleryman Clement Saussy of Wheaton's Battery (GA) wrote of his experiences with the retreating army:

> During our march through North Carolina by some mishap I lost my hat, and was bareheaded for two days. At that time, the Yankee prisoners were being removed from Salisbury in the box cars, with sentinels at each side door and on top of the cars. As comrade Jim Freeborn was also bareheaded, I suggested to him that we cut a long sapling so as to sweep the top of the train so as to knock off some hats from the sentinels. To this Freeborn agreed and we were soon ready for business. Very soon a train came in sight, and with a mighty effort we

made the sweep and down came several hats. There [sic] owners were completely taken by surprise and fired several shots at us. The motion of the train made their aim uncertain, and we escaped. When the train passed around the curve, we descended and got two or three fairly good hats.[26]

Charles W. Hutson of the Beaufort Artillery (SC) noted in his journal that his unit had absorbed other batteries, and that "this made us represent four town that were in the hands of the enemy: Charleston, Beaufort, Savannah, and New Orleans." It was depressing news for these artillerymen.[27]

The realities of the war interrupted their efforts to acquire badly needed supplies. The cavalry of General Dibrell moved towards Salisbury, and on the way, George Mitchell of the 9th Kentucky Cavalry learned from a civilian that Lee had surrendered. He wrote, "We did not believe it; but the third day we intercepted some of Lee's men on their way home. Then it was that gloom seized the boys. We marched as silently as a funeral procession. It was the first time I ever saw the 9th Kentucky march for one hour without some merriment breaking out in the columns."[28] A Georgia soldier agreed with the effect of the news, writing, "We found it out by seeing some of Gen. Lee's men on their way home. The announcement ruined the morale of Gen. Johnston's Army, as it was nothing more than a howling mob after that."[29] A soldier with the 60th North Carolina observed, "Paroled prisoners from Lee's army were passing for days past in a constant stream." The Army of Northern Virginia veterans were free to go home, while the Army of Tennessee soldiers were still fighting the war. The irony was not lost on the men.[30] Federal troops experienced the same phenomenon. At Goldsboro, Corporal Joseph Crowther of the 128th New York wrote, "Prisoners, deserters & stragglers is constantly coming into our lines. The most of them take the oath of allegiance and are free to go to their homes."[31]

The veterans of Lee's army noted the condition of things among their comrades in the Army of Tennessee as they passed through. Isaac G. Bradwell of the 31st Georgia observed that he was "surprised to see them everywhere engaged in gambling. I had never seen so many kinds of games of chance before. They all seemed well supplied with Confederate money, and it was changing hands pretty freely. But I suppose they were not so much to blame for this, as the money was worthless and it was a means for diverting their minds from their unfortunate situation."[32] Commanding the post at Greensboro, General Alfred Iverson wrote, "Large numbers of stragglers are constantly arriving. Most of the forces here are composed of men collected together for the emergency and are not reliable."[33]

General Collett Leventhorpe, the English-born commander of North Carolina's Home Guard, gave his view:

I perceived within a day or two a material alteration in the morale of the troops occupying the lines west of Greensborough. Desertions are becoming very numerous. About 200 men of one battalion abandoned their post last night, and the remaining men of this force state openly their intention to return to their homes. I am far from desiring to impute this design to a very many gallant men now under my command, but the fact of the demoralization of the majority, is, I fear, indisputable.[34]

From Lexington Colonel A.M. Boone wrote to General Leventhorpe and Governor Vance: "The men of my regiment are very impatient under the present excitement. They are men of means and their property in different counties has been plundered by raiders and tories. The army of Generals Lee and Johnston falling back, with discouraging accounts, renders it almost impossible for me to hold them together. Please instruct me what to do."[35]

James W. Albright and some comrades of the 13th North Carolina Light Artillery made their escape from Lee's army prior to the surrender at Appomattox. Making their way to their hometown of Greensboro, they arrived on April 16, Easter Sunday. Albright wrote, "The town was in a perfect uproar—Yankees expected every minute. Goods of the army are going in every direction—went in for my share and got a good deal. Met many friends." Albright remained with his family while events unfolded in Greensboro over the next few weeks.[36] David T. Copeland of the 3rd South Carolina Consolidated Regiment wrote of the absent men of his unit: "I expect a great many of them are on French furlough as we call them which in other words have runaway from their Regt without any furlough...."[37]

Unlike the Army of Northern Virginia, which was driven from Richmond and Petersburg and was hounded during its retreat to Appomattox, the Army of Tennessee moved at its own pace. Johnston's force had time to refit and reorganize, it was not harassed like the Army of Northern Virginia. This also meant that, unlike Lee's anxious troops, who fought until literally the last hour, Johnston's men had time to contemplate their situation and reflect on the war's obvious and imminent ending. Lee's harried veterans had no such opportunity, as days ran together in their exhausted and tormented minds. The men of the western army had time to reflect on their situation and greater ability to make their decision about staying or going.

General Alfred Iverson, commanding the post at Greensboro, reported:

I have the honor to report the desertion of numbers of the troops from the lines around the town, the Virginia troops generally leaving. I am pained to say that the disposition of the command is not good, there being much demoralization. Large numbers of stragglers are constantly arriving. Arrangements have been made to collect these men, but the difficulty is to keep them from deserting. Most of the forces here are composed of men collected together for the emergency, and are not reliable. I respectfully suggest that it would be best to remove these troops to some point where there is less confusion, and supply in their places with a well organized command. There is great want of cavalry, only fifty men being present of that arm.[38]

Captain Albert Ferry wrote that Captain Harris's Georgia Company of Palmer's Battery deserted one night: "I have ascertained that fifteen men left camp last night with as many horses.... I am informed that these men were the best soldiers of that organization and determined to leave Greensboro so as not to surrender with the Army...." The desertion of the men was bad enough, but the worse news was the loss of the horses, as the guns could not be moved without them. The horses from the other batteries would have to move the artillery of both batteries if orders came to move.[39]

Trooper O.P. Harris of the 1st Georgia Cavalry recorded his experiences during the final weeks of the war:

We again kept on fighting and falling back until our Cavalry reached Raleigh, N.C. There we was ordered to get corn at the depot and go on a few miles and feed our horses. We went out a piece from Raleigh, took off our bridles and fed our horses and while we were sitting around waiting for our horses to eat, our bugles called to mount quick and we sprang for our horses, and by the time we got into our saddles the Federal Cavalry was right on to us and every man had to take care of himself. It was the worst stampede I ever saw.[40]

His adventure was not yet over, for after the battle, "I missed my brother and couldn't find him. A good many of the company said they saw him in the charge but had not seen him since. I was about to conclude that he was either killed or captured but I kept up my search for him. At last I found him at a house with some other soldiers getting their canteens full of syrup."[41]

On April 14 the last combat between the two armies took place in Durham County. Seven Confederates ambushed and killed twelve Union cavalrymen in the southwest corner of the county. Farther to the west, troops under General Smith Atkins crossed New Hope Creek along the Stagecoach Road (now NC Route 54), pushing back Confederate troopers and killing three. About a mile to the north, the 9th Ohio Cavalry crossed the creek under fire. This action was the last battle of the war in North Carolina. Some of the fighting along the creek took place on the land of Richard Leigh, whose cousin Nancy was married to James Bennitt. The Bennitts lived about ten miles north, along the road from Hillsborough to Durham.[42] James and Nancy had already lost two sons and their son-in-law in the war, and were about to be drawn even deeper into its grip. Their home was a modest farmhouse and the family was typical of many that scraped by during the war.[43]

The commander of the post at Salisbury, Col. A.M. Moore, wrote that his men were becoming "impatient under the present excitement." He asked for instructions in regards to desertion, and the lawlessness of guerillas and deserters.[44] From Greensboro General Alfred Iverson reported a growing number of desertions among his command, especially Virginia troops whose homes were not too far distant: "I am pained to say that the disposition of the command is not good, there being much demoralization. Large numbers of stragglers are constantly arriving." It was "difficult to keep them from deserting."

On the 17th (the day that Sherman and Johnston met at the Bennitt house), Sumner A. Cunningham of the 3rd Tennessee Consolidated described the growing tension in his camp:

> We had eaten a hasty breakfast and were packed up and ready to march at daylight. But, no order to "fall in" or command to "forward march" came. The morning began to pass away, and still no order to march. What could it mean? The men began to collect in groups with wonder and anxiety depicted on every countenance, discussing the probabilities of what could be up. Late in the evening, rumors began to be current that negations were going on for our surrender.[45]

William H. Andrews with the 1st Georgia Regulars wrote, "All order and discipline was lost in the army when an armistice was agreed to. The camps are nothing more than a mob. Nearly all of the ammunition was destroyed, the men tearing up cartridges, putting the powder in sacks, and running the balls into bars of lead. The soldiers confiscated everything they could get their hands on, consisting of bacon, crackers, chewing and smoking tobacco, leather, and various other things."[46] He further observed, "Gen. Harrison's Brigade was camped in a grove near the railroad, and the saplings were all weighted down with sides of bacon. What a crazy camp we had. One morning I paid five dollars for one pound of tobacco, and before I had made up one pipe full, Cpls. Smith and Harris of my mess came into camps with as much as they could carry on an army blanket between them. Wild rumors of all kinds are flashing through the camps."[47] He also noted that "by night the soldiers will begin to call at headquarters in howling mobs asking our generals to enlighten them.... At night I can hear the tramp of soldiers' feet on the railroad leaving the army to go and make their escape homewards.... Men refused to stand guard duty or take on assignments from their officers, insisting 'they had done their last guard duty.'"[48]

Artilleryman James Albright, home from Lee's army, wrote, "[S]till great confusion, and all in the dark as to army movements. Spent the day trying to get clothing and provisions—got some—not much. The Quartermaster was as stingy as if he expected the war to last another three years. Slept in the barn again to save my horse."[49] Albright reported to General Beauregard to offer his assistance, but the general replied, "Well, sir, you were included in the surrender of the Army of northern Virginia, and you must take no part in the military transactions of the forces here or elsewhere, and if we evacuate Greensboro, remain here until legally paroled."[50]

In the camp of General Brown's Division men discussed going to Texas to continue the war. One soldier wrote, "Discipline is very loose. Everyone doing pretty much as he pleases...."[51] At Greensboro, Captain Nicholas Schenck wrote, "Before the Expiration of the Armistice our men began to leave — without leave — and desert in squads — as they had no idea of capture and prison life at Yankee Prisons.... My clerks ask permission to leave — I could not grant it but they took "leg bail" and departed.... It was necessary for a Negro servant to stay with the horse — night and day to keep the soldiers from taking him off — things broke loose and there was some looting of Government stores, food, and clothing."[52]

According to Daniel Dantzler of the 2nd South Carolina Artillery in Greensboro, "Rumor says that Gen. Johnson has surrendered his whole army." He later wrote, "We hear that negotiations are being made for peace, and that the war is at an end, on the basic of reconstruction under the United States Constitution. Great excitement prevails in the army. Some talking one thing and some another. A great many men are talking of quitting and striking out for home. Some have gone."[53] Charles Jones of the Chatham Artillery (GA) wrote, "A spirit of dissatisfaction prevailed in the army in anticipation of its early surrender; and numerous desertions occurred, accompanied by constant thefts of the transportation and artillery animals. A strong guard was posted for the protection of the battery."[54] Lieutenant Robert M. Collins of the 15th Texas described an incident in their camp between Raleigh and Greensboro:

> [W]e camped on a nice piece of woodland ... stretched our dog tents as if we were going to rest quite a while. The writer was standing at the head of the street we had made by our tents on either side, when he noticed ... Maxwell, coming out of the pine thicket, carrying a camp kettle. He beckoned to us to come. Says he, "Smell in the kettle." We smelled. It was about half full of apple brandy. We turned it up, drank as long as we could hold our breath, caught it and then drank again. The third breath was expended in the question, "Where did you find it?" He pointed over towards the pine thicket. By this time the boys were going that way in crowds. We followed on, of course. When we got there the boys had raised the forty-gallon barrel of apple brandy from the hole in the ground caused by the wind having blown a great oak tree up by the roots, and some old North Carolina fellow had used it as a grave for his pet barrel of brandy, which he was saving for his own use when the cruel war should end.... But be all this as it may, we can say with confidence that few barrels of brandy have ever made a more jolly crowd than ours was on that occasion. In a very short time the bulk of our brigade was "over there" around that barrel. By gen-

eral consent the writer was appointed to issue it out. A faucet was soon made from a boot-leg, cut to fit and twisted into the bung-hole. Then commenced the drawing of it off in canteens and camp kettles, and each canteen must need run too full, and rather than pour it out so the stopper would go in we would drink it.... All hands got drunk....

Along in the afternoon there came a big rain. When the big drops commenced striking us we looked for our dog tent ... we made a dive and went through to our waist at the other end. We were too weak ... to get out or back and, therefore, just lay there, and the hard cold rain pelted us good....

The next morning we were a hard looking set, and for the boys we plead as an excuse for this spree the peculiar surroundings.[55]

James Hawkins, a railroad worker with the Southern Express, recorded his impressions of Greensboro:

I staid in Greensboro NC 14 days amidst the greatest scene of confusion & excitement I ever beheld. Johns[t]ons army arrived there a few days after I did and lay around the 10 days truce or Armistice between Sherman & himself. The last of the CS Govt was also there a part of the time including "Jeff Davis," Benjamin, Breckenridge, Trenholm etc. nearly all the big men. ("Jeff Davis" and I suppose the balance have since been captured in Georgia).

The C.S. Govt had vast amounts of Stores there, 114 lbs [of] sugar alone, Bacon by the thousand, Corn and enough Army grey cloth to furnish a suit for every man in the Armies [of the] South. Nearly everything was carried off by the mob consisting principally of these NC woman (who beat everything I ever saw in the shape of Females) and Cavalry, Citizens & Negroes besides that they cleaned out trains loaded with stuff from Raleigh. At last I managed to get away the road having been fixed (where [Union cavalry Maj. Gen. George] Stoneman men had torn it up)....[56]

Greensboro was full of paroled men from Lee's army, deserters from Johnston's army, refugees, runaway slaves, and camp followers. Security was dubious. All of the soldiers and civilians were hungry and in need of clothing and supplies. It was well known that the city held vast stores of equipment and food. General Iverson, commander of the city, was worried about the growing number of shiftless men around him and being powerless to do anything. He wrote that "men are now waiting here for the opportunity to plunder."[57]

On April 15 the tension building in Greensboro finally broke when a mob of soldiers and civilians looted the state warehouse. The crowd gathered on South Elm Street and ransacked the Confederate Quartermaster Department's warehouse and another that held supplies for the state (near the corner of Market and Elm streets).[58] Among the rampaging mobs were deserters and stragglers from Johnston's infantry, cavalry that did not feel compelled to continue the retreat, paroled men from Appomattox who had drifted into

Elm Street looting site. None of the buildings in this view date to the Civil War, but this was the scene of looting by Confederate troops, civilians, and refugees.

town, civilians bent on getting their hands on supplies, runaway slaves, and every category of refugee and displaced person imaginable.[59] Among the goods looted were bacon, sugar, blankets, shoes, cloth, and corn. Many of the looters were Kentucky and Tennessee cavalrymen from General George Dibrell's Division. Just a few blocks away was President Davis and his party.[60]

The secretary of the navy, Stephen R. Mallory, did not have a favorable impression of the city:

> No provision had been made for the accommodation of the President and staff or for his cabinet; and to their surprise they found it impracticable to obtain these essentials, important alike to peasant and potentates, board and lodging. Greensboro had been a flourishing town, and there were many commodious and well furnished residences in and about it; but their doors were closed and their "latch strings pulled in" against the members of a retreating government. The President was unwell, and Col. Wood of his staff provided him with a bed at the limited and temporary quarters of his family, and the staff and cabinet, with other prominent gentleman, took up their quarters in a dilapidated, leaky passenger car. Here they ate, slept, and lived during the day. Among the generous people of Greensboro, a negro boy cooking their rations in the open air near them. Mr. Trenholm, who was very ill, and who found quarters at the large and elegant mansion of Gov. Morehead, was the only exception."[61]

Richmond & Danville Railroad Station. This is where President Davis's train arrived in the city (Greensboro Historical Museum Archives).

The mansion to which Mallory referred was Blandwood, an impressive home a few blocks from the heart of the city. Burton Harrison, secretary for Jefferson Davis, agreed with Mallory. He noted, "We observed indifference to what should become of us. It was rare that anybody asked one of us to his house; and but few of them had the grace even to explain their fear that, if they entertained us, their houses would be burned by the enemy, when his cavalry should get there. During the halt at Greensboro most of us lodged day and night in the very uncomfortable railway cars we had arrived in."[62]

Naval captain John Taylor Wood wrote of Greensboro: "Houses all closed. The people are afraid to take any one in; the Cabinet, General Cooper, and others are sleeping in the cars. Colonels Johnston and Lubbock we hear given beds on the floor." He added, "The surrender of General Lee and his entire army is confirmed. I can hardly realize this overwhelming disaster, it crushes the hopes of nearly all."[63] Wood, who was renting a house on Elm Street, offered it to Davis, who occupied it during part of his stay in the city. Although the secretary of the treasury, George A. Trenholm, stayed with former governor John M. Morehead at his Blandwood mansion, Harrison gave the reason he suspected:

> The possessor of a large house in the town, and perhaps the richest and most conspicuous of the residents, came indeed effusively to the train, but carried off only Mr. Trenholm, the Secretary of the Treasury. This hospitality was explained by the information that the host was the alarmed owner of many of the bonds, and of much of the currency, of the Confederate States, and that he hoped to cajole the Secretary into exchanging part of the "Treasury gold" for some of those securities. It appeared that we were reputed to have many millions of gold with us. Mr. Trenholm was ill during most or all of the time at the house of his warm-hearted host, and the symptoms were said to be greatly aggravated, if not caused, by importunities with regard to that gold.[64]

Blandwood. Home of former Governor John Morehead, the Confederate secretary of the treasury, John Trenholm, stayed here. Later, Union officers stayed at the home.

John Morehead, however, was known to be a generous philanthropist in Greensboro, contributing to educational schools like the Edgeworth Female Seminary. In fact, he had given shelter to Varina Davis, the president's wife, when she passed through the city.[65]

The Confederate cabinet's stay in the city was uneventful and lacked any physical comforts. Mallory graphically recorded their reduced state of affairs:

> The times were "sadly out of joint," just then, and so was the Confederate government. Here was the astute "Minister of Justice," a grave and most exemplary gentleman, with a piece of half broiled "middling" in one hand and a hoe cake in the other, his face bearing the unmistakable evidence of the condition of the bacon. There was the clever Secretary of State, busily dividing his attention between a bucket of stewed dried apples, and a haversack of hard boiled eggs; here was a Postmaster General, sternly and energetically running his bowie knife through a ham, as if it were their chief business of life, and there was a Secretary of the Navy courteously swallowing his coffee scalding hot that he might not keep the venerable Adjutant General waiting too long for the coveted tin cup. All personal discomforts were borne not only with cheerful philosophy, but they were made the constant texts for merry comment, quaint anecdote or curious story. State Sovereignty, Secession, foreign intervention and recognition, finance, and independence, the ever recurring and fruitful themes of discussion, gave place to the more pressing and practical question of dinner or no dinner, and how, when and where it was to be had; and to schemes and devices for enabling a man of six feet to sleep upon a car seat of four.[66]

The Wood house site. The Wood house, where President Davis stayed, stood in the center of the photograph.

Robert Herriot of Bachman's Battery (SC) observed of the city,

Greensboro at this time was quite a depot of military supplies. The quartermaster's was packed with uniforms, blankets, and shoes. The depot was guarded by a portion of the North Carolina Regiment. Some of Wheeler's Cavalry, belonging to Dibrell's brigade, took a notion to rush the depot of supplies, but the garrison fired on them, repulsing, killing, and wounding several. It was a tragic and unfortunate affair, as the war had just about drawn to a close. As I saw one of the cavalrymen lying on the side of a hill with his head downward, just as he was shot from his horse, I thought of the good work done by the Wheeler and Hampton cavalry in protecting the marching columns of infantry and artillery.[67]

James Cole of the Home Guard had been assigned by Governor Vance as chief quartermaster, a thankless job that spring. Cole wrote that he was to

... take charge of all the goods, and property belonging to the State at Greensboro, and distribute the clothing to the soldiers, State and Confederate. This property filled several large warehouses and was probably worth a million dollars. There were probably 20,000 soldiers of the various armies in the town and round about, and Lee's paroled soldiers were arriving daily. The soldiers, rendered desperate by misfortune and defeated and insubordinate to all command, were storming houses, breaking into military stores, taking horses and wagons, and a general riot and mutiny was threatened and several men were killed. Under these circumstances I took charge and after several days of hard work,

assisted by a score of earnest assistants and guarded by 300 soldiers and thousands of men from all parts of the Confederacy went away from Greensboro on
their way home clothed by the State of North Carolina by order of her great Governor. The soldiers were disbanded and returned to their homes and my last
service to my country was performed at my own home in helping to clothe our
brave, ragged soldiers.[68]

During the riot he wrote of what he saw:

> The avarice of men, the insubordination of reckless soldiers who had lost every-
> thing, the fears that all these valuable goods, of which they stood in so much
> need, might fall into the hands of the "Yankees," all wrought upon the soldiers to
> such an extent that riot and plunder and storming of horses were followed rap-
> idly upon each other. Cavalry galloped over the streets campfires were built on
> the sidewalks. Guards and sentinels were posted across every street and at every
> corner. The main streets and by-streets and yards and houses were crowded with
> desperate soldiers who were reckless because of their final defeat.[69]

Cole noted that the mob "destroyed everything in one house, overturning
the guard. They were headed by a huge Kentuckian who shouted, 'Kentuck-
ians, charge the house!' Not a man stirred. 'Tennesseans, charge the house!'
No one responded. 'Wheeler's Cavalry!' shouted the gigantic warrior on
horseback, 'charge!' A yell, a scuffle and the guard was overpowered and the
house sacked."[70]

Also observing the chaos was President Davis's executive secretary, Burton Harris, who noted, "A formidable attack was made by men belonging to
a cavalry regiment upon one of the depots where woolen cloths were stored.
They charged down the road in considerable force, with yells and an occasional shot; but the 'Home Guards,' stationed at the store-house, stood firm,
and received the attack with a well directed volley. I saw a number of saddles
emptied, and the cavalry retreated in confusion."[71] Stephen Mallory also wrote
of the chaos:

> Hundreds of armed men, swarming like locusts into well filled warehouses,
> struggling, cursing, yelling, every one for himself, in utter disregard of all
> authority, & to the destruction of a great amt. of property each seizing upon
> whatever he chose.... Many a bronzed, weather beaten veteran was seen to
> emerge from such a crowd, strangely burdened with more plunder than he could
> take care of. Seated upon a new saddle over his old one, with a bag of flour or
> meal tied behind him, a huge bundle of blankets & cloths in front of him, & a
> couple of pairs of brogans hung around his neck, and a side of bacon strung
> under the animals' neck & resting against his breast & legs, he would make his
> way out.[72]

About twenty men of Company F of the 27th North Carolina (known as the

Perquimans Beauregards) responded and fired into the crowd. Corporal Joseph Mullen Jr. recalled that the cavalry "drew their pistols and fired ... without hurting anybody. We immediately returned the fire with a better effect than they had. We killed two men and one horse and wounded one other man. Then they took flight, running off at the quickest possible speed in every direction. This quieted them down and we were not bothered any more by them."[73]

The 27th North Carolina was one of many Confederate regiments that had a presence at both major surrenders. The bulk of the unit (the other 9 companies) were with the Army of Northern Virginia at Appomattox (where 105 men surrendered). Company F had been detached and sent to assist Johnston's army, along with other commands from Lee's army.[74] Other detachments from the 7th, 15th, 46th, 48th, and 55th North Carolina regiments arrived. Again, these units were assigned to Greensboro from Lee's army in Virginia. The troops ordered the mob to disperse. In response the leader of the rioters fired a pistol, and the troops returned fire. The leader fell dead from his horse.[75]

James Harris of the 7th North Carolina recalled "we dispersed a considerable body of mounted men claiming to belong to Wheeler and Vaugn's cavalry commands who were plundering the government stores, and recovered twelve cart loads of good stake not by them."[76] A witness wrote that "for a few minutes the crack of musketry was rapid and deadly, both sides battled, but soon the desperate mob fled over fences, through yards, and back streets, and as far as the eye could see a huge sea of heads appeared running and rapidly disappearing from the fatal glance of the guard. Four men were shot down and slain in the melee — all belonging to the mob." These would be the last shots of the war for these soldiers, shots they fired into a crowd of civilians and fellow soldiers.[77]

Corporal Joseph Mullen, Jr. of the 27th North Carolina wrote of his unit's action that day: "Quite early we had orders to get ready to move immediately. It was raining.... When we got up town we found that the soldiers had charged the Quartermasters Department and it was for this that we had been hastened from camp through the rain. We immediately went to work to suppress the riot. We had orders to take everything belonging to the Quartermasters Department from the soldiers unless they could show some receipt for them."[78] A trooper in the 8th Tennessee Cavalry recalled the retrograde movement from Smithfield and the looting in Greensboro afterwards:

> On the 12th of April we crossed the Neuse River at Battle's bridge, and then learned the truth of Gen. Lee's disaster in front of Petersburg, which Sherman's men had been hallooing to us for two days before, but we did not believe it. Moving up to Raleigh that evening we were ordered to march as rapidly as we

could to Greensboro, eighty-five miles distant, and report to President Davis. Starting just before sundown, with the little Kentucky and Tennessee brigade and Wigger's Arkansas battery, we made the march to Greensboro in two days and nights, a very hard march. Arriving at Greensboro, N.C. about twelve o'clock at night, we reported in person to Gen. Breckinridge, Secretary of War, and President Davis, and received orders and instructions as to our future movements. Our men and horses were fatigued, and needed rest after the hard march. On the next day Greensboro was full of soldiers from Gen. Lee's army, together with a great many stragglers, State troops, and others, all of whom were greatly demoralized, and many solders were drinking. It was said there were some supplies in the town that the soldiers wanted, and the authorities in charge were destroying vast quantities of alcohol and other supplies. In the evening some of the cavalry had got into the crowd, and to disperse them all a certain cowardly Leiut. Molloy, of the North Carolina State troops, ordered his men to fire upon the others, which they did, killing James Brown, of Co. D, Eighth Tennessee Cavalry, and wounding one other soldier. This was the last death in the regiment and his death was a cold-blooded murder, perpetuated by order of Lieut. Malloy, and caused great indignation with the cavalry, as Brown was an extra good soldier and a popular young man.... On account of this affair the command that evening, with President Davis and his staff, moved out six or eight miles and camped for the night.[79]

This trooper obviously had a different point of view on the looting than the generals did. The 8th Tennessee Cavalry was among the units that accompanied Davis and his party as they moved into South Carolina and Georgia.

Later that day in Greensboro the mob appeared at another warehouse, and General Beauregard ordered Home Guard troops to assist the officer in charge there. Beauregard, who appeared "nervous" and spoke "rapidly," gave instructions that an entire brigade could be called on if that were not enough, and if more help was needed still, authorized artillery to be deployed in the streets with grapeshot. General William Brantley's brigade of Mississippi, Alabama, and North Carolina troops, camped nearby, moved into the center of the city and deployed to guard warehouses. It was the day before Easter.[80]

Arriving later in the city to help restore order was the 24th Mississippi Consolidated Regiment. According to Private Robert A. Jarman of that unit, "[W]e arrived on April 16th and went into camp around the Court House, and here on the doors we saw on guard over all public property, both Confederate and State of North Carolina, and to keep down all rioting and disorders of every character. We kept the streets around the different supply depots guarded day and night, permitting no one, unless with a pass, to come in. I even saw what was said to be the gold and silver, in boxes and kegs, loaded in wagons and under strong cavalry guard, start South."[81] Also marching into Greensboro that afternoon was the 37th Georgia. Hezekiah McCorkle noted "numbers of the N. Carolina reserve troops going to their homes. All confusion about the town also."[82]

While the religious holiday itself was quiet, the following day, Monday, April 17, another large group assembled in front of a warehouse. Many women were among the agitated crowd. James Cole wrote that "the old women from near and far who had been charging over the guards and taking advantage of their sex believ[ed] the guard would not fire upon them." In addition, the women were "urged on by the men who desired to follow after they broke the line." Cole issued orders to shoot anyone trying to break in, "on the spot."[83] Confederate troops stood guard with bayonets leveled at the civilians and deserters. After Major William Brantley gave orders for his Home Guards to shoot anyone who tried to break in, the mob dispersed. Thus, as with the North Carolinians of McAllister's command, the last military service performed by Brantley's men was to guard supplies and stare down civilians and deserters in the streets of Greensboro.[84] This was the only instance of mob violence by southern civilians at the war's end in a Confederate city. Two days later looting also broke out in the towns of McLeansville and Graham, east of the city. Whiskey, molasses, cloth, leather, and other goods were taken by these mobs. Drunkenness became rampant.[85]

In Chapel Hill the Confederate cavalry under General Joseph Wheeler pulled out of the village that was home to the University of North Carolina. Only one senior graduated that spring of 1865. In fact, there were only about a dozen students at the university. Like most schools across the South, its students, and many professors, were off in the war.[86] Chapel Hill resident Cornelia Spencer wrote of the cavalry's withdrawal:

> We ... waved our last farewell to our army. A few hours of absolute and Sabbath stillness ensued.... The groves stood thick and solemn, the bright sun shining through the great boles and down the grassy slopes.... [A]ll that nature can do was still done with order and beauty, while mens' hearts were failing them for fear, and for looking after those things which were coming on the earth.
>
> We sat in our pleasant piazzas and awaited events with quiet resignation. The silver had all been buried — some of it in springs, some under rocks in the streams, some of it in fence corners, which, after the fences had been burned down, was pretty hard to find again.... There was not much provision to carry off — that was one comfort. The sight of our empty store-rooms and smoke-houses would be likely to move our invaders to laughter. Our wardrobes were hardly worth hiding — homespun and jeans hung placidly in their accustomed places. But the libraries ... the buildings of the University — all minor selfish considerations were merged in a generous anxiety for these. So we talked and speculated, while the very peace and profound quiet of the place sustained and soothed our minds. Just at sunset a sedate and soldiery-looking man, at the head of a dozen dressed in blue, rode quietly in by the Raleigh road....[87]

Captain Rawlins Lowndes rode from General Wade Hampton's head-quarters at Hillsborough with Johnston's note for Sherman. Lowndes entered Union lines near Morrisville and was admitted to General Judson Kilpatrick's headquarters. While waiting for Sherman's response, Lowndes and Kilpatrick had a lively conversation.[88] At first their discussion was pleasant but it went downhill quickly when they began discussing the recent campaign. Kilpatrick's cavalry had been ambushed at Monroe's Crossroads, near Fayetteville, and he still simmered over it. Kilpatrick countered, with very little effect, that if he hadn't been surprised he would have been victorious.[89] Lowndes then challenged Kilpatrick and 1,500 picked cavalrymen to a saber-only battle with 1,000 Confederate cavalrymen. The idea never went anywhere but it reveals the determination of many southerners to keep fighting.[90]

At Chapel Hill, Union cavalry occupied the town with orders that private property was to be respected. Civilian Charles Mallett recorded that Michigan troops were sent to guard "evry house that desired it."[91] He also noted that as the time passed under occupation by Union troops, "I felt much like the monotony of prison life." He also wrote of worrying about hidden supplies: "Our meat having lain so long under ground that we began to fear it would be spoiled."[92]

Davis and the cabinet had left Greensboro on Easter morning (April 16). Later that day Johnston arrived to inform him that Sherman had accepted his invitation to meet. Finding the president gone, and somewhat surprised that he had not bee informed of his departure, Johnston returned to his headquarters at Hillsborough and prepared to meet his opponent.[93] Beginning that same day and continuing for the next few days, the Army of Tennessee arrived in Greensboro and began to set up camps in and around the town, as well as at Jamestown, High Point, and elsewhere. Johnston established his headquarters in the center of the town. Some troops camped at the site of the present North Carolina A&T University, most (Lee's and Stewart's) were east of town along the Burlington Road at Buffalo Creek (modern US Route 70). The city of 2,000 found itself amid about 40,000 troops. In addition, thousands of refuges, runaway slaves, and deserters flooded into the area.[94]

Hardee's Corps moved to New Salem, in northern Randolph County. Their march took them along what is now NC 62, through Alamance and Guilford counties, paralleling Stinking Quarter Creek. At New Salem the commands dispersed and set up camps. The 31st North Carolina set up camp at Bush Hill (now Archdale) in northern Randolph County. Men of the 17th and 42nd North Carolina were not far away at Center Church, a colonial house of worship and an important local landmark. What was left of the 58th North Carolina camped at Jamestown for a week, then moved on to Greensboro.[95]

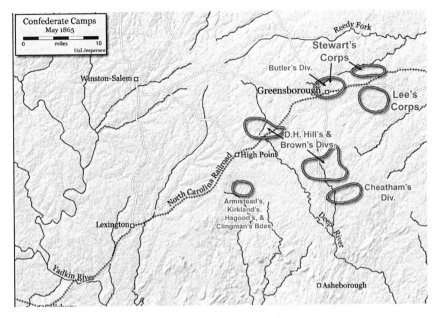

Confederate Campsites (Map by Hal Jespersen).

Delphina Mendenhall, a widow living in Jamestown, wrote, "There is much suffering for bare bread in this country — women & children just ready to perish — I have very little to spare them...." The arrival of detachments from the Army of Tennessee further strained local resources.[96] John Hiatt of Jamestown wrote to his sons that Confederate troops camped on his farm for several days, ruining his wheat and oat crops. Of 160 acres, he estimated that only 10 or 12 were salvageable.[97]

W.J. Armfield recalled seeing Davis and his party ride through Jamestown on their way south: "I saw this cavalcade as it passed through ... and it was a very impressive sight, for the horses were fine and well-groomed, the ambulances looked new and shining, and formed a strong contrast to the poor, half-starved horses and equipment of the Confederate soldiers, to which we were accustomed."[98] The coming of so many Confederate soldiers was not welcome news to the residents of Randolph County either. An army's presence was always hard on civilians, even those who supported the cause. Roads were clogged, fences torn down for fuel, crops and animals taken for food, and wells drunk dry. Yet in the central counties of the Tar Heel state, large numbers of Moravians, Quakers, and other pacifists opposed the war. Many had even fled, but those who remained were determined in their opposition to the war.[99] In fact, Randolph County in particular had acquired a reputation for harboring deserters and draft dodgers. Many of its citizens, poor whites

Richard Mendenhall store. This was owned by a Quaker family in Jamestown. Confederate troops camped nearby and used the road running in front of this landmark.

living on hardscrabble farms, had no vested interest in the fate of the Confederacy. Throughout the war, Home Guard units patrolled the county, attempting to cajole, entice, and force men to serve in the military.[100]

Not only did the region's small farmers oppose secession and the Confederacy, as did Moravians and Quakers, the Underground Railroad had been active in the region before the war; and during the war years runaway slaves, draft dodgers, and military deserters hid out in the area's woods.[101]

As in other areas of the Confederacy, the civilians were severely impacted by the war. Shortages of salt forced some to dig up dirt from smokehouses and boil it for salt. Malnutrition made the population more susceptible to diseases like smallpox, diphtheria, and dysentery. Citizens had been subject to conscription and taxes, and when cash was not available to pay taxes to the government, tax in kind—in the form of sheep, hogs, corn, and other crops—were taken.[102] Inflation, skyrocketing food prices, and shortages of everything from medicine to cloth to shoes to new tools affected daily life. Bacon for example, jumped from 33 cents a pound in 1862 to $7 a pound by April 1865. In the same period, a pound of potatoes went from $1 to $30, and corn and wheat saw similar increases. Many goods were not available at any price.[103]

Mana D. Foust of Randolph County wrote to her children that spring of her "troubles." They "have almost pushed me into the earth," she wrote. "I feel that I can bear but few more and but for my two unprotected daughters I would pray to be at rest, but for their sakes I try to live. All I can say is that I have had all the armies pass and camp around here for the last few weeks and you can form some idea of my situation." A few lines later she writes, "How I am to live God only knows, but I must try, if I was younger and able to work I would not feel so bad...." In what may have been a reassuring act, a soldier from Massachusetts agreed to deliver her letter.[104]

Discontent was so strong in this central part of the Old North State that a strong antiwar movement emerged by 1863. Residents held public meetings throughout the region, and largely voted for a peace candidate for governor.[105] The region was one in which the runaway slaves, draft dodgers, military deserters, passive resistance to the Confederacy, and more organized militant resistance all intersected. "Outliers," those on the run from the law, hid in the area's woods and hills from the "Hunters," members of the Home Guard and county sheriffs who were authorized to arrest them.[106] The tight-knit Quaker families assisted each other during these difficult times. One local doctor assisted deserters who hid in, and made their escape through, the area. Levi Cox cut grain for the women of the area, even after being told by authorities not to help them.[107]

The rhythms of regular life were interrupted by the war, and more so by the arrival of the Army of Tennessee that spring. Few of the people could attend regular religious meetings. Women had to take on extra work when husbands were drafted or arrested. School attendance declined because of the additional demands placed on families and the lack of teachers.[108] J.W. Norwood, an Orange County resident, noted, "First our county has been stripped of horse, and then all the roads are filled with Wheelers and other cavalry and wagons going on to join their commanders, who seize all the horses they can lay hand on ... to say nothing of our own deserters."[109] The once prosperous Quaker community of New Garden, south of Greensboro, was described that spring: "Horses all gone, few cattle ... merest pretense at farming; tools worn out; harness mostly rope; buildings dilapidated; roofs leaking ... fences gone, mostly burned ... houses and properties destroyed by fire; no sugar, or tea, or coffee, drank warm water with sorghum sweetening; little boys with the help of their mothers did some farming and gardening; no stores at which to buy anything ... roads in bad condition; bridges in disrepair; thread and needles scarce; mending a problem."[110]

In March Confederate troops were directed to search the area for "deserters, absentees, and recusant conscripts." The troops were "empowered to impress citizens for guides" and if the locals refused to help, they were authorized to "administer punishments as you may think necessary to protect you from betrayal." One Confederate officer carrying out these orders wrote, "No quarter will be shown; they will be shot down wherever found."[111]

The Confederate Home Guard used vicious tactics to root out deserters and draft dodgers. One pregnant woman died as result of being strung up by her thumbs when she refused to divulge the location of her family's missing men. Other women were tortured and harassed in Home Guard efforts to track down deserters.[112] Some women took matters into their own hands. Martha Sheets of rural and mountainous Montgomery County wrote to Sheriff Aaron Sanders:

> Dear Sur
> I can tell you the truth but I dont reckon that you want to her hit. If you dont send me too bushels of wheat and too bushels and a peck of corn in the corse of tenn days I will send enuf of Deserters to mak you sufer that you never suffered before. And send me good grain if you want to live. Pepel tell me Whow mean you was before I went to see you But I found you wors than ther told me and athout a grate alterrashen you will go to the Devile and that soon. Ther you have got all of your suns at home and when my husband is gon and he has Dun Work for you and you try to Denie hit and When this ware Brake out you sad goe Boys, ill spend the Last doler for your famelys and Drat your ole sold you never have dun athing for the pore Wiming yet, you nasty old Whelp. You have told lys to get your suns out of this War And you dont care for the rest that is gon nor for ther fameleys, now you ma depend if you dont Bring that grain to my dore you Will sufer and that Bad
> This from Martha Sheets[113]

J.M. Worth of Asheboro wrote to his son: "There is no spot upon this earth more completely subjugated than Randolph County. There is not a day or night that passes but what some one is robbed of all the parties can carry away ... unless it is stopped we shall be utterly used up."[114] At one point fifty deserters had ransacked the home of Mrs. I.H. Foust, a widow. She and her daughter Sallie watched as the men tore through the home, taking several thousands of dollars.[115]

As the Army of Tennessee entered Guilford and Randolph counties, it came into a region bitterly divided by the war and whose civilians had practiced everything from passive resistance to flagrant violations of military drafts and orders. No doubt the area's civilians watched with anxious concern as thousands of hardened veterans came into their midst.[116]

Family histories of the region recall the impact of the war: depredations committed by both Confederates and anti-secession guerillas, and soldiers from Johnston's army begging for food and water.[117]

The troops of Johnston's army were not static once they arrived in the

Greensboro area. Some units moved to thwart Stoneman's cavalry, others shifted position for various work assignments. The 58th North Carolina Consolidated stopped near the depot in downtown, then left for Jamestown. On April 26, they were ordered back to Greensboro.[118] Hardee's Corps initially camped at the rural community of Redcross. The troops set up camp along both sides of New Salem Road and along Providence Church Road. The North Carolina Junior Reserves were camped near Bethel Church in Randolph County. Many artifacts have been found near the church, including a number of artillery shells. A grave stands today along New Salem Road, that of J.L. Froneberger of the 2nd North Carolina Junior Reserves, who was killed by a lightning strike in camp. It is one of the few reminders of the massive camps in this area. Otherwise there is no indication of the thousands who marched and camped here amid the modern fields, woods, and subdivisions.[119]

Alfred Tyler Fielder of 2nd Tennessee Consolidated noted, "About 3 oclk. P.M. a very heavy cloud arose with sharp lightning, heavy thunder and a strong wind and a very hard rain. One man was killed in camp with lightning."[120] According to one of the unit's officers, he was killed "within ten steps" of the regimental headquarters along the road. Froneberger was from Cleveland County, near Charlotte.[121]

Some of Hardee's troops camped around Center Meeting House, along modern NC Route 62. The camps extended up Davis Mill Road, where artillery was parked. Among these troops were the few North Carolinians of the army.[122]

General Hardee initially made his headquarters at the Jarrell Inn in the center of town, which still stands. He later moved his command post to Trinity College, making his headquarters at the home of Dr. Braxton Craven. Officers' wives used the second floor, while Hardee and his staff took over the first. The general's wife and daughter joined him there. All around the campus troops set up camps.[123] Mrs. Craven had a run-in with one of the soldiers at her home. Apparently ordered to gather firewood, a soldier began to cut an oak tree in the front yard of the home. Horrified, Mrs. Craven rant out and accosted him. General Hardee apologized, and the soldier found firewood from another source.[124]

Early in the war, Dr. Craven organized the Trinity Guard, composed of young men from the school. His hope was that this volunteer company would be used for local defense, and he could keep his students from going off to fight far from home. The Trinity Guard in fact did just that. They were guards at the Salisbury prison, and later the men were assigned to other units.[125] Confederate officers established their camps among the trees on the north side of the college building, while the troops were camped for six or eight miles along the road from Archdale to Freeman's Mills. The college later moved and is now known as Duke University.[126]

Nearby Davidson County also felt the impact of war. Hospitals in the Lambeth Tobacco Company warehouse and in the yard of the Thomasville Methodist Church cared for over 2,000 men. The dead were buried in Thomasville City Cemetery. The Lexington Home Guard had been called out to help guard the railroad.[127] The bulk of the army, however, camped in Guilford County. General Stewart's Corps set up camp along the old Burlington Road, modern US 70. The campsite straddled the road and is now bisected as well by the intersection of I-840 and US 70. Stewart's troops camped on high ground overlooking Buffalo Creek.[128]

William A. Johnson of the 2nd South Carolina wrote, "General Stewart's ... headquarters just across the road from our camp. Suppose we are to be the guard of his quarters." The general occupied the Fountain McLean House, later owned by Bate Donnell, near the junction of today's US 70 and Willow Lake Road. The house no longer stands.[129] Campfire rings could be seen here as recently as the 1980s, until modern development obliterated them. Just to the west, across Buffalo Creek, was the campsite of General S.D. Lee's Corps. The campsites covered the area around modern Clapp Farm Road, Hooper Road, and Mount Hope Church Road. In fact, a local farmer nicknamed one field "mini ball field" for all the bullets he found there while plowing. Other units of Lee's command were widely scattered.[130]

Robert H. Dacus of the 1st Arkansas Consolidated Regiment recalled that his brigade arrived and set up camp at Jamestown, where they waited for news of their fate. The Georgia Brigade of General Robert Henderson camped in Salisbury.[131] George Harper of the 58th North Carolina Consolidated Regiment noted that his unit camped about a mile and a half west of Greensboro. The wartime city was a small area in the center of the modern town, and this campsite would have been in what is now the modern eastern city limits.[132]

A veteran with the 72nd North Carolina (3rd North Carolina Junior Reserves) recorded the following after the war: "We reached Red Cross, twenty miles south of Greensboro late on April 16. Here we stayed until the following Easter Sunday.... Next morning after a scanty breakfast we made ready to resume the march but received no orders. We waited till noon then all afternoon then night and still no orders. The next morning we heard that General Johnston had surrendered. We camped at Red Cross for a few days."[133] Another North Carolinian with the 17th Regiment noted, "[A]s we tramped along the rough stony road, I noticed eggshells of various colors—red, yellow, green, blue, etc., and woundered [sic] what they meant. I was told it was Easter Sunday. I didn't know what that meant, for up to that time Easter had not been observed or even mentioned in any part of the State I had lived or visited. The part of the State we were then traversing had been settled by Moravians, and they had preserved their Easter customs."[134]

Grave of J.L. Froneberger. This young soldier of the 2nd North Carolina Junior Reserves was killed by a lightning strike.

Some of the men with the army were natives of Greensboro or Guilford County, and found themselves camped near their hometowns and farms. Private Peter Lopp of the 76th North Carolina (6th Reserve Regiment) was a 42-year-old blacksmith and farmer who arrived in the city in March with his unit to protect the supplies there.[135]

In Greensboro General Johnston's headquarters was a tent at the present site of North Carolina A & T University. He later moved to site now within the grounds of UNC-Greensboro. An observer wrote that it was in a grove on a hill "with a small stream of water crossing at its front. In the rear of the General's and staff officers' tents, were scattered the smaller tents of the attaches."[136] With his army safely out of harm's way for the moment, and supply lines established with the rail line running down to Charlotte and into South Carolina, Johnston prepared for his next move.

To make matters worse, paroled men from the Army of Northern Virginia began moving through upper North Carolina on their way home. These men, now off the hook and free to return home, had a negative impact on the soldiers of the Army of Tennessee, who had to remain in the field. In the camp of the 7th South Carolina Consolidated Regiment along the Burlington Road outside of Greensboro, desertions reached epic proportions. Officers of

Campsite along New Salem Road. One of the many Confederate campsites in the area, virtually unknown today.

the regiment posted guards at night to stem the tide. Private George Bussey, one of the guards, wrote that the evening the news of Appomattox arrived was a "trying night," as he was horrified at orders to shoot his fellow soldiers should they try to escape. The next day he stood guard over three deserters who waited by their coffins, waiting to be executed. When news of Appomattox arrived, they were released. Despite what Davis and some commanders felt, it was obvious to everyone in the ranks that the game was up.[137]

Among the men of the 3rd Tennessee Consolidated (formerly in the 19th Tennessee) at High Point, Private William J. Worsham noted, "The news of Lee's surrender and Johns[t]on's negotiations produced a feeling of sadness throughout the army. Although we were anxious for the war to end, yet we were hardly prepared for surrender. We had not calculated and looked into the depth of a surrender, the giving up as lost that for which we had fought for long and for which so many had given their lives, was indeed hard, and the idea grated like a harsh thunder, on our nerves."[138] Captain Foster of the 1st Texas Consolidated noted as follows in his journal over those few days:

> Still in camp. Clothing issued today. No one knows what Genls Johns[t]on and Sherman have done, yet all suppose it is a surrender.
> Everything very quiet. All hands talking about how they will go to Texas; and by what route he or they expect to go....

Davis house near Center, one of the few surviving wartime structures.

Discipline very loose. Everyone doing pretty much as he pleases; but if Genl Johns[t]on issues an order they will be on hand.

Still in camp. More clothing issued today, but still not enough. Had Battalion drill today just to see if the men would drill. Various rumors afloat in camp. Lees men from Virginia are passing us every day....[139]

One Confederate officer reported to army headquarters that "the whole of the 3d regt of the State Force has disbanded at Lexington, and gone home without orders. Of the two regiments here not a handful of men are left."[140] Private William A. Fletcher of the 8th Texas Cavalry (Terry's Texas Rangers) wrote, "In a few days there were about one hundred fifty of us started for home, without permission or parole. We rode out of the army lines at night — we had a Lieutenant as commander, and passed over country in some places that knew nothing of the ceasing of hostilities."[141]

Another Texan wrote to his sister: "This is a very critical time with us up here — we have no hope much of getting out of this place. Our army is nearly surrounded by overwhelming forces— For the last few days we have been expecting Genl Johnston to surrender this army. There is no other hope for it but to surrender.... I am firmly convinced of that fact."[142] He went on to state, "Night before last I attempted to make my escape through the lines— got ready about 2 o'clock at night, mounted my horse and started, but after-

The Craven House, General Hardee's headquarters, Trinity College. The home stood at the center of a vast Confederate campsite, all traces of which are gone.

wards changed my notion and concluded to wait one day longer to see the final issue of affairs...."[143] He added, "Thousands of the army have already left — men still going every night. About thirty of our boys have gone. The night I got ready to leave about sixty of the Company prepared to go with me but when I backed out and concluded to wait a day longer ... about half concluded not to go then also, while the remaining half went on."[144]

In the camp of Company C of the 13th North Carolina Artillery a unique drama unfolded. Company C consisted of two sections, one of which was with Johnston's army, the other with Lee's. A group of men made their escape from Appomattox before the surrender, coming south through Lynchburg and Danville to rejoin their comrades near Greensboro. Now it seemed that they had made the arduous trek for nothing. These men, knowing that Lee had surrendered, debated whether they were included in those terms. If they were, then they were paroled and free to go home. Moreover, if they continued to fight, it was a violation of their parole. In the end they decided to leave camp and go home, while their comrades in the other section of Company C watched them depart.[145]

South Carolinian William A. Johnson, camped along the Burlington Road near Stewart's headquarters, wrote, "More men going home. The army greatly demoralized. Still talk about surrendering. General Stueart [*sic*], pleads with the men who are leaving, as they pass his headquarters, to remain until they have orders to act upon. They refuse to remain or to fight anymore. For the past three days the road has been full of armed men leaving their commands and going home. No power to stop them short of a fight with them."[146]

Officers tried to maintain discipline and a sense of normalcy among their anxious troops. Musician William J. Worsham of the 3rd Tennessee Consolidated Regiment (formerly of the 19th Tennessee), camped at High Point, wrote of "daily drills and inspections to quiet the unrest."[147] Artilleryman Charles C. Jones of Savannah wrote:

> A spirit of dissatisfaction prevailed in the army in anticipation of its early surrender, and numerous desertions occurred, accompanied by constant thefts of the transportation and artillery animals. A strong guard was posted for the protection of the battery animals belonging to the Chatham Artillery, and in honor of the vigilance and the patriotism of this company be it remembered that during these darkest days of impending ruin, of privations, and of horrid suspense, there occurred not a single desertion from its ranks, or the loss of a battery animal.[148]

In the 40th Alabama, Sergeant John Cury observed great demoralization was manifest, especially among those so near to their homes as the Carolinians."[149] Sergeant Walter Clark of the 1st Georgia Consolidated (formerly of the 63rd Georgia), wrote from their camp at High Point that rumors were current that the army was to be surrendered and numbers of the troops left their commands, unwilling to submit to the seeming humiliation."[150]

General Alfred Iverson wrote from Greensboro that commanders reported to him of the "almost entire desertion of their troops" and stated most of the rest were "ready to desert." He continued: "I have no longer any more troops than are barely sufficient to guard stores. No further arrangements therefore can be made to organize stragglers."[151] He asked that "the first Brigade of organized troops arriving be put upon the duty of arresting all men without commands and that the officers along the road in rear to telegraph and to stop and organize all men leaving the army. The further to the rear this is done, the more success will be obtained."[152]

If the men of the Army of Tennessee hoped for relief or good news, they were to be bitterly disappointed. While they gained some much needed rest in their new campsites, and were, for the moment, out of reach of Sherman's forces, a growing mental strain, combined with lack of resources, conspired to make their last encampment anything but pleasant.

4

Funny Drunk, Gentlemanly Drunk, and Dog Drunk

General Johnston had successfully concentrated scattered forces from across the South, and across military boundaries, to strike Sherman's army at Bentonville, and pieced together an army from various commands. In the weeks afterwards he also took steps to improve the army's organization, transportation, and supply situation. Yet none of that mattered now as he prepared to meet his counterpart, General William T. Sherman. After obtaining permission from President Davis to meet with Sherman, Johnston prepared the following note:

> The results of the recent campaign in Virginia have changed the relative military condition of the belligerents. I am therefore induced to address you, in this form, the inquiry whether, in order to stop the further effusion of blood and devastation of property, you are willing to make a temporary suspension of active operations, and to communicate to Lieutenant-General Grant, commanding the armies of the United States, the request that he will take like action in regard to other armies— the object being, to permit the civil authorities to enter into the needful arrangements to terminate the existing war.[1]

Sherman received Johnston's note on the 14th and replied that he would meet with him. They agreed that they would each ride out from their lines on the morning of April 17th and meet on the Hillsborough Road.[2]

While the generals went to confer, unrest grew in the Confederate camps, as Captain William E. Stoney of General Hagood's South Carolina Brigade near Greensboro noted:

> Early in the day it was reported our army was to be surrendered. This rumor was at first disregarded, but presently began to assume shape and force. The wildest excitement seized the troops.... Colonel Rion immediately ordered the brigade into line and urged them not to leave. The enemy were now supposed to be not only in rear, but on both flanks, and it would be difficult to escape; that if any

considerable number left it might compromise the terms given to those that remained. The men seemed at this time ready to do anything that their officers advised, to march that night in the effort to cut their way out, or to remain and abide the issue where they were. All the afternoon the cavalry were passing us saying they "were going out." The infantry soon became almost frantic, and in every direction were rushing to beg, borrow, buy and steal horses.

Disorganization was complete. Horses carried off after plundering the wagons. The divisions supply train was thoroughly stripped. The flags of the brigade were burned by the men in the certainty of surrender. About dark an order came from army headquarters to keep the men together, but with that day the army perished — a mob remained.[3]

An artilleryman with the Beaufort Artillery (SC) reported that he and some others "planed to steal battery horses and join another command somewhere across the mountains, rather than surrender." Their plan was foiled when guards arrived to watch over their horses.[4]

In their camp at High Point, William Dixon of the 1st Georgia Consolidated noted the following:

Things seem to be drawing to a close. Rumors of all kind prevail today. Col Olmstead called the commanding officers together today stating from information received from Gen Smith, negotiations were now going on between Gen Johnston and Sherman for the surrender of our army, but nothing official was yet known. It is supposed the same terms granted Lees Army will be fixed upon. Nothing is now left us but the Trans Mississippi Dept. all the states east ... of it is over run by the enemy. Large lots of shoes and clothing were issued today. Each company was furnished with all the clothing and shoes they wanted so that we all look respectable now. All seem to wait patiently the result....[5]

Rumors also reached General Hardee, and he reported that morale was deteriorating rapidly in his corps. Many of his troops near New Salem, in northern Randolph County, were deserting, some taking horses with them.[6]

Both Union and Confederate troops took advantage of the cease-fire to rest and attend to that most important business of any soldier: scavenging for food. In Orange and Alamance counties, foraging parties often bumped into each other. Both groups having the same goal, they often assisted each other. Union troops also noted the large number of Lee's soldiers moving south through the region.[7] Major William C. Stevens of the 9th Michigan Cavalry wrote to his sister describing what he saw: "There are quite a number of confederate Officers here from Lee's army, and could you see them visiting and riding out with our Officers you would hardly believe they had been opposed to each other in deadly warfare for four years." William G. Bentley of the 104th Ohio agreed, noting, "It seemed odd to be on such good terms with them when each party were armed...."[8]

Union troops entered Raleigh and recorded their impressions of the city, the sixth Confederate state capital to fall to Sherman's troops. Nelson A. Pinney with the 104th Ohio noted, "Raleigh we found to be a very pretty and pleasant city, situated on high, rolling ground, with wide, clean streets, completely shaded by rows of beautiful dark-green oaks."[9]

In the meantime, Sherman left Durham Station with a small cavalry escort, riding west. They eventually met gray troopers from Hampton's command, escorting Johnston. Here the generals met and decided to go to a nearby home that Johnston had recently passed, the farm of James and Nancy Bennitt. Although both men had served in the army before the war, this was the first time that Joseph E. Johnston and William T. Sherman, long-time adversaries, had met in person.[10] While their escorts waited outside (and in the course of conversation, nearly came to blows) Sherman and Johnston sat down to work. Sherman began by informing Johnston of President Lincoln's assassination, which Johnston described as "the greatest possible calamity to the South" and assured Sherman the Confederate government had nothing to do with it.[11]

They were alone in the house and Sherman informed Johnston that as the Union government did not recognize the existence of the Confederate government, there could be no negotiations for peace by civil authorities. Affirming that he also wished to see the destruction and violence end, Sherman offered the same surrender terms granted to Lee the week before at Appomattox. The Confederate general countered with a broader, and quite radical, proposal — a general surrender that would end the whole war.

In Johnston's words, "[I]nstead of a partial suspension of hostilities, we might, as other generals had done, arrange the terms of a permanent peace." Believing that he was acting in the spirit of Lincoln's hope for a quick and smooth transition to peace, Sherman agreed. Both officers concurring, they decided to meet again the next day after Johnston informed President Davis of the results of the conference.[12]

During the night in Hillsborough, Johnston, along with General John C. Breckinridge, Postmaster John C. Reagan, and Governor Zebulon Vance, discussed terms to propose to Sherman. They produced several key points that would not only end the fighting here but end the war as a whole, restore peace, and keep the current state governments running. Not wishing to merely surrender, they took pains to propose terms that would end the war and restore the South with no punishment.[13]

When they met again on the 18th, Breckinridge accompanied Johnston at the Bennitt House. At first Sherman objected to a member of the Confederate government, but Johnston explained his role was not as secretary of war, but as a Confederate general. As they got down to business, Sherman

The Bennitt house. The reconstructed house commemorates the site of the meetings between Johnston and Sherman.

became agitated with the demands and conditions the Confederates placed on the terms. At one point he asked, "See here, gentlemen, just who is doing the surrendering, anyhow?"[14]

Sherman then wrote out terms he felt were appropriate. They allowed the southern army to march home and deposit their arms in their home states, recognized existing state governments, reestablished federal courts in these areas, and guaranteed property and political rights of the citizens. They were wide and sweeping terms. It was everything the two Confederates hoped for and more. Johnston readily agreed and both commanders signed off on these terms. After departing, Sherman sent a copy of his agreement to Washington for review by President Andrew Johnson, while General Johnston did the same, sending his news to President Davis.[15]

On the 18th more rumors began to spread among the Confederate soldiers about the meeting between Johnston and Sherman. Officers began to request confirmation from their superiors, "in view of the fact that there are many faithful men and officers who think they should have the information, so that they may consult their own judgment whether to accept the terms or not."[16]

William Fletcher of the 8th Texas Cavalry (Terry's Texas Rangers) wrote of the mood among his fellow troopers: "[A]ll hopes were gone, and the thought of returning home, defeated, seemed to be depicted on each face, and for a few days I don't think I saw a smile."[17] Captain W.H. Andrews with the 1st Georgia Regulars observed, "The 18th day of April, 1865, General Johnston was in command of a well disciplined army who had but a short time before at Bentonville fought one of the hardest battles of the war, but on the 19th his army was a thing of the past, so far as discipline was concerned."[18]

Upon hearing the news, artilleryman Charles W. Hutson wrote, "I am sick at heart. The whole thing seemed sometimes a fearful dream too horrible to be real. Still we must bear our fate manfully & keep ever ready to renew the struggle, when the right moment comes. Many of us have been deliberating as to whether it would not be best to escape."[19] He "had decided with Bill Colcock to make our way out on one of the battery horses before the surrender; but the horses have been put under an infantry guard, & that intention is knocked in the head. Keith & I then cast our eyes upon the mules; but they have also been put under a guard."[20]

One soldier in the 2nd South Carolina Consolidated wrote simply in his diary, "men demoralized." Upon learning of the details of the surrender in their camp along the Burlington Road outside of Greensboro, he wrote, "We must be in a sorry plight when our leaders agree to such terms."[21] D. Augustus Dickert of Kennedy's Brigade wrote, "The thought of grounding their arms to an enemy never before entered their minds, and when the news came of a surrender the greatest apprehension and dread seized all." He added, "Men began to leave the army by twos and by squads. Guards were placed on all roads and around camps, and the strictest orders were given against leaving the army without leave.[22]

Sumner Cunningham of the 3rd Tennessee Consolidated described the reaction in his camp:

> By night, the excitement became intense. We had never before heard any mutterings against Johnston. Before, everything that he did was right, but now it was different. That Johnston would dare surrender us to Sherman and without a fight, and when he was not compelled to, and when we had whipped him and could do it again.... They would then collect in crowds and go to the different General quarters, and those from Arkansas and Texas were the most sought after, and protest against being surrendered, and demanded of them to lead them across the Mississippi. This was kept up until midnight and probably past.
>
> The Generals would advise and urge them to be calm and await events; that Johnston would do right; that there was no treachery in his nature; that they themselves did not know what was being done, but they would abide by whatever Johnston did. That they had full confidence in his integrity, and knew that

The graves of George Ashley, 44th Tennessee, and George Mims, 10th Tennessee, at New Providence Church. These men died while camped nearby. The graves are one of the few reminders of the large campsites in the area.

he would do what was for the best, and would tell them that it was their duty to abide by the action of their commander.

The next morning all were more calm and not so much excited, but would collect in large crowds, and go to the different Generals, to learn the news, and what was being done, and many of those who on the day before were most violently opposed to surrender, began to see it in the proper light, and commending the wisdom of Johnston in seeking the opportunity to surrender without the further sacrifice of life. Further strife was useless.

In two or three days more, the news was received that we were surrendered, and the terms were made known to us. All were surprised and gratified at the liberality of the terms. Johnston has always received the credit and gratitude of the army and people for suggesting those terms.[23]

Captain Stoney of South Carolina recorded his impressions after receiving news of the cease-fire:

No one who has not seen and mixed with demoralized troops will be disposed to credit my statement that this announcement appeared unwelcome to many of the men. They regretted to have to remain in camp a few days longer, although the difference was between going home as prisoners of war on parole or as freemen under an honorable peace. This was undoubtedly the prevailing sentiment with the mass. Others drew high hopes from the expression underscored in the official copy, "the two governments." Recognition of independence was deduced from it, whatever minor terms might be agreed upon, and when later in the evening a courier from corps headquarters reported the news ... that peace was declared, and upon the most favorable terms, we were in the highest spirits. The impression prevails that the United States has become embroiled with France in the matter of Mexico, and that our independence is recognized on condition of an alliance offensive and defensive between the North and South.

The next day he wrote, "Nothing definite as to the terms of the impending peace. The universal sentiment of the brigade is opposed to anything like submission or reconstruction of the accursed Union. The feeling, I noticed the other day, I am sure arose from no desire of giving up the Cause, but going home as prisoners of war included in their minds the sequence of exchange and renewal of the struggle."[24]

Louisianan Taylor Beatty wrote in his diary it was "rumored that Grant has assumed the Dictatorship of U.S. and will settle with us—said he has recognized us. Day before & yesterday were very cold days, nearly enough for a frost. Today is warmer." He continued:

For last week we have hear daily sorts of exciting rumors—that peace was made & we are to return to Union—question of slavery to be left to Southern States—that this has been rejected by Andy Johnson—Prest. of U.S.—that France & U.S. have gotten into difficulty & that an engagement had taken place in Gulf of Mexico—in which French were successful—Now we have it that Genl. Johnston has surrendered or disbanded his army—I expect that this will take place—We have not means of continuing this contest this side of Miss. River—But over in the West the contest can be prolonged. It looks to me as if our government is paralyzed—No orders have been issued of late.[25]

He wondered, "What am I to do—The terms promised protection to all prisoners who will obey law in force where they reside—What laws are in force in La.—I don't know."

Johnston himself wrote that "the armistice ... produced great uneasiness in the army. It was very commonly believed among the soldiers that there was to be a surrender, by which they would be prisoners of war, to which they were very averse. This apprehension caused a great number of desertions between the 19th and 24th of April—not less than four thousand in the infantry and artillery, and almost as many from the cavalry; many of them rode off artillery horse, and mules belonging to the baggage—trains." After returning from the meeting, Johnston announced the news to the army in General Orders #14.[26] Lieutenant Edwin Rennolds of the 5th Tennessee wrote of it:

I have never witnessed such a scene as that which presented itself, when it became fully known that we were to lay down our arms. All phases of human feeling were exhibited. Some raved and swore that they would never submit to it. Some paced back and forth like caged lions. Some seated themselves on logs and buried their faces in their hands. Some wept like children, and the faces of others took on a look of stolid and stoical submission, and others still looked on at this unusual exhibition of emotions with feelings of wonder and astonishment.[27]

April 18 also saw paroled men from Lee's army beginning to pass through the camps of the Army of Tennessee on their way home. The men of the 12th Louisiana demanded an explanation of the rumors. A soldier with the 58th North Carolina, camped east of Buffalo Creek along the Burlington Road, wrote that the "regiment was melting away." Johnston himself estimated the desertion losses at 8,000 men; it is impossible to know for sure.[28] Captain Stoney of South Carolina wrote on this day, "Demoralization ... is utter and complete; there is no spark of fight left in the troops. Our remaining supplies of commissary and quartermaster store are fully issued but forage for the animals is failing."[29]

News of the impending surrender granted one lucky soldier a reprieve. Colonel Larack P. Thomas of the 42nd Georgia recalled the incident:

A soldier (his regiment and name I have forgotten) had been tried by a court-marital for desertion. He was a young fellow, and had not been long with his command; but the strictest discipline was necessarily in force, and the sentence was death. He was to be executed that very day near Greensboro. The detail of men had been made, the time and place selected where he was to be legally executed (shot to death) under military order. His position had been taken, the soldiers were drawn up in front to do the firing, when a dashing young officer from the army headquarters was seen in the distance riding at breakneck speed and waving the pardon from the general commanding just in time to save the life of the poor fellow.[30]

William Pollard of Tennessee summed up the feeling of many troops when he wrote, "Oh, the suspense! I am miserable thinking of our future."[31] An artilleryman from Stewart's Corps recorded that the soldiers debated their options, and many chose to "endeavor to make our way home and thence to Texas without being hampered by the Paroles."[32] Musician Albert Q. Porter of Mississippi wrote from his camp about five miles from Greensboro: "A great many Souldiers have left the army and gone home. One whole Brig. and a Regt. left yesterday. There was an appeal read to the souldiers to day from Gen. Louring to not take any ill advised measures, but to stand by their colours intact and that their higher officers would see that they had their rights. He begged them not to desert the flag that they had been fighting [for] so gallantly during 4 long years."[33]

While the officers met and discussed strategy and options, the common soldiers faced boredom and nerve-racking uncertainty. They also endured the miserable spring weather. William Dixon of the 1st Georgia Consolidated noted the effects of a storm one evening: "Had a heavy blow and rain which carried away the most of our temporary shelters. It lasted about one hour." No doubt the strong storm drenched the men, turned campsites into quagmires, and soaked everyone's equipment. For the men without shelter it was a miserable night.[34] Some of the misery was man-made. Bromfield Ridley recorded, "a band of marauding soldiers visited our camp this morning and coolly helped themselves to some leather and goods that we had quietly secured from the Quarter Master's Department." No doubt there were hundreds of similar instances of theft and robbery.[35]

J. A. Wilson of the 3rd Tennessee Consolidated (formerly the 24th Tennessee) was one who didn't hesitate to make his decision. He wrote, "I left the army at Greensboro, N.C. intending to cross to the west of Mississippi river and join Kirby Smith." Wilson did not make it all the way, as he explains: "A citizen friend of mine told me I was making a fool of myself, for me to go back ... to Tenn." He did so, getting a parole on the way.[36] Lieutenant Colonel James W. Brown of North Carolina wrote, "The report of our having to capitulate is now believed, and it is immense desertion to avoid the humiliation.... The men are terribly depressed, and since dark have been calling on all their comd'g officers for speeches to tell them of the situation."[37]

General Beauregard wrote to Johnston that should his negotiations result in the army's surrender, he should try to arrange for the right of the troops to march home, be mustered out, and deposit their regimental flags in the state capitals.[38]

Lieutenant Halcott P. Jones, with the 13th Battalion, North Carolina Artillery, was moving north with his unit to join the Army of Tennessee, having evacuated their coastal fortifications. As they moved up through the wake of Sherman's march, they encountered refugees and separated soldiers. He wrote, "Rumors of all kinds were very plentiful on the entire march after leaving Cape Fear."[39] Morale plummeted among these men who were traveling blindly through the countryside and facing uncertainty. Nineteen men deserted a few days after this entry.[40] That night Tennessean Alfred Tyler Fielder wrote that he stayed at the home of a friend he knew before the war. It was a restless night, as "I stood guard until midnight to keep the solders from breaking into my friend Garrett's slave houses."[41]

Early on the 19th Johnston arrived back in Greensboro, where he learned that the money of the Confederate treasury was present in the city. Davis had left instructions for the $39,000 to be sent on to Charlotte, where he was headed, but Johnston felt it was only right to pay the men who had labored so long without compensation.[42] The commanding general also occupied himself with overseeing the setup of supply depots at the railroad stations between Charlotte, North Carolina, and Augusta, Georgia. Several hundred wagons arrived from Georgia, and Johnston made efforts to reestablish a line of supply and repair the depots, bridges, and rail yards along his line of supply to the southwest.[43]

Other issues plagued Johnston's already over-taxed mind. Governor Vance wrote to complain about the looting committed earlier that week. Over half of the supplies of pants, jackets, blankets, cloth, socks, and leather "was violently seized or issued miscellaneously under the threat of the mob...." He also noted that "the books, papers, and private property of the quartermaster were stolen and destroyed."[44]

Looting was not confined to Greensboro, for in Graham a mob of soldiers took 6,000 pairs of pants, 7,000 pounds of leather, over 2,000 blankets, and 2,000 yards of jean cloth. Citizens also participated. The governor witnessed the attacking of a train at McLean's Station, by soldiers "laden with blankets and leather.... The woods were crowded with soldiers staggering under heavy loads of the plunder."[45] Vance appealed for protection for the state's citizens and for the state's supplies. He feared for the protection of the state's treasury, archives, banks, and railroad property. The looting was so bad, he said, "it seems impossible to stop them." Johnston responded by placing guards at the railroad facilities at Company Shops (modern-day Burlington).[46]

In the meantime, uneasiness and rumors continued among the soldiers. Captain James Tillman of the 16th & 24th South Carolina wrote that "rumor yet walks majestically through the army." Captain Stoney of Hagood's South Carolina Brigade reported:

> There being reason to think that many of the brigade were contemplating leaving for home, Colonel Rion issued a circular advising them to remain to the end. Immediately the whole command collected at headquarters to hear more fully from him. He addressed them at length. He stated the position of affairs, as far as known to him, and urged that their departure would be a violation of the truce, compromising their personal safety, compromising General Johnston, and finally compromising their personal honor.

Despite this plea, the next day he noted, "Seven men of the Seventh battalion and fifteen men of the Twenty-seventh regiment left for home yesterday and today. The division is being rapidly reduced in this way. They are going in large bodies and at all hours without an effort being made to stop them." Later he noted, "Desertion on the increase throughout the army. Thirty men and one officer ... of our brigade, left yesterday."[47]

In Greensboro, Presbyterian minister Jacob H. Smith reported that deserters were "steadily passing all day from east to west through town" on the Salisbury Road. Smith spent nearly every day visiting the Confederate camps and preaching to the soldiers in their camps scattered around the county or to the wounded in hospitals. Smith also visited General D.H. Hill and preached to his headquarters south of town.[48]

William Pollard of a Tennessee unit wrote, "I went to the first consolidated Arkansas regiment on dress parade, as I thought it would be my last opportunity to see a confederate regiment on dress parade. As I thought of the past and looked into the future, I could scarcely keep back the tears." He later added that they were "guarding our horses to keep them from being stolen."[49] Captain Samuel Foster of the 1st Texas Consolidated Regiment recorded his thoughts and observations over these few days:

> Another report is we go back into the Union and free all the slaves in ... years.... All hands talking politics and making peace.
>
> Soon after we arrive at our new camp today some of our men found two barrels of Old Apple brandy buried under the root of an old pine tree that had blown down. One barrel of it was brought to Our Brigade and tap[p]ed — Every one helped themselves, and of course some get funny, some get tight some get gentlemanly drunk and some get dog drunk, of this latter class are all the officers from our Maj up. Kept up a noise nearly all night, but no one gets mad — all in good humor.
>
> Rumor today says we are to go back into the Union, but as that is not the kind of news we want to hear, we don't believe a word of it. What have we been fighting all these years for? Oh no — no more Union for us.[50]

Over these same days a South Carolinian noted events in the camp of the 2nd Consolidated Regiment: "Fifty men left our regt. last night for home." Another entry noted, "45 men left our regt. last night."[51]

Some troops were employed in routine duties and managed to stay busy during this time period. The 7th North Carolina, according to one soldier, "was sent to repair the railroad bridge across Deep River at Jamestown, recently burned by Stoneman's Raiders."[52] The North Carolinians camped along the Salisbury Road, now Lexington Avenue in High Point, not far from today's High Point Museum. Artifacts have been found in the vicinity, including unfired minie balls, buttons, silverware, coins, heel plates for shoes, knapsack hooks, horseshoes, and other small metal items.[53] The variety of items are typical of what would be found in a camp. Among the North Carolina and Confederate buttons were United States eagle buttons. This is expected, as Confederates used captured Union clothing throughout the war.[54] Also of interest, a mechanical pencil was found here. Evidence of what soldiers did in camp may be found in a button made from melted lead. Some holes had many minie balls, one had fourteen, suggesting that the Confederates dumped out their ammunition before departing.[55]

Other Confederate troops camped further along modern Lexington Avenue, where High Point University now stands, and near the railroad depot

Railroad bridge over the Deep River at Jamestown. Men of the 7th North Carolina repaired this bridge during the anxious days of April 1865.

in town. High Point, like Greensboro, was flooded with refugees. Many fled there from New Bern and other eastern areas that had fallen to Union forces.[56] While no doubt the presence of the soldiers caused tension and anxiety among the civilians, some troops showed kindness to the residents. Confederate soldiers shared their food with one local boy who visited the Confederate camps along Lexington Avenue.[57]

About this time news of Lincoln's assassination reached the Confederate troops camped around Greensboro. William Dixon of the 1st Georgia Consolidated wrote, "The assassination of Pres Lincoln US and Secretary W.H. Seward US at Washington Theater is reported today."[58]

Captain William Stoney of South Carolina noted "a strange rumor in camp that Lincoln has been assassinated." Texas Captain Samuel Foster wrote, "We hear it reported on very good authority that the President of the U S M Lincoln was killed a few nights ago in Washington, and that about the same time Seward was shot at and mortally wounded."[59] Musician Albert Porter with the 33rd Mississippi wrote on the 20th, "The news in regard to the death of Abraham Lincoln is confirmed." (That evening the band was invited to serenade some women who lived six miles from camp and one mile beyond Greensboro. He wrote of the event, "We passed through Greensburrow on

Burlington Road campsites. Elements of General Stewart's Corps camped here.

our way. It is a very pretty place. On our way back we stopped at a Gentleman's house in town and played several tunes. He gave us some of as good peach brandy as I ever drank after which we came back to camp, getting in at 12 o'clock."[60])

The news of the assassination enraged the Union troops spread out across North Carolina. Corporal Joseph Crowther of the 128th New York noted on the 21st, "Today we received the official news of the assassination of President Lincoln and the attempts of Secretary Seward and Son. As soon as the news reached here nearly every house in Goldsboro was dressed in mourning. It seemed to affect everybody. On the receipt of this news the soldiers all seemed to be more anxious for the war to keep on than to have peace, until every traitor in the country was slayed. A number of guerillas came to our lines today and give themselves up." The next day he noted, "Guns was fired every half hours at this place for 24 hours for the death of President Lincoln."[61]

More bad news was in store for General Johnston, for in the meantime the terms of surrender had met with disapproval in Washington. Secretary of war Edwin M. Stanton condemned them, noting that Sherman had exceeded his authority by engaging in political issues, rather than purely military affairs. He had no authority, argued Stanton, to discuss the reentry of states into the union, and the status of their governments, courts, and other nonmilitary issues. The bitter mood in Washington following Lincoln's death did not help matters.

By now the deserters from the Army of Tennessee were well on their way home. Col. David G. MacIntosh noted from Charlotte he "met also constantly squads of men from Johnston's Army mostly cavalry who were rambling about, said that they were on their way home, that Johnston's Army was surrendered or disbanded." The steady stream of deserters moving southwest brought news of the chaos, and despair to regions that had yet to get official word of actions and negotiations at Greensboro.[62]

On April 23 Sherman had a surprise visit from his friend and commander, Ulysses S. Grant, with news that his terms were not approved. Grant arrived in Raleigh, having come from Washington to directly oversee Sherman's negotiations with the Confederates. General Sherman was shocked that his terms had been disapproved, but the real outrage was his treatment in the press. Sherman was a victim of bad timing, for his lenient terms met with outrage among a people and Congress still in shock from Lincoln's assassination.[63] The next day Johnston received word that Davis had approved of the terms, just as Sherman was preparing to inform him that his government had rejected them. Sherman and Johnston communicated again, suddenly realizing that the war was back on, as the cease-fire was ended.[64]

In the camp of the 1st Georgia Consolidated, William Dixon noted, "It has been clear and pleasant after a heavy white frost last night. Had Battalion Drill. There was a little rebellious spirit evinced today, the men not wanting to drill. It died out. They think of nothing but going home. Col. Olmstead spoke to them at Dress Parade and it had a good effect."[65] The next day he noted,

> Company Commanders were notified to day that Gen Sherman had notified Gen Johnston that the cessation of hostilities ceased tomorrow the 26th inst at 11 oclock. It is the first we know of the limit of the armistice. We are ordered to be ready for any move. It has caused a great excitement in the Brigade. I would not be surprised to hear of a great many diserting as they say they are going home. I am satisfied that the army would not make a half right if brought to it such is the demoralized condition of it. Allmost the whole of Hokes NC has gone and many other command in the same fix. My firm believe is that if hostilities are resumed the army would be lost in the first fight. Long faces are plentiful as their dreams of home seem to vanish. Ammunition was distributed to all. Any quantity of grape vine [rumor] afloat…. After Brigade inspection I done a little washing as my clothing needed it badly. Dress Parade finished the day.[66]

Dixon's prediction proved to be true, as he recorded: "Each night crowds leave stealing all the mules and horses they can lay their hands on, so that a guard has to be kept over the stock. We lost four men from the regiment last night and it will continue as they get nearer their homes. I feel sad when I see the turn things are taking as they cannot continue in the present state long."[67]

Orders went out from both headquarters to prepare for hostilities to resume. William H. Andrews recalled the situation of the 1st Georgia Regulars:

[We] marched six miles beyond Greensboro where we went into camps. While on the march thousands of men left their guns by the roadside. Could have followed the line of march by the abandoned guns. The march was simply a rabble. No order, ranks scattered from one side of the road to the other. When we halted at night, the men were notified that all without guns would be arrested. That did not have any effect. Orders were then issued that all men without guns would not be allowed to draw rations. That order cooked their goose and you ought to have seen them making back for a gun.[68]

In the 3rd Tennessee Consolidated, Sumner Cunningham wrote:

Our surprise can only be imagined, when one morning we were ordered to march; and that Jeff. Davis would not approve the terms of surrender, and that hostilities must be again commenced. It is strange to contemplate the sudden changes that men can undergo in their views and opinions. Only a few days before, the army would not think of surrender, and now we would have thought that they would have rejoined at the prospect of continuing hostilities, but not so.

Jefferson Davis was cursed on all sides, and it was not until the next day that we learned the true cause of the rejection of the cartel, and about the same time we received the news of Lincoln's assassination. We considered it a great calamity to us.[69]

The 1st Georgia Consolidated moved out, and William Dixon recalled their movements: "The truce expired at 11 Oclock at which hour we were all ready moving off on the Greensboro road, then on the Jamestown road, from there to the Saulsbury road on which we marched the rest of the day 13 miles bivouacking at dark. The roads were dusty but in good condition. Plenty of grape vine [rumors] afloat but nothing reliable, but it serves to make the men worse and worse."[70] Captain W.H. Andrews of the same unit noted that, "Any one who saw the troops march through Greensboro could have told we no longer had an army."[71] Captain William Stoney noted, "Informed that the truce would terminate at 11 o'clock tomorrow. Received orders to be ready to move at that time. Men still leaving in crowds. Our brigade lost thirty-nine, all from Seventh battalion."[72] Artilleryman D.E. Huger Smith noted from his camp near Greensboro that "the rank and file of Johnston's army did not intend to do any more fighting." He observed soldiers placing percussion caps along the rails that exploded when trains ran over them.[73]

At 7 o'clock in the morning Major Archer Anderson of General Johnston's staff sent out orders to Generals Hardee, S.D. Lee, and Stewart informing them that if the truce was renewed, "I will let you know immediately." In the meantime they were to march out of camp at 11 o'clock and prepare to engage.[74]

Once those orders came, the army lurched into motion. But from their camp at High Point, Captain Stoney recalled seeing the following:

> Marched at 11 A.M. May I ever be spared such a sight as I witnessed when the order to move was given. Whole regiments remained on the ground, refusing to obey. In the last ten days desertion had reduced Kirkland's brigade from 1,600 to 300 men; Clingman's and the brigade of junior reserves from the same cause were each no stronger; Hagood's and Colquitt's brigades had suffered, but not so much. Now not more than forty men in each brigade followed Kirkland and Clingman from the ground. Officers as high as colonels, not only countenanced, but participated in the shameful conduct. Major Holland, of the North Carolina troops, formerly attached to our brigade, went off with all his men, and officers of higher rank did the same. Hagood's brigade here left forty men; Colquitt's about two hundred. These command being from South Carolina and Georgia, are willing to hold together while movement is towards their homes. I fear a march in another direction would equally reduce their numbers. For all this demoralization I must hold our higher officers responsible. All the sensational reports which have so loosened the band of discipline originate at their headquarters, and many of them are playing first hands in the shameless appropriation of public property that is going on. This last remark applies principally to General Hardee's headquarters, and much feeling is elicited among the troops by the appropriation there of supplies intended for and much needed by them. Halted on the Trinity College road five and a half miles from Trinity, having marched ten miles.[75]

In Greensboro, South Carolina artilleryman Daniel Dantzler recorded that, upon learning of the failed truce, "the men are all gloomy and despondent." He did manage to obtain food from the Bumpass family, whose large home still stands on Mendenhall Street.[76] Dantlzer wrote about roaming the streets of town begging for food. At one imposing house they had good luck: "We did not want to go in, we were so dirty. But they insisted and took us into a nice parlor and entertained us in royal style ... and invited us in the dining room where a nice lunch was spread with hot coffee."[77]

Lieutenant Joseph F. Waring of the Jeff Davis (MS) Cavalry noted that the news did not sit well with his troopers. "The bullet dodgers are rampant," he recorded.[78] In the Chatham Artillery (GA), Charles Jones wrote, "In anticipation of a renewal of hostilities the Confederate army was put in motion on the morning of the 26th, and while upon the march some four miles from the village of Greensboro, the news of the surrender of the Confederate forces

The Troy Bumpass house. Several Confederate soldiers received food here.

under Gen. Johnston was received. The column halted, and the Battery was parked."[79] Captain Foster of the 1st Texas noted the report is that we go to fighting again, that Genl Johnson can't make any terms but submission reunion free negroes &, and we have been fighting too long for that. I have not seen a man today but says fight on rather than submit."[80]

Civilians observed the army staggering into motion. Recorded one:

> Immediately the Confederate army was put in motion and moved from the eastern part of the town where it had been principle encamped. We thought the "horrid front" of war was again about to present itself to our afflicted vision and that this part of our country overrun by both armies. But the army only moved one day and camped some distance west of the town. As the army moved through the streets with streaming banners and martial music — cheering and joking, the old war-worn veterans seemed determined to put on the best face they could — and as they passed by me one of them bade me adieu by saying "Good-bye Mister! If I never return this mule's yourn."[81]

Yet Johnston's army was almost beyond fighting; the men were demoralized and it had yet to experience combat in its newly minted state. Having passed so many trials already, and devastated by the news of the fall of Richmond and Lee's surrender, most were simply not willing to risk their lives one more time. Both Johnston and Sherman realized that they needed to act quickly to establish another truce and renegotiate. Not wanting the war to continue, in subsequent letters the two commanding generals agreed to meet the next day at the same location.

On April 26th, back at the Bennitt farmhouse, there was no doubt as to what the terms would be. With no room to negotiate, Johnston agreed to the terms that Grant had written at Appomattox. While satisfied, Johnston had some unresolved concerns that these points did not address. General John M. Schofield, who had accompanied Sherman, suggested some amendments and they were quickly agreed on.[82] The Supplemental Terms to the Military Convention of April 26 stated the following:

1. The field transportation to be loaned to the troops for their march to their homes, and for subsequent use in their industrial pursuits. Artillery-horses may be used in field-transportation, if necessary.

2. Each brigade or separate body to retain a number of arms equal to *one-seventh* of its effective strength, which, when the troops reach the capitals of their States, will be disposed of as the general commanding the Department may direct.

3. Private horses, and other private property of both officers and me, to be retained by them.

4. The commanding general of the Military Division of West Mississippi, Major-General Canby, will be requested to give transportation by water, from Mobile or New Orleans, to the troops from Arkansas and Texas.

5. The obligations of officers and soldiers to be signed by their immediate commanders.

6. Naval forces within the limits of General Johnston's command to be included in the terms of this convention.[83]

The terms were similar to those given at Appomattox, allowing officers to keep sidearms and men to retain their horses and private property, but they were also more generous in allowing the soldiers to keep a portion of their weapons and use the army's wagons for transportation. The agreement not only saw to the disbandment of the army, but also to the transportation, protection, and supply of the men as they journeyed home.[84]

Lieutenant Albert B. Coleman of General Sherman's staff wrote the final copies of the terms. He managed to get the pen, holder, and inkstand that the generals used. He also tried to purchase Mr. Bennit's table, "but the old fellow could not be induced to part with it."[85] Grant, waiting in Raleigh, approved these terms and made for Washington with the news. Sherman soon departed for Raleigh, Wilmington, and other points as he dealt with issues regarding the occupation of the Carolinas. In his absence Major General John Schofield assumed command and oversaw the surrender proceedings.[86]

One of Sherman's first orders upon returning to his headquarters was for 250,000 rations readied to be sent to the Confederates. The major obstacle was the poor condition of the railroads running through that part of the state. In areas already under Union control, northern troops were issuing rations to "destitute" civilians, who had to prove they were in need of relief.[87] Following this agreement, orders came out from Confederate headquarters setting the process into motion. Archer Anderson, Johnston's aide, who had sent out marching orders at 7 o'clock, sent out new instructions from Beauregard at 1:30 that afternoon, telling the corps commanders to "halt and go into camp on the ground most convenient for receiving supplies."[88] More detailed instructions soon followed:

> Corps commanders will immediately send to the Ord. Officer at Greensboro under charge of Ord. Officers four-fifths of the small arms, accoutrements and ammunition....
> The field transportation of the army belongs to the Troops and at the end of the march will be fairly distributed amongst the Officers and men of each organization.
> By order of General Johnston[89]

The first Confederate soldiers to hear of the new agreement were the cavalry of Butler's division at Hillsboro, who learned of it as Johnston returned on the evening of the 26th. Men had been deserting for days, and now it looked as if all order would be lost.[90]

Cobb's Legion, along with the Jeff Davis's Legion, Phillips' Legion and 10th Georgia Cavalry, were camped just outside of town. According to Sergeant Charles Hansell of the 10th Georgia, "a rumor gained currency in our camp that we had all been surrendered as prisoners of war unconditionally. Many of the men began making preparations to leave and were nearly ready to start for home."[91] Sergeant John S. Wise of Virginia wrote of it:

> The spirit of Johnston's men was much finer than, under the circumstances any body would have expected. They were defiant, and more than ready to try conclusion with Sherman in a pitched battle. Many expressed disgust and indignation when the surrender of the army was announced. An epidemic of drunkenness, gambling, and fighting prevailed while we were waiting for our final orders. Whatever difficulty General Breckinridge may have experienced in procuring liquor, the soldiers seemed to have an abundance of colorless cornwhiskey and applejack, and the roadsides were lined with "chuck-a-luck" games. The amount of Confederate money displayed was marvelous. Men had it by the haversackful, and bet it recklessly upon anything. The ill-temper begotten by drinking and gambling manifested itself almost hourly in free fights."[92]

Catching wind of the situation, Colonel Gilbert J. Wright, commanding Young's Brigade of Cavalry, assembled the men and gave firm orders against any more desertion. Sergeant Hansel wrote, "That settled it, for the whole brigade was more afraid of him than of the Yankees. Those who had gone so far as to saddle up slipped quietly back, took off the saddles, and 'didn't intend to go, noway.'"[93]

Later that evening they moved out under orders, and Hansell recalled that the town clock in Hillsborough was striking eleven o'clock. At Company Shops, they dismounted and gathered around Wright. Here he told them that wagons were ready, and those who wished to go on to the Trans-Mississippi to continue fighting could go with him. General Wade Hampton then rode up, and again gathered the men, explaining he had tried to exempt the cavalry from the surrender but it could not be done. Riding on to Greensboro, the men were "dead for sleep." Outside of Greensboro on May 2 at noon they received paroles. Before leaving for home they attempted to find pasture for the horses, there being no feed to be had.[94]

Hampton did his utmost to gather a force and move west to continue the war. J.W. Evans with Phillips' Legion recalled that he "made a speech, called for volunteers to cross the river and join Kirby Smith, but said any who wished might remain and be paroled, which most of them did." At the time, General Kirby Smith commanded Confederate forces in the Trans-Mississippi Department, consisting of Arkansas and Texas. It was assumed that Davis, and anyone else who wanted to make a stand, was headed that way.

Evans and his comrades intended to leave and fight on. He wrote, "Our plans were to go in squads, not over five or six in a squad, and meet Hampton on the Etowah, near Rome, Ga., and there he would take command and push on to join Smith and fight it out." His plans were foiled when their group was captured by Union cavalry.[95] George Guild of the 4th Tennessee Cavalry at Hillsborough wrote that the men were "dazed" by news of their surrender. They had been camped there for ten days, waiting for news or battle orders. The downtime gave the men a chance to ponder their situation. Guild wrote, "In the meantime the men took time to reflect, and had about settled down to the conclusion, often weighing all the facts, that this was about as favorable as they could expect."[96]

The men from the far corners of the Confederacy decided to leave and fight on. Guild noted that most of the 3rd Arkansas Cavalry, and 8th and 10th Texas cavalries left: "They tried to persuade the Fourth Tennessee to go with them on account of the ties of true comradeship that had existed between them so long and during such trying scenes as they had shared together. A few did go, but better counsels prevailed, and the body of them remained." The Tennesseans spent the rest of their time exchanging addresses and thinking of home.[97] Cavalryman Lieutenant Clay Reynolds wrote of the uncertainty he and his man faced:

One night they came to my camp, a place where we had stopped for several days, and told me all that they had heard about the probability of the surrender. They feared that they would lose their horses and arms, as was experienced with other unpleasant treatments. I assured them that, if I saw surrender was about to take place, I would move with them myself. I reminded them that I had as much and even more to fear than they, and promised I would find out the next day if there was anything in these reports. I went to General Wheeler's quarters the next morning, and there learned that he with several officers had gone to the front for some purpose; no one could tell me what. So that night my men came to me again, more uneasy still. I again went in search of General Wheeler — also General Allen. They both assured me that they would not surrender: and General Wheeler remarked that, if this army surrendered we'd go cross the Mississippi River and join the troops over there and continue the fight. I told him that we'd go with him but that we could not afford to stay here and surrender. At that time my scouts had a large fine wagon with six fine mules hitched to it in which we carried our baggage. All, even the driver, had been captured from the enemy. After seeing the alarm of my men, I proposed to them that we should quietly withdraw from the place the army was now lying and go back some distance and camp until we saw what could be done.[98]

David M. Sadler of the 11th Texas Cavalry recalled his experiences of that day:

We had been on rear guard for three or four days and nights, and on the morning of April 26, 1865, just at dawn of day, a scout came into camp. They had found a barrel which contained some gallons of apple jack and had put some in a water bucket and the balance in a wash tub.

We had camped along a hedge row, into which we had crawled to sleep. We were not up when the scout came in and called out "Apple Jack!" but we were very soon out, and before the cups had gone around the outer pickets fired. Of course, we could not pour the jack out ... so we drank it in a hurry, and mounted our horses. The enemy was on us, and the scrap began. We divided our command into two squadrons — about fifty men each. The squadron next to the enemy would stay in line until the enemy would charge. Each man would empty one six-shooter, then fall back behind the other squadron and take a position. We were more or less exhilarated — probably more than less. The enemy came up vigorously, swift, and strong, in charge after charge — for we did not have to wait long for them. Business was good.

In the course of an hour there developed a third squadron, which was more than exhilarated, fairly lubricated; for, when a squadron would fire, which would always check the enemy, the lubricated squadron would countercharge, and sometimes in close six-shooter range.

My squadron took a position behind a small field on the left-hand side of the road — the field was, say 150 or 200 yards wide. We were on a hillside, six miles from Chapel Hill. We had waited longer than usual, when a Yank hallooed on the other side of the field: "Hello Johnny; don't shoot! We want to make peace with you." We hallooed back, "All right." Then he rode out in the fence corner in plain view and hallooed: "Johnny, what command is that?" "The Eleventh Texas." He hallooed back: "What is the matter with you boys this morning?" "We are drunk and reckless and if you want to fight come over!"[99]

He continues:

> In a few minutes we turned out of line and went back. Soon we came to General Wheeler and other officers, and went into camp on a hillside among small trees. Toward night word came that General Johnston had surrendered and that in the morning we would have to stack arms. Our camp was turned into a camp of mourning; men and officers mingled their tears together. Old, weather-beaten and battle-scarred soldiers who had prided themselves their six-shooters, horses, and valor as soldiers, threw their belts aside as something to get rid of, and wept like whipped children.[100]

Staff officer Bromfield Ridley of General Stewart's staff noted, "The eagerness of the men to get to their home now is beyond picture." He noted that his command was near a copper mine not far from Hill's Point.[101]

Here, as elsewhere in the camps of the Army of Tennessee, men found hidden supplies of liquor. Guild observed, "The pine woods of North Carolina were flooded with old applejack, and the soldiers, of course, got their full supply of it."[102] The chaos and uncertainty in the Confederate camps must have been immense. In twenty-four hours they had gone from bracing for combat to surrendering and going home. One moment they were soldiers, the next, civilians. The transition, even for the most accepting, was not easy. Alfred Tyler Fielder of the 2nd Consolidated Tennessee Regiment commented:

> We were almost heartbroken to think of being defeated after the terrible struggle and returning home conquered. We were yet subject to orders and had to wait until all things were ready before we could start. We decided to go to General Cheatham's quarters and call on him for a few words of encouragement. He finally consented and addressed fellow Comrades and advised us to return to our dilapidated homes, obey the laws, made good, true loyal citizens to the Untied States government as we had to the Confederate Government on many battle fields.[103]

Unfortunately the news of the final surrender traveled unevenly. George P. Wilson of the 1st Tennessee Consolidated wrote that Colonel Hume R. Field had ridden forward and was returning to the unit's picket line when the guard fired on him. The ball struck him in the thigh, "mangling and shivering the bone and mutilating the flesh frightfully." Ironically this was the last shot by a soldier of the 1st Tennessee, a case of friendly fire.[104]

General Johnston returned to Greensboro by rail from Hillsborough to meet with President Davis, but found that he had moved south. Upon receiving the news of the rejected terms, Davis ordered Johnston to take the cavalry and light artillery, and mount as many infantry as possible to "re-assemble at a place named." In other words, take the most mobile forces south and continue the war. Johnston had an open line of retreat to the southwest, through Salisbury and Charlotte.[105] Despite the fact that Davis rejected the terms of surrender, Johnston disobeyed orders and carried them out anyway. In meeting with Sherman again and agreeing to a surrender, Johnston had directly violated his orders from his commander in chief, President Davis. Yet he did it with the sense that Davis's orders were unrealistic, and that the war was clearly lost. It is a rare example of a military commander disregarding the orders of his civilian commander-in-chief.[106] Davis argued that Johnston had more men than Lee, a better supplied army, and a clear line of retreat. He was not surrounded as Lee was at Appomattox and had a supplies flowing in from South Carolina.[107]

Following up on Davis's advice, General John C. Breckinridge suggested taking the cavalry with the best horses, and the light artillery, and moving to the southwest to continue the war in Texas.[108] As he made his way south towards Charlotte, Breckinridge noted increasing chaos and disorder. The train he was expecting to take had been most likely seized by stragglers, forcing him to order another locomotive and cars with armed guards.[109]

Back in Greensboro, General Johnston was in a difficult position, as his army was slowly disintegrating, he could not control it, supplies were nonexistent, and he had to keep an army together that was waiting only for its end. Johnston wrote to Governor Vance on April 24: "[O]utrages are committed on your people by Confederate soldiers, I know, but they are the disbanded men of the army of Northn Va. I regret this as much as you do, but can not, with my little force, prevent it. Indeed this army has probably suffered as much, proportionally as the people of the State. For crowds of these disbanded soldiers seize our subsidence stores wherever they find them."[110]

Sherman correctly recognized that Johnston's army was "powerless when Lee was defeated," and this fact was what led him to pursue negotiation. He also observed that North Carolina was a "pandemonium."[111] Upsetting to Johnston was the fact that much of the cavalry ignored the terms of the agreement and fled to keep fighting. He wrote, "I regret the movement of these troops, fearing it may embarrass me." He added he had "no means to stop the cavalry." Not only did it compromise his integrity, which Johnston held sacred, it undercut his authority and made the lawless situation worse.[112]

General Wade Hampton, who had been away at Charlotte during the negotiations, did not want to be included in the surrender. Thus he informed

Johnston that he did not feel bound by it and gave orders to his cavalry commands to leave.[113] Hampton wrote to Davis:

> My own mind is made up as to my course. I shall fight as long as my Government remains in existence; when that ceased to live I shall seek some other country, for I shall never take the "oath of allegiance." I am sorry that we paused to negotiate, for to my apprehension no evil can equal that of a return to the Union.... If you will allow me to do so, I can bring to your support men of strong arms and brave hearts— men who will fight to Texas, and who, if forced from that State, will wreek refuge in Mexico rather than in the Union.[114]

This letter failed to reach Davis, yet Hampton moved southwest with what remained of his loyal command. He sent out an order calling for men to join him:

> All officers and men of the Cavalry Corps of the Army of Northern Virginia who have escaped capture, and are not now on parole, are earnestly called upon to join me at once, mounted or dismounted, and strike another blow for the defense of their country. And now particularly should the men of my North Carolina Brigade assemble, and prove that the valor which has triumphed upon a hundred fields, is undiminished, and that blows as heavy as those of yore can again be struck. Our cause is not desperate, if our men will rally around and cling to the old battle flags that so often have led them to victory.[115]

Hampton encouraged others to continue the war, as illustrated when he met with some troopers going home. M.M. Buford, Charles Witherspoon, and Sanford Welborn of the 5th South Carolina Cavalry left after the surrender was formalized and made their way to Charlotte, where they encountered General Hampton. Buford recalled "we rode for three or four miles together, when he turned off into another road.... We promised him we would meet him at Due West, S.C., five weeks from that day and go with him to join Gen. Kirby Smith's army beyond the Mississippi.... But before the time appointed rolled around everything had gone to pieces."[116]

The day following the final meeting with Sherman, Johnston issued orders for the troops to remain in their present camps until further notice. At Hillsborough he directed Confederates to establish a receiving office for telegrams from Union forces in Raleigh, thus ensuring good communication with his Union counterparts.[117] It is difficult to state with certainty how man men were in Johnston's army at the time of surrender. The total number of men included in the surrender, including the Carolinas, Georgia, and Florida, has been estimated at about 89,000 men, making it the largest troop surrender of the war. There were also troops from every Confederate state (and including Missouri, Kentucky, and Maryland) with the Army of Tennessee.[118]

A total of 36,971 men of the Army of Tennessee received paroles, and records indicate that 32,174 got their final pay. Thus, accounting for at least a few thousand desertions, perhaps close to 40,000 men initially arrived in the Greensboro area in early April. Private Sam Watkins of the 1st Tennessee observed that his regiment, which was consolidated with the 27th Tennessee, had only 65 men, and well over 3,000 had served in the unit during the war. The 20th Tennessee Regiment had only 34 men; Company E was reduced to one man.[119]

As expected, North Carolina units were particularly hard hit by desertion. The 58th North Carolina Consolidated had 92 men present at the end, the 61st had only 14 men by the time of the surrender, and the 66th Regiment counted only 32. The old 60th Regiment, which had 73 men at the end of March, had only 3 men left when it stacked arms as part of the Consolidated 58th Regiment.[120] Lieutenant Oliver P. Bowser of the 18th Texas Consolidated wrote "of the eight Texas regiments there were not exceeding six hundred paroled."[121] Some South Carolina regiments were extremely depleted, the 27th had seven men, the 25th five, the 11th sixteen. None of them had their battle flags; these had been captured at Weldon Railroad, Virginia, the previous fall.[122]

Charles Inglesby of the 1st South Carolina Artillery wrote, "As I have said, the companies were skeleton companies, and when the surrender came ... there were only eleven officers and about one hundred and twenty-five men to be paroled. It had gone into the field two months before, with forty-five officers and over one thousand men.[123] Lieutenant Edwin Rennolds of the 5th Tennessee noted, "Of the 1,300 men who followed the flag of the regiment to the front, only thirty stood under its folds at the last scene of all."[124]

In the old 15th Tennessee Regiment, now part of the 4th Tennessee Consolidated, were three men of the original members of Company G. Theirs is perhaps one of the most unusual aspects of the surrender. A number of Company G men hailed from southern Illinois, the land that bordered the slave states of Kentucky and Missouri. These men had such strong Southern sympathies that they fled their homes and enlisted in a Confederate regiment early in the war. Now they stacked their arms near Greensboro.[125]

5

All Was Confusion and Unrest

From the time of the army's arrival in North Carolina in March to the first week of May it had been a rollercoaster of emotions, full of highs and lows. The various rising of expectations and dashing of hopes was mentally exhausting for the Confederate troops. Not only was their own fate in constant fluctuation, but the news from the outside was no better. The Army of Tennessee received three major pieces of bad news in April, starting with word of the fall of Richmond. Next came the unthinkable, news of Lee's capitulation at Appomattox. The final blow was the reality of their own surrender.[1] Nor was this last transaction a neat and simple process. Laden with rumors, men were beside themselves for accurate news. Once an armistice was confirmed the soldiers had to wait, only to learn that the war was back on. Suddenly, as quickly as the news changed, it changed again, with word of a final surrender.

Whatever optimism may have existed among the ranks in the army that spring dissipated with these successive blows. Huddled around their campfires and in their makeshift shelters, the men pondered their fate. The stress of the last few weeks, and the last few days in particular, was taking its toll. After several years in the army, these soldiers had become accustomed to the routine of military service. Yet the difference was that, before, there had been positive expectations. Many had endured periods of tedium and boredom when first enlisting, waiting to be assigned to a unit and drilling. During the course of the war itself each campaign had a "hurry up and wait" aspect to it. Their past experiences had been long periods of quiet, monotony, and anxious waiting, followed by short, sharp instances of sheer terror.

Short rations, long days of waiting, the mind-numbing monotony of drill and inspections are tolerable by soldiers who know what lies ahead. That was not the case here in the camps scattered around Greensboro. At each point in the past, the men had known that they were going to join the army and march away, going into battle or going to forage for supplies. Here they were waiting without knowing the end result. The difference was crucial. Now they were waiting to find out what their fate was: were they going home, were they going to prison, were they fighting again, were they surrendering?

One local soldier wasn't about to wait to be told to go home. Oliver J. Lehman, a cornet player from a North Carolina regimental band, left the army before the surrender was finalized. He returned to his home at Bethania and noted the unfamiliar landscape: "And Oh what a change since we left our old home nearly four years ago. No one here but old men and the women. The state government had been overthrown. All laws were a thing of the past.... Banks all closed and bankrupt, no money and but few of the necessities of life could be had. Under these circumstances what was to be done? It was root hog or die."[2]

Major Bromfield Ridley of General Stewart's staff wrote, "Around the campfires the surrender was discussed. Confusion and unrest prevailed with the stern realization that the Southern army had finally been subdued."[3] Captain George Brewer of the 46th Alabama near Salisbury recalled how he shared the news with his troops. Speaking of himself in the third person, he said, "His voice at times choked so that the words could hardly be heard and tears ran down his cheeks and that of many of the men, as these sad, humiliating words were heard. We thought of the desolation of our land, the poverty of our people, the multitudes of widows and orphans of our comrades sleeping in the dust. Lives and families sacrificed, and for what?"[4] Henry M. Holmes of the 6th Florida recalled men much demoralized, desertions in large no's, every night carrying off large no's of horses & mules."[5]

Carroll Henderson of the 1st Tennessee Consolidated wrote from his camp near Greensboro: "We were in rags, and with empty haversacks, and discouraged." Of the surrender he said, "I was glad and sorry too. Glad the war was over and sorry we had to give it up." In his diary he also recorded "all was quiet in the line many brave boys shed tears." James Ritchey of the same unit wrote, "Yes, if our cause is wrong I pray to God to pardon us. We have ever believed that it was right and have always acted accordingly.[6]

A Tennessean of the 3rd Consolidated Regiment observed that his comrades "raved and swore that they would never submit to it. Some paced back and forth like caged lions." Others, he noted, quietly shed tears.[7] In the old 9th Tennessee (now part of the 1st Consolidated Regiment), Sergeant N.S. Caruthers took a branch from the tree under which the unit stacked their rifles. He made a walking stick of the souvenir and carved into it the following inscription:

NS Caruthers, 9th Tenn Regt, May 1865, also the battles of Shiloh, Perryville, Murfreesboro, Chickamauga, Mission Ridge, Cat Creek, Resaca, Adairsville,

Rocky Face, New Hope, Kennesaw Mt, Dallas, Peachtree Creek, Atlanta, Jonesboro, Lovejoy, Dalton, Franklin, Overton Hill, and Nashville.

He also carved the initials of several comrades, including Privates J.H. Layton, J.M. Bell, William Hilliard, G.W. Carmack, Sergeant R.W. Davis, Lieutenant R.J. Dew, and Corporal T.J. Latimer.[8] Another Tennessean, Alfred Tyler Fielder of the 2nd Consolidated Regiment, wrote that "the boys stacked their Enfield rifles near Greensboro in the piney woods." He continued: "About 12 oclk the assembly was sounded and every man was ordered to buckle on his cartridge box and get his gear and all were marched a short distance to the ordnance train and every fifth man was ordered to retain their accoutrements and all the rest were ordered to stack arms and cartridge boxes after which all were marched back to their respective camps and ordered to break ranks."[9]

Robert Jarman of the 24th Mississippi Consolidated wrote, "We stacked our arms around the Court House at Greensboro, and marched out and gave possession to the Federal advance guard. While here it was necessary to keep a strong guard at the government stock yard to prevent the mules and horses from being stolen, and there was a detail of 20 men from our regiment for the purpose, and ... each of them was given a horse or mule to ride home."[10] Jarman also recalled that there was a large map of the country hanging in the courthouse, and "I daresay it was consulted oftener while we were there a few days than it had been in as many years before; the men with strings and straws trying to compute or measure the distance to be traveled to reach their respective homes again."[11]

The chaplain of the 17th North Carolina, Doctor Alexander D. Betts, wrote of scenes in their campsite at Bush Hill:

> The night following the tidings of our contemplated surrender was a still, sad night in our camp. In little, sad groups they softly talked of the past, the present, and the future. Old men were there, who would have cheerfully gone on, enduring the hardships of war and protracted absence from their families, for the freedom of their country. Middle aged men were there, who had been away from wives and children for years, had gone through many battles, had lost much on their farms or stores of factories or professional business; but would that night have been glad to shoulder the gun and march forward for the defense of their "native land." Young men and boys were there, who loved their country and were unspeakably sad at the thought of failure to secure Southern Independence.
>
> Rev. W.C. Wilson and I walked out of the camp and talked and wept together. As I started back to my tent ... I passed three lads sitting together, talking softly.... I paused and listened. One said, "It makes me very sad to think of our surrendering." Another said, "It hurts me more than the thought of battle ever did." The third raised his arm, clenched his fist, and seemed to grate his teeth as he said, " I would rather know we had to go into battle tomorrow morning."

There was patriotism! There may have been in that camp that night generals, colonels, and other officers who had been moved by a desire for worldly honor. Owners of slaves and of lands may have hoped for financial benefit from Confederate success. But these boys felt they had a country that ought to be free![12]

Colonel Olmstead of the 1st Georgia Consolidated camped at High Point remarked that they "lay down at night in security and peace," a sentiment probably shared by many of his weary comrades.[13] William Dixon of the same unit recalled, "We are doing nothing now but lying about loose in camp. I made out my muster roll and handed it in. We are rich now and don't seem to care which way the wind blows having receive one dollar and twenty five cents in silver apiece."[14]

At Lexington James Harris of the 7th North Carolina wrote, "At 9 o'clock, A.M., we turned over to the United States authorities four fifths of the arms and retained one fifth. Officers were allowed their side arms."[15] D.E. Huger Smith of Parker's Battery (SC) wrote, "There was no formal surrender, but one morning the drivers harnessed up and took the guns to Greensboro, where they were parked, and they turned loose the horses into a huge pen or field where they remained for a time with a lot of others without food."[16]

Private Duncan McLaurin of the 3rd South Carolina wrote, "Johnston then only had 30,000 men at Greensboro, so many had left after the battle of Bentonville. His army was badly disorganized; the men knew the war was about over and many threw down guns and left saying they would not fight any more. We were paroled and discharged in three or four days and everybody started for their homes." He added, "The Yankees gave us plenty rations enough to last us to get home and gave every regiment wagons and mules to haul their rations and for the sick to ride."[17] E. Funderburk of South Carolina, without food for two days, was guarding a wagon in the woods when he learned of the surrender. So angry was he that he beat his rifle against an oak tree, bending it double, rather than surrender the weapon.[18] Another South Carolinian, Col. Benjamin Smith of the 16th & 24th Regiment, wrote, "The consolidated [regiment] behaved well until the unhappy surrender. Very few deserted, the men standing by their guns to the last."[19]

A few men of Lee's army managed to join Johnston's forces. While many of the men who were at Appomattox and discussed sneaking away, only a fraction actually did. Of those who got away, a small number reached the Army of Tennessee in North Carolina. South Carolinian Berry Benson recalled his journey out of Appomattox:

When we were about to surrender at Appomattox, I went to my brigadier, General McGowan, and told him that I had been in prison once, and I was not going again; that I would escape through the enemy's lines if I could and march to

Johnston's army in North Carolina. He asked me to wait till we were sure it would surrender. I did, and then my brother and I crept through the enemy's lines (at times on our hands and knees in the running ditches, hidden by the blackberry vines) and marched with our guns to Johnston's army, where we joined the 7th South Carolina.[20]

Of course, once the Benson brothers reached Greensboro, they learned they were to be surrendered anyway. Their story is illustrative, for many accounts of soldiers at Appomattox mention thinking of escaping to Johnston's army. Of those who considered it, only a fraction actually attempted it.

G.H. Baskette of the 4th Tennessee Consolidated Regiment (formerly in the 18th Tennessee), camped at High Point, wrote,

It would be impossible fitly to describe the feelings of the officers and men who after so long and heroic a contest were now called upon to lay down their arms. Into the past four yeas, so fraught with momentous events, were crowded the memories of untold privations and hardships, and of battlefields upon which thousands and thousands of their comrades had offered up their lives in a grand but unavailing obligation of blood.

The paroles were sent to the different regiments signed by the officers, and distributed among the men. The brigade moved slowly and sadly out into an open field where officers sheathed their swords and the men silently stacked their guns. Then the unarmed command moved out of sight.[21]

A soldier in the 12th Louisiana wrote, "All is confusion and unrest." The Louisianans, the only regiment from that state with the army, had endured a long road to Greensboro. The unit had fought on both sides of the Mississippi, beginning the war in Missouri. It had also already surrendered once, at Island Number 10 on the Mississippi in 1862.[22]

Samuel Foster of Brown's Division probably expressed the feelings of many when he wrote that "we feel relieved. No more picket duty, no more guard duty, no more fighting, no more war. It is all over, and we are going home."[23] Captain Stoney wrote, "Still in camp. Rumor seems to have tired of her occupation. The stern reality of accomplished defeat is upon us. Famine begins to threaten us."[24] Later he recorded his thoughts, and they reveal the boredom, suspense, tension, and uncertainty shared by the men of the army:

Still here, disorganized, dissatisfied. No right acknowledged now except might, no property safe which is not defended with pistol and rifle. Regimental and higher commanders ordered to High Point to receive paroles. Colonels sign for their regiments, brigadiers for their staff, and colonels, major-generals for their brigades and so on. Paroles are not to be issued to individuals until we reach the end of our journeys to our respective States.

Our horses have for a week been reduced to one quart of corn per day, while the mules get no grain and but a handful of long forage. Expected issues from the

Federal authorities have not been received. The days' rations of bacon are in the brigade commissariat and no meal. No orders have been received, but with famine staring us in the face, General Hoke consents to our starting. As it might, however, turn out a serious step, in the event of our not being able to get food on our route, the question of waiting for the Federal issue of supplies, or of starting now was submitted to the men. Of course, they voted to go. They would go with the certainty of starving. Received General Hoke's farewell address to his division. It is full of feeling.[25]

Captain William E. Stoney wrote of his brigade's departure on May 3rd: This morning at 8 A.M. our brigade started upon its last march. The Twenty-seventh led the column with seven men it its ranks; the Twenty-fifth followed next with five; the Seventh battalion, which had not suffered so much in battle as the other regiments, had near a hundred men in ranks; the Twenty-first not quite so large and the Eleventh regiment, numbering sixteen in all told, was the rear guard. We stopped at Hoke's headquarters to pay him our respects and say good-bye. He and his staff seemed to feel the occasion deeply, and their expressions of regard and good will were very grateful to us all.[26]

At his camp in High Point, Captain John Blair of the 3rd Tennessee Consolidated (formerly in the 35th Tennessee) noted, "The terms were agreed on and now we drew rations from the Yankees and the boys began to be lively; money in our pockets, bacon and crackers in their haversacks and home in their heads."[27] Artilleryman Clement Saussy wrote of the miserable conditions for the soldiers: some were covered with lice, and all were hungry and ill-clad. Many troops wandered the streets of Greensboro, looking to steal cloth, food, and whatever else could be useful to them.[28]

In one of the few Virginia regiments with the army, the 63rd, a soldier reported that "the company seeing the war at an end ... made their escape the best way they conceived to be possible, and many were not present to be surrendered."[29] The men of the 54th Virginia, guarding the railroad bridge over the Yadkin River near Salisbury, apparently agreed. Being so close to home, many left without getting their paroles. This regiment had lost its battle flag at Bentonville, one of the last banners lost in combat by the Army of Tennessee.[30]

Southern soldiers noted that the rations given them by the Union army went a long way towards improving their morale and reinforcing the notion that the future held the promise of recovery. Although bitterness lingered, some began to accept the situation and prepared to move on.[31] Samuel Foster of the 1st Texas Consolidated Regiment, however, wrote despondently, "As for our own Company, Regiment, and Brigade, they can be found at Arkansas Post; at the Prison cemetery of Camp Springfield, Illinois, at Chickamauga, at Missionary Ridge, at New Hope Church, at Atlanta ... at Jonesboro ... at

Franklin and Nashville...."[32] Others, like William Stoney, summed up their view of the war and their service: "[We had] done our duty as we saw it. We felt that we had been loyal to our State and our country and had lain down our arms only at the commands of our beloved leaders, Lee and Johnston. We were not ashamed of our defeat as we knew, and the whole world knew, that we had been simply overpowered and starved out by far superior forces in numbers and not in quality. We were welcomed home by our sweethearts and wives as heartily as if we had come out conquerors."[33]

William H. Andrews of the 1st Georgia Regulars wrote of what he saw was a major defect during the war:

While it is a bitter pill to have to come back into the Union, don't think there is much regret for the loss of the Confederacy. The treatment the soldiers have received from the government in various ways put them against it. The army has been half clothed and half starved, besides they have reached little of the worthless money due them. Numbers of Confederate soldiers who went home to aid their starving families and were afterwards shot for desertion would most likely be with us today if the government had fulfilled its contract by paying them off so they could have sent the money home to their needy families.[34]

Captain Samuel Foster of Texas wrote of their last day in the Army of Tennessee: "After turning in our guns, and getting our paroles, we feel relieved. No more picket duty, no more guard duty, no more fighting, no more war. It is all over, and we are going home. HOME after an absence of four years from our families and friends."[35]

At Trinity College, one observer noted "arms were thrown in piles, their cannon abandoned, and all the paraphernalia of war left to be turned over to the enemy. On breaking camp, they formed a line of marching order, which reached for miles through town and country. Their gladdened shouts at the thought of peace, and home, and friends, made the welkin ring."[36] Georgia Artilleryman William Talley wrote,

The Yankees were very kind to us. They let our captain have three wagons and teams for the use of our men to carry our baggage and cooking utensils. The teams and wagons [were] to be turned over to the Government when they reached Perry, Ga. The Capt. informed us that if we stuck together he would see that we got home without any expense. A lot of our boys had picked up a horse apiece when the Yankees were not looking. I, suffering with boils, was not able to forage for a horse so I had none. Early one bright morning we loaded the wagons and hitched up and began our mournful tramp for home.[37]

Captain James J. Hawthorne of the 3rd Alabama Cavalry described the end of the war for his unit: "Here many of the soldiers, among whom I was one, left their command without the formality of surrender or parole and started for their homes."[38]

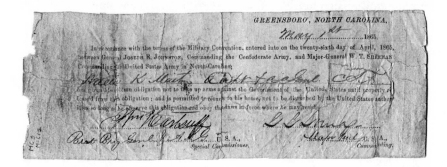

Parole pass. Similar to those issued at Appomattox, these passes were printed for the soldiers of the Army of Tennessee in Greensboro (Museum of the Confederacy, Richmond, Virginia).

As with the surrender of the Army of Northern Virginia, some regiments hid their battle flags, while others chose not to turn in their flags. These flags were cherished symbols of what the men had fought for, and their value to the men cannot be understated. Various regiments hid, destroyed, or cut up and divided their flags. This was a different situation from Appomattox, for there were no Union troops to oversee actions of the surrender. Free to keep their weapons, wagons, and flags, many Confederate troops marched home as organized soldiers rather than as surrendered troops.

A reporter with the *New York Herald* observed the chaos unfolding in Greensboro: "We have got in but very few battle flags or horses. All of them have been either destroyed or carried off. We have got about fifteen thousand stand of small arms, with about one hundred and ten or twenty pieces of artillery."[39] Piecing together the fate of the various battle flags reveals numerous examples of reverence for their flags among the men of the Army of Tennessee, although unfortunately the fate of most of the army's flags cannot be determined.

Color Sergeant John H. Reeding hid the 20th Alabama's flag under his clothing at Salisbury and gave it to his regimental commander, Col. James M. Dedman. He took the flag home and it stayed in his family until they donated it to the Alabama Department of History in 1943. Their flag was an Army of Tennessee pattern (rectangular shape) flag, issued in the spring of 1864.[40] Captain Needham Hughes left the camp of the 33rd Alabama at Greensboro and went off into some nearby woods and wrapped the flag around his body under his uniform to hide it. Hughes took the flag home and today it remains in the family of his descendants. This is a Hardee pattern flag with no numbers, words, or battle honors.[41]

Major John N. Slaughter hid the flag of the 34th Alabama, which was camped in the High Point/Jamestown area, an Army of Tennessee pattern flag they had received the year before.[42] Ensign Joseph Tillinghast hid the flag of the 36th Alabama by wrapping it around his body and hiding it under his jacket. He took the flag home and it remained in the family until donated to the Alabama State Archives. The flag of the 36th was an Army of Tennessee pattern, with crossed cannon battle honors in the center of the blue cross, for capturing some artillery guns near Atlanta.[43] In their camp at Greensboro, Lieutenant Colonel William F. Slaton hid and took home the flag of the 37th Alabama. It was an Army of Tennessee pattern flag, most likely one issued in the spring of 1864.[44] In the 40th Alabama, camped near the Yadkin River bridge near Salisbury, Lieutenant Colonel Ezekiel S. Gulley asked his brigade commander, General Edmund Pettus, what to do with flag since the unit had been consolidated with the 19th and 46th regiments. Pettus simply told him he could keep it, and Gulley did, safeguarding the banner during the surrender and trip home.[45]

Color sergeant Degan Foley camped at Jamestown, hid the flag of the 9th Arkansas, and took it back with him to Pine Bluff, Arkansas. This was a rare Third National flag; very few units had this banner as their battle flag.[46] The color bearer hid the flag of the 7th Florida and took it home, where it remains in the family today. All of the Florida troops were camped at High Point. They marched south and disbanded at Augusta, Georgia, on May 14, making their way home from there.[47] The men of the 1st Georgia not only kept their flag, but openly flew it as they marched home. Charles Olmstead wrote, "The Regiment marched back to Georgia with its colors flying, and disbanded at Augusta. I brought the flags home with me and returned them to the Regiment some years afterward when it had reorganized." Their flag was a Department of South Carolina, Georgia, and Florida pattern (a square flag with a white border, having thirteen stars and a colored sleeve).[48] From Olmstead's journal it may be wondered if any of the units in the 1st Georgia Consolidated, including the 57th and 63rd regiments, turned in their flags. He also noted, "The troops were marched to a certain point and there laid down their arms. Officers however kept their swords and each Regiment retained its colors."[49]

The fate of the flag of the 41st Georgia, issued to unit in 1864 and believed carried until its surrender at Greensboro, remains a mystery. This was an Army of Tennessee pattern flag, and it was discovered in Yonkers, New York, by the United Daughters of the Confederacy and given to the Museum of the Confederacy in 1935. At this time it is unclear if the flag was hidden and taken back to Georgia, then transported to New York, or if it was turned in, and a New York soldier took it home as a souvenir.[50]

At High Point in the camp of the 42nd Georgia, color bearer William F.

Edwards, removed the flag from the staff and hid it under his coat and took it home. A photograph in 1912 shows him and his granddaughter holding the flag.[51] A remnant of the flag from the 43rd Georgia, a piece kept by Captain Joseph Storey, indicates that this flag may have been cut up and divided by the men. Further investigation is needed on this, however. The regiment was camped at High Point, along with other Georgia units.[52] Captain Ben S. Williams of the old 47th Georgia (the unit had merged with the 1st Georgia Regulars on April 10th) wrote:

> I was present for duty with Johnston's army when Johnston had made ready for surrendering but I did not surrender. In the evening of April 25, 1865 I cut the bullet-riven shell-torn, old battle flag of my regiment from the improvised staff — (our first staff was shot to splinters on the field of Chickamauga) — folded it in my saddle blanket, girthed my saddle tightly up on it and mounting my horse, accompanied by two other young officers — well mounted — started to wend our way to our trans-Mississippi Department and join General Kirby Smith.... We didn't get there. But I did save our old battle flag, presented to the regiment by my mother and other noble women of Savannah; under and around which I had seen comrades fall "like leaves in wintry weather."[53]

This flag had been made by the wife of Colonel G.W.M. Williams and presented to the regiment upon its formation. It served throughout the entire war, and by 1865 had 32 bullet holes. This was probably one of the few flags with the army that had been through the whole conflict.[54]

In the only regiment from Louisiana, the 12th, Leonodias Polk wrapped the unit's flag around his body and hid it under his shirt. He took it home on the 900-mile march from Greensboro. Regimental commander Col. Graham, unable to find the flag, was "much incensed but his threats and appeals ... were unavailing." This was a Second National pattern flag (a white banner with the crossed battle flag pattern in the corner) with thirteen stars.[55]

The men of the 7th North Carolina, a local unit, cut up their flag rather than surrender it. Fragments with battle honors "Sharpsburg" and "Hanover" are housed in the North Carolina State Museum of History today. The unit later moved on to the Lexington/Jamestown area. They spent a week repairing the railroad bridge over the Deep River. The war had come home for the men from Company A of the unit, as they were from nearby Burlington and Alamance counties.[56]

Private Able Thomas hid the tattered remnants of the 17th North Carolina's flag while camped at Bush Hill in northwestern Randolph County. A Second National pattern, the regimental flag had lost most of its white field by this time; only the battle flag in the cannon and some shreds of white survived.[57] Apparently Maj. George Washington Finley Harper of the 58th North Carolina cut up his regiment's flag and kept the "58" and "NC" of the banner for himself. Others received additional parts of the banner. The men cut up the flag in their camp along the Burlington Road not far from Mount Hope Church. In the 1920s Harper's daughter donated the fragments to the North Carolina Museum of History.[58]

Color bearer Anton W. Jager of Bachman's Battery (SC) wrapped the battery's flag around his body to hide it under his coat and brought it home to Charleston. The unit, comprising of Germans from Charleston, had fought in both theaters, seeing action from the Seven Days to Gettysburg, then transferring later to the Army of Tennessee. The unit's guidon had several battle honors, including Cockpit Point, West Point, Mechanicsville, Gaines' Mill, Fraser's Farm, Meyer's Farm, Second Manassas, Suffolk, Boonsboro, Gettysburg, Fredericksburg, and Sharpsburg. It had carried this banner all through the war since 1862.[59]

When the men of the Pee Dee Light Artillery from South Carolina turned in their guns and equipment, R.C. Nettles hid the unit's flag under his jacket and brought it back to Louisa McIntosh of Society Hill, one of the ladies who had made the flag four years earlier. Amazingly, this banner had survived the entire war.[60]

According to Private O.G. Thompson, the men of the 3rd South Carolina hid their flag at the surrender. Lieutenant A.W. Burnside took the banner home with him.[61] In General Hagood's South Carolina Brigade, commanded by Lt. Col. James Rion, some of the men burned their regimental flags. Captain William Stoney of the brigade kept a diary and noted on April 17, "The flags of the brigade were burned by the men in the certainty of surrender." Unfortunately he does not specify which units burned their flags. In the brigade at the time were the 11th, 21st, 25th, and 27th South Carolina Infantry regiments, all camped at High Point.[62] Hagood's headquarters flag, a First National pattern with the word "Hagood's" in the white stripe, was cut up by the men at High Point.[63]

From their camp in Greensboro, B. Wallace Wright took the regimental flag of the 7th South Carolina home with him.[64] The 10th and 19th South Carolina had been consolidated, with the flag of the 10th being the new unit's colors. When leaving High Point after getting their paroles, Captain Robert Z. Harlee handed a package to James Sullivan, telling him not to open it until he was home. When Sullivan finally did open it, he found the flag of the 10th Regiment.[65] Major B.B. Smith of the 24th South Carolina brought his regiment's flag home, along with that of the 16th South Carolina. Both units had been consolidated. Many stars were cut off of both flags, as evidenced by square holes and missing stars, suggesting that the men may have cut souvenirs from the flag before departing.[66]

The color bearer of the Lafayette Artillery in Kanapaux's Company (SC) hid their battle flag and took it home to Charleston. The unit was camped near Bloomington, in northern Randolph County.[67] In Parker's Battery (SC), camped near Greensboro, gunner D.E. Huger Smith noted a party of us took our battle flag from its place by the Captain's tent and cut it up, each man keeping a fragment. I have one white stare before me now."[68]

Private Sam Watkins of the 1st Tennessee wrote that his regiment "was indeed a sad sight." Of their stacking of arms, he said, "a mere squad of noble and brave men, gathered around the tattered flag that they had followed in every battle through that long war. It was so bullet-riddled and torn that it was but a few blue and red shreds that hung drooping while it, too was stacked with our guns forever."[69] A member of Company A of the 3rd Tennessee "took part in the last battle of the Confederacy at Bentonville, N.C., and was paroled at Greensboro, N.C. Wrapping the blood-stained, bullet torn flag under his clothing, he marched from Greensboro to his home, in Tennessee, where he gave the flag to Mrs. Calvin H. Walker, widow of the Colonel of the 3rd Tennessee who had been killed just prior to the surrender...." This was an Army of Tennessee Dalton pattern flag.[70]

Color bearer J.B. Harrell of the 6th/9th Tennessee Regiment hid the unit's flag and took it home. The unit was camped near High Point.[71] A soldier named Roberts hid the flag of the 20th Tennessee. He took it home and kept it. It was most likely an Augusta Depot pattern Army of Tennessee flag.[72] William Belew of the 31st Tennessee hid the regiment's flag under his coat and took it home with him. It was an Army of Tennessee pattern flag issued at Dalton with several battle honors on it.[73] While in Charlotte, James Nance, color bearer of the 4th Tennessee Cavalry, took the unit's flag home with him, and later his wife made an apron out of it for their daughter.[74] Major General Matthew C. Butler commanded the army's cavalry. His headquarters flag, a Second National pattern, had been in use from 1863 until end of the war. Major Henry B. McClellan of his staff saved the flag while at their Greensboro campsite.[75]

There appears to be no rhyme or reason as to which flags were surrendered or saved, or what the men did with them. No clear-cut pattern can be seen among commands or units from the same state. Unlike the men of Lee's Army of Northern Virginia, they faced no Union troops during their ordeal and were free to hide or destroy their flags. It seems that the fate of a regiment's flag was often decided by the troops in the ranks, gathered around their gloomy campsites that May.

Aside from the fact that they were going home, the other thing on the minds of most Confederate soldiers was food. Numerous diaries and accounts mention the unceasing quest for a good meal. Charles W. Hutson of the Beaufort Artillery (SC), camped east of Greensboro, wrote that "Willie Hutson,

Charley DeSaussure and I have just got back from a jaunt in search of a supper. We first succeeded in getting more buttermilk than we could drink & then, after walking a few miles further we were supplied with a fine supper, refreshed by the presence of butter in abundance. This is a noble country & the people cannot be surpassed in kindness."[76] Over the next few days Hutson and his comrades would make many excursions into the local countryside for meals. He also noted that "no one around here will take Confederate money."[77]

Boredom, frustration, and uncertainty prevailed in the Confederate campsites. In addition to looking for clothing and food, the soldiers occupied themselves with carving bullets. Relic hunters have found numerous examples of artwork from campsites near Red Cross, including carved bullets. The soft lead ammunition has been found carved into practical things like bottle stoppers, chess pawns, and decorative pieces like acorns, urns, thimbles, and the like.[78] Some soldiers also melted lead minie balls into sheets and carved animals and figures on them. Examples include a dog three inches long, and a donkey head with holes punched out for its eyes. The carved and melted bullets indicate an attempt to pass the time during the stressful days camped around Greensboro.[79]

With so much time on their hands, perhaps some of the troops reflected on the course of the war. A few of the units in the Army of Tennessee were at the Confederacy's first major victory at Manassas in 1861. The 1st Arkansas, and 2nd and 3rd Tennessee regiments fought there, having been hastily transferred to Virginia upon their formation. When the imminent Union threat abated in Virginia, these western troops were shipped back to the other theater of the war and fought at Shiloh. They remained in the west, serving out the rest of the war there. These were the only Confederate regiments to participate in the first great battles of both east and west.

Ironically, Generals Johnston and Beauregard, architects of the first major victory at Manassas, now oversaw the surrender of the Confederacy's largest remaining army. Although a handful of other officers were also at Manassas, they spent the majority of the war in the west: James Fagan, William Bate, John Vaughan, and States' Rights Gist.

6

The Yankees Arrive

After returning from the second meeting with Sherman, Johnston telegraphed the governors of North Carolina, South Carolina, Georgia, and Florida, informing them of the news. His last sentence clearly articulated his views at the time: "I made this convention to spare the blood of this gallant little army, to prevent further sufferings of our people, by the devastation ... from ... invading armies, and to avoid the crime of waging a hopeless war."[1]

While the meetings at the Bennitt house were important and had been full of drama, the real work of arranging the surrender now began. It would be a time-consuming and challenging process for the Confederate high command to dismantle the army that they had spent weeks building up. Details of the surrender included designating officers to oversee various tasks, arranging for transportation home, issuing parole passes, overseeing the relinquishing of weapons and ammunition, and countless other mundane tasks.

Johnston ordered his aide, Archer Anderson, to send messages to the far-flung detachments and posts in his command. Telegrams went out to units in Charlotte, Chester, and other areas informing them of the surrender and clarifying that they were included in it. Orders also went out to secure supplies and maintain order in their local districts.[2]

The end of fighting did not ease the burden of work on the commanding general. For Johnston, it was simply replacing one set of priorities with another. General Beauregard sent a messenger to General Horatio Wright, commanding the Union army's Sixth Corps at Danville, Virginia, informing him of the surrender. Wright's troops had marched south from Appomattox to link up with Sherman's army. Union messages also arrived turning Wright's men around.[3] After arriving back at his Greensboro headquarters, Johnston issued a flurry of orders to begin the process of collecting weapons, organizing the men to march home, maintaining security, collecting transportation, and a host of other pressing issues. Orders went out for artillery to move to Greensboro to place their guns, caissons, forges, horses, harnesses, and ammunition, all "under charge" of responsible officers.[4] As agreed on, Johnston sent trains loaded with cotton toward the Union lines. They were to proceed to Morehead City on the coast, where they would pick up 200,000 rations for the Confederates.[5]

With a new agreement in place, General Johnston ordered his troops to remain in their present positions. The men were officially informed on the 27th. Artillery guns, caissons, forges, and horses were to be sent to Greensboro for collection. He also ordered his corps commanders to send four fifths of their weapons to an ordnance officer.[6] Johnston issued further orders that specified that the field transportation of the army (wagons, carts, horses, mules, etc.) belonged to the troops, and that it would be used for their journey home. Upon arrival, it was to be "fairly distributed" to the officers and men.[7]

Commanders began to take inventory of the arms and ammunition of their troops. The men in General S.D. Lee's Corps, for example, had over 150,000 rounds of ammunition in their cartridge boxes. The corps' eleven wagons had another 89,000 rounds. The corps also had 87 wagons and 30 ambulances available for transportation.[8]

Sherman issued orders that included the following details. Captain Jasper Myers, an ordnance officer, was designated to receive the arms and artillery of the Confederates. He also instructed his commanders to loan civilians any captured horses, mules, wagons, and other vehicles that could be spared. Officers were to encourage civilians to engage in their "peaceful pursuits." Lastly, he ordered that "foraging will forthwith cease" and that if it became necessary to gather supplies from civilians, the civilians be paid "on the spot."[9] With other business in his Department to attend to, Sherman left for Savannah to oversee the surrender of forces there. Writing of the difficulties faced by his adversary in carrying out the surrender, he noted that "General Johnston had fulfilled his agreement to the very best of his ability."[10] Sherman himself noted that, "the greater part of the North Carolina troops had gone home without waiting for their papers.... [A]ll of them would doubtless come into some one of the military posts, the commanders of which are authorized to grant them."[11] Of the notorious Confederate cavalry that had fled and was rumored to be headed for Mexico—and had established a reputation for brutality and lawlessness—he said, "I would sincerely advise that they be encouraged to go and stay; they would be a nuisance to any civilized government."[12]

The supplementary terms allowed the Confederate troops to keep their transportation (wagons, horses, etc), allowed each brigade or unit to retain arms equal to one-fifth of its strength. This last point might seem odd, but the situation was so volatile in the North Carolina piedmont that it was felt the troops should have some way to protect themselves and stop bandits should they need to The weapons were to be turned in to local authorities once the men reached home. It also specifically stated that horses and property of officers could be retained by them. Water transportation was made available to troops from the Gulf Coast areas.[13]

In Sherman's army news was received "with enthusiastic cheering through the camps. A celebration a la Fourth of July, succeeded, and the night was made most noisy with the discharge of fire-arms, and brilliant with the discharge off fire-works."[14] Private John C. Arbuckle of the 4th Iowa wrote of the news reaching the Union army:

> When on the evening of April 26, 1865, we were officially notified that terms of surrender had been agreed upon and signed; the whole army went wild with rejoicing; flags and banners were all unfurled; the drum corps were called out; guns were fired; bonfires were kindled,; we paraded the camp; gathered at the various headquarters of the commanding Generals and were entertained with thrilling and eloquent speeches.... It was a night never to be forgotten; not until the small hours of the morning did we lie down to dreams and sweet sleep.[15]

William G. Bentley of the 104th Ohio wrote that "nothing else is talked about among the men scarcely but Peace & Home."[16]

Construction crews began repairing the railroad from Hillsborough to Greensboro, and Union troops of the Army of the Tennessee made ready to march north toward Washington. General Oliver O. Howard, commanding the army, issued orders that "promiscuous foraging is prohibited" and advised civilians to "remain at your homes as much as possible while the columns are passing by." He insisted that thieves would be punished by their officers, and that commissaries of his army would pay civilians for supplies.[17]

General John D. Kennedy's South Carolina brigade kept its wagons, since it moved into Greensboro to serve as provost guard for the supplies and weapons stockpiled in the town. Over 2,000 army horses grazed in a field at the edge of town, and ammunition was stored at the railroad depot.[18]

That night the men of Terry's Texas Rangers, the 8th Texas Cavalry, debated their options. J.K. Blackburn of the unit noted:

> Captain Doc Mathews ... visited General Hardee's headquarters to learn what he might about the current events of the day. He told Mathews of the situation pending ... and that while he had nothing official on the subject, he felt satisfied the army would be surrendered right there. He also advised Mathews to take his regiment away from there and join Dick Taylor's army then at Mobile, Alabama, and by thus adding strength from different sections to that army, under the providence of God, victory might finally come to the Southern cause, and added, "I don't want to see your regiment surrendered to the enemy."[19]

Perhaps General Hardee was fond of these Texans since his son had served with them and had been recently killed in action at Bentonville while defending Confederate headquarters. Blackburn continues:

> Captain Mathews returned to camp at midnight and had the bugler sound the assembly call for the regiment, and when it was assembled he delivered Hardee's information and advice and concluded his remarks with these words, "I am too young a man to assume the responsibility of such an undertaking, but I now offer my resignation as commander of the regiment," asking each company commander to take charge of his company. "Hold a council to determine your course, and each company decide and act for itself regardless of what others may do."
>
> Company F, my company, returned to quarters, held its conference and decided unanimously to go to Dick Taylor and to start at once. Some of the company, including the commissioned officers, were absent on police or scout or other duties or on account of sickness, and were not in this conference and hence were left behind when we started to leave. C.D. Barnett, our orderly sergeant, agreed to be commander and I agreed to be "counselor" for the expedition. I never did learn definitely the course the other companies pursued, but had the impression fixed upon me that most of them made their escape and were never paroled until after all Confederates had surrendered, and some of them were never paroled at all, but are still to say, soldiers of the Confederate government.[20]

It seems that perhaps only a handful of the 8th Texas Cavalry remained to surrender weapons and receive paroles in North Carolina.[21]

Soldiers fortunate enough to be guarding supplies had access to goods that many men did not. Private George Bussey of the 7th South Carolina wrote, "The day before the surrender our company was put on guard of a train load of bacon, with the privilege of giving away some that was tainted. We were not very particular and gave a great deal of it to soldiers and civilians."[22]

On April 27, Union forces began splitting up and moving on to their next assignments. The Armies of the Tennessee and of Georgia began their march north into Virginia and on to Washington, DC. The Tenth and Twenty-third corps remained as occupation troops in North Carolina. This rapid redeployment of Federal troops, so soon after the surrender, meant that while the Confederate army remained in place, the Union troops were mostly leaving. As with the surrender at Appomattox, when the end finally came, there were more Confederates than Federals on hand.[23]

Johnston performed one more act of defiance against Davis's wishes. The Confederate treasury had $37,679.96 in Mexican silver coins, and Davis had directed that it be sent on to him in Charlotte. Instead, on April 28 Johnston's men were paid $1.17 each, and records indicate 32,174 were present. It was distributed as evenly as possible, with every seventh man getting an extra one.[24] One Georgian recalled getting $1.16 In the 20th Tennessee the men got $1.25 each. Those in the 12th Louisiana got $1.15; one man recalled that he got four quarters, a nickel, and a dime.[25] Soldiers in the 20th Tennessee each got $1.25. Col. William Butler, a cavalry officer, received $1.75. Some men got $1.80. Soldiers in the 16th & 24th South Carolina received $1.29.[26]

George Washington Harper of the 58th North Carolina Consolidated recorded the payment of his regiment: "At Greensboro the regiment was paid in Mexican silver dollars—one dollar and fourteen cents to each officer and enlisted man present. There being no means of making change for the cents, the men, in groups of seven, drew for the surplus dollar. This pitiful amount was the only payment received for months, and was the first coin seen by many of the men during the war."[27] One soldier recalled that as the soldiers began the march home they sang, "One dollar and fifteen cents for four years' service."[28] George W. Bussey of the 7th South Carolina wrote,

> While here the remnant of silver money on hand was divided among the men. The amount each private received was $1.60. This was the first money we had received in a long while. I should have kept it all my life, but boylike I soon spent it. There were three old half-starved horses to be given to each company, and I drew the first choice and got a large nick-tail bay, which would have been a fine horse if I could have rested him up and fed him. In a short time we started for home. I buckled all the belongings of our company on my old horse that I could get on him and mounted him and started for home. But my experience of the first day taught me that I could not get the necessary forage for my horse and at the same time keep up. There was but little forage in the country to be had, so I sold him to an old citizen for $2.00 in North Carolina money, which was never worth one cent to me. As we came on, I got into a government store and got me three splendid pairs of shoes.[29]

Captain Stoney wrote of the payment: "The brigade was paid today one dollar and a quarter in silver per man, the last I suppose, of the Confederate treasury. I shall have mine made into a medal to keep and value as received from the dying hands of my government. It is the greatest earthly satisfaction and my only consolation now, that I entered her service on the day of the inauguration of this war; was never absent from my command expect by authority or from wounds, and continued in the field until the last day."[30]

Samuel Foster of the 1st Texas Consolidated noted, "This evening Muster Rolls are made out and all hands including officers and men draw 1.25 in silver—the first silver larger than a dime I have seen in a long while."[31] A soldier in the 1st Tennessee recalled that they were "paid off the same morning, each man receiving an old silver Mexican dollar, and there being an extra dollar for every seventh man, we cut the cards for the odd dollar."[32]

The differing amounts are hard to reconcile. They may be the result of a faulty distribution system, stealing, different distribution systems or simply failing memories among those who wrote about the event. As the money went out to the widely spread out commands, officers of the various units chose to distribute it differently. The distribution of the money was not without jealousy and controversy. General Benjamin F. Cheatham, one of Hardee's division commanders, accused General Robert F. Hoke of taking more than his share of the funds. Hardee intervened and ended the disagreement. It appears to have stayed at the headquarters level, for no soldier's accounts mention the accusation.[33] As with the other events of late April, rumors surrounded the treasury, its value, its distribution, and its eventual fate. One Greensboro civilian recorded the following:

> It was reported that there was about thirteen millions of dollars in specie on some cars which had been brought from Richmond, and the naval Brigade was guarding the treasure. Nearly all of this money belonged to Virginia banks and had been sent south to prevent its falling into, the hands of the enemy. Eventually, after leaving Greensboro it was stolen, lost, and a portion recovered by the banks while that part of it which belonged to the Confederate States Government was divided out to Johnston's men used in purchasing forage.[34]

Also that day the men turned over weapons to ordnance officers, who would turn them over the Federal troops. From his Greensboro headquarters Johnston wrote to General John Schofield that he was collecting arms and ammunition under guard, but asked that no Union troops be sent to Greensboro yet as he was not ready to receive them and turn over control.[35] Corporal Bromfield L. Ridley wrote about his experiences leaving the army at Greensboro. On April 28 he and a fellow staff officer, Lieutenant R.C. Stewart, "concluded to get ahead of the disbanded army ... so we could find forage for man and beast." He wrote that "we left camp last night with three headquarters wagons ... and one ambulance. Rode all night and are now in camp, seven miles from Lexington, on the Danville Road." The next day he noted "a great many people visited us to exchange forage for spun thread; that is our currency now." Here he sent a messenger to General Stewart to bring his parole.[36]

Governor Vance issued a proclamation on the 28th that urged citizens to "abstain from any and all acts of lawlessness." He also instructed "good and true soldiers of North Carolina, whether they have been surrendered and paroled or otherwise, to unite themselves together in sufficient numbers in the various counties of the State, under the superintendence of the civil magistrates thereof, to arrest or slay any bodies of lawless and unauthorized men."[37] The governor had been using the one-story brick building office building of attorneys W.L. and Levi M. Scott. It stood near the courthouse on Market Street.[38]

General Beauregard came upon a group of men rummaging through a railroad car and tossing papers outside onto the muddy ground. Upon learning that these were official papers of the Confederate government, he ordered them out of the car, and posted guards over it.[39] Despite the war's end for the army, Beauregard still followed up on one important issue: commissions for his staff. He telegraphed Adjutant General Samuel Cooper in Charlotte, asking that his aides and those of General Johnston be promoted in recognition of their service. Beauregard felt justice would be served them by promoting them before releasing them to return home. Cooper replied that President Davis had already left Charlotte and was unreachable. Thus nothing could be done, and Beauregard and Johnston had enough other concerns at the moment.[40]

Commanders in the Army of Tennessee spent the next few days in routine paperwork. No matter what an army did — fight, march, or surrender — muster rolls, receipts, and orders had to be filled out as usual. Officers took roll calls, filled out reports on arms and ammunition, tools and supplies, and prepared their commands for the journey home.[41] Along the railroad corridor that linked Greensboro to the south military activities continued. On April 29 a regiment went to guard supplies in Chester, South Carolina, and another proceeded to do the same at Catawba Bridge, North Carolina.[42] Things were deteriorating further to the south as well. An officer informed General Johnston that the railroad depots in South Carolina had been plundered by "fugitives and country-people, who thought, apparently, that, as there was no longer a government, they might assume the division of this property." He also noted that supplies in Charlotte "had either been consumed by our cavalry in the neighborhood or appropriated by individuals"[43] Near Greensboro the 2nd South Carolina left camp at sunrise and marched into the center of town to guard horses. William A. Johnson wrote, "I have about 2,000 horses to guard. People from the surrounding country are hourly besieging and beseeching the guards to sell or let them have horses. This keeps me up night and day on the watch, and I am compelled to walk the guard lines around the coral [sic] all the time to prevent any one from getting any of this stock."[44]

Part of the agreement at the Bennitt place called for parole passes to be issued to the Confederate troops, as was done at Appomattox. General William Hartstuff, inspector general of Schofield's staff, went to Greensboro from Raleigh to begin working with a local printer to produce them. As he passed through Hillsborough and entered Confederate lines with a few staff members, "it was with a curios, [sic] half-uneasy sensation that I thus for the first time found myself on the wrong side of the Confederate outposts without having driven them in by a hostile advance. It was not easy to orient one's

Greensboro Patriot Office. The parole passes were printed here (Greensboro Historical Museum Archives).

self at once with the new condition of things, and it would hardly have been a surprise to find that we had been entrapped by a ruse."[45]

The paroles were printed in the offices of the *Greensboro Patriot*, at 218 Market Street. During the war this office had also printed a series of Confederate primers for youth, authored by James W. Albright, Richard Sterling, and James D. Campbell.[46] One of those who helped print the paroles was Albright, who had made it away from Appomattox before the surrender. Using a hand press and working with his brother Robert, also a paroled soldier from the Army of Northern Virginia, they used paper supplied by the Union army, as there was none to be had in Greensboro.[47] Albright recalled, "[W]e went to work with a will, and the way we turned out paroles was really marvelous — considering our slow press.... But we kept ahead of the officers after first thousand was delivered. I never asked Maj. Worth what he would pay me — indeed he might refuse to pay me anything — so you may know how I felt good when he asked me if $125 would pay me for the work. I said 'yes, sir, with thanks, also.'"[48]

On April 30 the printed paroles were ready and General Hartstuff oversaw their distribution the next day. General Schofield arrived in Greensboro and made his headquarters at Blandwood, the elegant home of former governor John Morehead.[49]

In the meantime General Jacob D. Cox chose the 104th Ohio, a veteran regiment and one known for discipline, to move into Greensboro. They had seen their fair share of action: Knoxville, Chattanooga, Atlanta, Franklin, Nashville, and Fort Fisher. The unit was also distinguished by its various mascots — a pet cat, raccoon, and two dogs, a Newfoundland and a white bulldog named Old Harvey. Harvey wore a tag that read, "I am Lt. D.M. Stearns' Dog, Who's Dog Are You?" Cox also ordered that they take their brass band and drum corps, in order to perform garrison duty in the presence of the Confederates "with all the honors." When they arrived on the afternoon of May 1, they would be the only Union troops there for some time. Cox accompanied them, assigned as commander of the Greensboro Military District.[50]

General Cox boarded a train at Durham Station and it proceeded west. At Hillsborough General William Hardee met him and accompanied him the rest of the way to Greensboro. Hardee had been sent by Johnston to meet with Union commanders and ease the transition from Confederate to Union military control.[51] Next their train stopped at Company Shops (now Burlington) for wood and water. Here they were "hailed with gladness" by the civilians. "The ladies waved their handkerchiefs, the band played, the soldiers cheered, the darkies danced, and all seemed lighted and overjoyed."[52] James Gaskill of the 104th Ohio wrote of the journey:

> General Schofield ... and General Cox ... with their respective staff officers, accompanied by our regiment board a train made up partly of flat cars and after a few hours run we arrive at Greensboro ... where for a few days Jeff. Davis established migratory headquarters of the Confederacy.
>
> Here we leave the cars and form in line in the midst of about thirty thousand defeated and disheartened Confederate soldiers, many of whom rejoice with us that the contest is ended. We are soon surrounded by thousands of our late enemy whose appearance and equipment plainly show the exhausted and impoverished condition of the Confederate forces and we know that braver boys cannot be found on this continent for they have been our adversaries during the past year, facing privations and dangers with but scant hope of success.[53]

The men of the 104th Ohio remained near the station until other arrangements could be made. While sending only one regiment into the heart of the Confederate army's camp may seem unwise, Schofield's goal was to send only enough men to guard the arms and supplies, hoping not to provoke conflict. The Buckeye troops must have felt uneasy, standing amid the heart of the enemy army with no support available. Ohioan Nelson A. Pinney wrote, "We landed right in the midst of twenty thousand rebel soldiers. They immediately marched to a large field east of the city where they stacked arms and parked their wagons and artillery."[54] He continues:

> The 104th was then divided into three reliefs and put on guard, one over the railroad property and the remainder over the war matériel. They turned over one hundred forty six pieces of artillery, over three hundred wagons, forty-one thousand stands of small arms, over two hundred stands of colors, two-hundred forty five locomotives and more than one thousand cars, with an immense amount of commissary and ordinance stores. It was a time of excitement and judgment on our part. The rebel commander could turn over his war matériel, but as to the soldiers, it was another matter. Feeling themselves no longer under the restraint of military discipline, thousands of them had hid their weapons and were "Raising Cain" in town and in the camps, some of them less than half a mile away.[55]

A fellow soldier in the unit, William G. Bentley wrote, "We found the town full of rebels who were still guarding the rebels stores. Our Regiment was the first force of Yankees in the place and it looked a little squally for awhile, as a great many of them were drunk and inclined to be impudent but we got along first-rate considering, we relieved the rebel guard that evening and have been on duty ever since."[56]

The Union officers and troops had arrived on a Sunday, and Reverend Jacob H. Smith wrote, "Several Federal officers arrived today and attended church and heard Mr. Fountain preach." He also wrote of the Union officers "sitting on Jno Sloan's porch and Mr. Wood's apart.... They have come to issue paroles, take charge of the surrendered property and resolve the matter."[57] The Ohio troops set up their camp north of town, in an area now within modern-day Greensboro. Private Bentley wrote that he had "a *good bunk* for five of us, covered with *Confederate documents* which make a first-rate bed and are living in fine style."[58]

Among the stores now in Union hands were over one hundred artillery guns and 341,000 rounds of ammunition. The bulk of these materials stood at the railroad yard near the center of Greensboro. Here were thirty-three buildings that included a wagon shop, offices, five hospital buildings, and four warehouses, liveries for mules and horses, and barracks. Other supplies were scattered in Greensboro, Jamestown, Charlotte, Salisbury, Hillsboro, and close to a half dozen other widely separated points.[59]

Upon arrival, General Jacob D. Cox proceeded from the depot to Confederate headquarters, where he noted Johnston's camp conditions:

> His tents were pitched in a grove in the outskirts of the town, and he waited for us there. It seemed to us, as we approached, that the little encampment was not quite so regular and trim as our own custom required. The wall tents did not sit quite so squarely upon the ground, and the camp was not laid out with regular-

Confederate supplies in warehouses. An example of the many warehouses full of Confederate supplies in the city (Greensboro Historical Museum Archives).

ity. The general indirectly apologized for some of these things by saying that we could not expect the discipline in his army to be fully maintained when all knew that it was on the eve of being disbanded

Cox also noted the "breakdown of discipline which was rapidly going on." Officers had to guard their own horses, in fact Johnston himself was the only one of his headquarters staff not in the guard duty rotation.[60] Cox added, "The moment the blue-coated sentinels began to pace their 'beats' around the warehouses, parks of artillery, etc, the submission of these men ... was most complete. They were scrupulously respectful in their bearing and language, and the groups of them who gathered about ... would obey the slightest direction of the sentry with a cordiality ... in contrast with the sort of ... defiance they showed their own officer."

    That same day, General Judson Kilpatrick, the Federal cavalry commander, reported from Durham that Confederate deserters, in groups of twenty or more, were committing "depredations" in the region, including stealing mules and horses.[61]

    Some Confederates put their worthless money to good use, as it became prized among Union soldiers for souvenirs. One South Carolinian from the

General site of Britton Hotel. This important landmark stood near the center of this photograph.

Army of Northern Virginia recorded his experiences passing through Greensboro on the way home. He noted, "Our clothes were rough and ugly, what were we to do five hundred miles away from home with nothing to eat and no means to buy with. Our supply of food lasted until we got to Greensboro, N.C. There Mr. M. McCoy's greenbacks and mine that we got for our Confederate money which we sold to those Yankees for relics to take home, were used to get us some flour that did us to Charlotte N.C."[62]

On May 1 General Hartstuff, with three other Federal officers, began to issue paroles in downtown Greensboro. In a further show of cooperation and true to his sense of duty, General Johnston allowed only the men present to receive paroles. These four Union officers worked at their task with the assistance of Confederate staff members. As the 104th Ohio had not yet arrived, they were the only four Yankees in the city.[63]

Hartstuff opened his office at 8 o'clock at the Britton Hotel on Market Street. The building no doubt suffered from the same lack of upkeep that nearly every structure had with four years of neglected maintenance. It was described by one traveler as "dumpy." He added that the "row of circular brick columns which support the porch have lost much of their plastering," and the floor was of "rotting plank, which look as though a load of Wheeler's

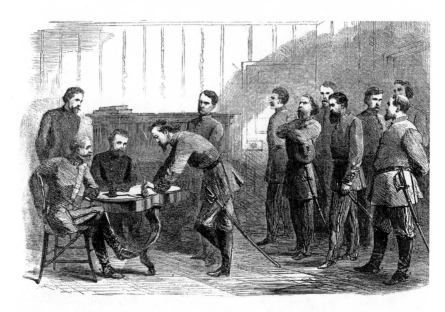

Confederate officers receiving paroles. This scene took place in the Britton Hotel (Greensboro Historical Museum Archives).

cavalry had left their starving brutes to make a meal there." Unfortunately the exact location of the hotel is not known, but it sat on Market Street in the heart of downtown.[64]

The first to arrive at the office was an anxious Admiral Raphael Semmes. He had good reason to be first in line as he was fearful of being tried for piracy for his raiding on the high seas during the war (Semmes had the distinction of being the only Confederate to hold the ranks of both admiral and general).[65] He wrote in his diary that he met General Hartstuff at 8 o'clock, and that "there were four of the Northern men present." The paroles were ready to be filled out, and Hartstuff reviewed the muster roll that Semmes brought, counting the names of his command. Hartstuff then handed Semmes the correct number of blank paroles. Semmes replied, "I prefer, if you have no objection to have it filled up and completed here in your presence." Thus Semmes filled out his parole and had it witnessed by the Union officers, no doubt feeling a sense of relief that he was now protected by the parole.[66]

Later that day the stock of paroles ran low as they were being issued, and Hartstuff contracted with local printer James W. Albright (who had escaped from Appomattox) for 15,000 more.[67] Writing at the time, Johnston said that he "tried faithfully to carry out the terms of agreement ... but the terribly disorganized condition of his army, resulting from its being hastily disbanded, rendered it exceedingly difficult for him to control it. I think it would have been entirely disorganized but for the anxiety of the men to receive their paroles before going home. As it was, a large number did go home before they were paroled." On a good note, however, he also said, "I am satisfied ... that the number of arms carried way was not greater than was allowed by the terms of agreement."[68]

Nelson A. Pinney of the 104th Ohio recorded events of their first night in Greensboro:

> All night they made the region about us resound with their drunken brawls, and the vicinity extremely dangerous with their wild and reckless firing, as they sauntered through town and country, committing crimes and ravages of the most horrible nature. Probably twenty-five percent of those thirty-thousand or more men marched or rode off into the country in bands from five to fifty, committing robberies, murders, arson, and every crime known. For several weeks the helpless inhabitants of central and western Carolina lived under a perfect reign of terror. The guard lines were made as strong as possible with so few men, yet scattered as we were obliged us to be, we would have been unable to stand before an attack by these forces, such as might have been precipitated by any false or unwise step on our part. Happily, all such trouble was averted by our patience and forbearance under the most trying insults, threats, taunts, and insinuations from the drunken and desperate characters by which we were surrounded.[69]

Captain Nicholas Schecnk observed of his commander, "The worst whipped man — of the entire army — that I saw was Gen. Beauregard, as he was sitting on a crosstie with his hands at his face and an expression of despair — Exchanged kind words with officers of an Ohio command. Everyone seemed happy at the words, 'Peace and war over' one officer said to me — 'we are just as tired of this thing as possible and glad it is over.'"[70]

On the 2nd Hartstuff sent word that the Confederates were "dissolving and raising the devil." Cox realized the situation was too much to handle for the 104th Ohio alone, no matter how good a unit they were, and he sent for another regiment. Old Harvey and his comrades would not be alone for long.

That same day, Charles F. Vanderford reported 8,467 weapons turned in at that point, yet not all Confederate units, such as Kennedy's and Pettus's brigades, had turned in weapons yet. He also noted that the number of arms-bearing men seemed to be smaller than allowed, perhaps as low as 2 or 3 percent. He also notes that many weapons must have been taken by deserters starting on April 27. He goes on to note "the ordnance officers of the commands have faithfully discharged their duties, as far as was possible under the circumstances."[71]

Yet, as with so many other aspects of the disbanding, not all went according to plan. General Hoke's Division, for example, turned in only 170 of the nearly 4,000 weapons they possessed.[72] Among the items turned in were weapons of various calibers, including a wide variety of rifles and muskets, 411,000 cartridges, cartridge boxes and belts, cap pouches, waist belts, bayonets, scabbards, 216,000 percussion caps, and hundreds of gun slings and other leather goods.[73] Captain George Pepper of the 80th Ohio took stock of the artillery that had been turned over:

> We obtained 108 pieces of artillery, which were parked near the town, with limber-chests, caissons, and running gear, but little or no ammunition and nor horses or mules, or wagons. All these were needed by the paroled army to carry their rations, private property, etc.
>
> All the valuable horses were, of course, the "private property" of somebody, and were appropriated. Such was the scramble for horses and mules, that the officers had to keep a strict watch over their horses to prevent them from being stolen, but many lost their animals notwithstanding every precaution. Every horse or mule that could carry a man or any other burden had been gobbled up.[74]

Johnston realized that the dispersed nature of his forces, combined with the poor state of the army's transport, high rates of daily desertion, and the anxiousness of the men to leave all prevented the arms and property from being centrally gathered in Greensboro. Thus he had officers sent to receive it wherever men "chose to throw them down."[75]

Reporter T.C. Wilson of the *New York Herald* noted of the Confederate camps he visited on May 2nd, "There was nothing like the same order and neatness in the rebel camps that mark the federal. No nicely laid out streets. No shaded pavilions for headquarters, but it looked like a bivouac, or if there was a heavy shower of dirty tents, and there they stood, higgledy piggledy, bit and little, as they fell."[76]

Paroles continued to be issued on May 2, with the Confederates leaving Greensboro on May 3. All told, 36,971 men received paroles. It was no secret among both Union and Confederate officers that thousands of troops had simply left without paroles. North Carolinians, especially, were deserting in large numbers, being so close to their homes.[77] From April 27 to May 2 Johnston had ordered his men to stay in their camps and wait patiently. For many it was just too much after the weeks they had already waited.[78]

Men of the 6th North Carolina Cavalry, posted at Salisbury, disbanded and went home "as best they could afoot and on their badly famished horses." Most did not bother to wait to get their paroles. A number of this unit were also paroled in Athens, Georgia, having moved that far south in the weeks after Bentonville.[79] Captain Isaac Bailey of the 58th North Carolina Consolidated wrote later that the unit was "paroled on 2 May 1865, the fragment of noble, battle-scarred veterans who breasted the storm in each of these battles, and intervening skirmishes. Now and hereafter the question may be asked, why did we not succeed? The answer is: They who justly deserve success, do not always win it. Braver men never fought or died, but overpowering numbers and munitions of war were against us."[80] Captain David E. McKinney of the 2nd North Carolina Junior Reserves, camped at Bush Hill, noted "the mule teams were divided among the members of the regiment to which the wagons belonged."[81]

For many who did receive them, the paroles were valuable proof that they had served, and were present right up to the end. Said one soldier, "When the roll is called way up yonder, I'll be there. I have my parole, dated April 26, 1865, Greensboro, NC." Another man's pass was kept by his children, who called it his "certificate of honor."[82]

General Robert F. Hoke prepared a heartfelt farewell address to his troops, delivered on May 1:

Soldiers of my Division:

On the eve of a long, perhaps a final separation, I address to you the last sad words of parting.

The fortunes of war have turned the scale against us. The proud banners which you have waved so gloriously over many a field are to be furled at last; but they are not disgraced, my comrades. Your indomitable courage, your heroic fortitude, your patience under sufferings, have surrounded them with a halo which future years can never dim. History will bear witness to your valor and succeeding generations will point with admiration to your grand struggle for constitutional freedom.

Soldiers, your past is full of glory! Treasure it in your hearts. Remember each gory battlefield, each day of victory, each bleeding comrade. Think then of your future. "Freedom's battle, once begun

Bequeathed from bleeding sire to son

Though baffled oft, is ever won."

You have yielded to overwhelming forces, not superior valor. You are paroled prisoners, not slaves. The love of liberty, which led you into this contest, burns as brightly in your hearts as ever. Cherish it. Associate it with the history of your past. Transmit it to your children. Teach them the rights of freedom, and teach them to maintain them. Teach them the proudest day in all your proud career was that on which you enlisted as Southern soldiers, entering that holy brotherhood whose ties are now sealed by the blood of your compatriots who have fallen, and whose history is coeval with the brilliant record of the past four years.

Soldiers, amidst the imperishable laurels that surround your brows, no brighter leaf adorns them than your connection with the late Army of Northern Virginia!

The star that shone with splendor over its oft-repeated fields of victory, over the two deadly struggles of Manassas Plain, over Richmond, Chancellorsville and Fredericksburg, has sent its rays and been reflected wherever freedom has a friend. That star has set in blood, but yet in glory. That army is now of the past. The banners trail, but not with ignominy. No stain blots their escutcheons. No blush can tingle your cheeks as you proudly announce that you have a part in the history of the Army of Northern Virginia.

My comrades, we have borne together the same hardships; we have shared the same dangers; we have rejoiced over the same victories. Your trials and your patience have excited sympathy and admiration, and I have borne willing witness to your bravery. It is with a heart full of grateful emotions for your services and ready obedience that I take leave of you. May the future of each one be as happy as your past career has been brilliant, and may no cloud ever dim the brightness of your fame. The past rises before me in its illimitable grandeur. Its memories are part of the life of each one of us. But it is all over now. Yet, though the sad, dark veil of defeat is over us, fear not the future, but meet it with manly hearts. You carry to your homes the heartfelt wishes of your General for your prosperity.

My comrades, farewell![83]

Hoke's command had obviously fought much of the war with General Lee's army before transferring to the Carolinas. His address includes many themes common to that of General Lee's General Orders Number 9, issued at Appomattox. It includes many concepts later found in the "Lost Cause" mentality that surged through the postwar South.

The same day, Schofield telegraphed Sherman that the paroles were being issued, but that "utter confusion and anarchy had resulted from a want of understanding on minor points, and on the political questions that had to be met at this instant."[84] Schofield also reported the total number of prisoners paroled as 36,817, and the total number of men surrendering in Georgia and Florida at 52,453. Thus the total of Johnston's force officially paroled for the entire Department was 89,270. The last returns of the Army of Tennessee, taken May 3 when paroles were issued, showed 27,749 men present. The week before, however, over 28,000 were paid. It must be remembered that much of the Confederate cavalry had left.[85]

Charles Hutson, an artilleryman from Stewart's Corps, recalled that many men decided "to make our way home and thence to Texas, without being hampered by the Paroles." His unit, the Beaufort Artillery, was camped about five miles below Greensboro.[86] One North Carolina soldier set out for home through a "devastated country, made so by the ravages of the enemy, until it was so poor that a 'jaybird' would starve flying over it, unless he ceased his rations."[87]

All across the region, various units began to turn in the required arms and prepare for the journey home. At Jamestown Lieutenant Robert M. Collins of the 1st Texas Consolidated (formerly of the 15th Texas) described the surrender:

We boys walked up to the place designated, signed some sort of a document, got our paroles, and one dollar apiece in silver. We were not required to stack arms nor to ground our arms in the presence of the enemy. The fact is, we did not see a Federal soldier during the whole proceedings. Many of the boys left their guns in the woods where we were camped. The writer drove his little Confederate sword out of sight into the earth, and it is there yet if some North Carolina farmer has not plowed it up.

The struggle was now over, and we felt relieved after so many years, months, and days of waiting and watching suspense, and early on the morning of the 3rd of May, we started for our homes....[88]

In High Point Colonel Charles Olmstead of the 1st Georgia Consolidated Regiment described the various emotions he felt during the stacking of arms. No doubt many others had similar thoughts:

The troops were marched to a certain point and there laid down their arms. Officers however kept their swords and each Regiment retained its colors. You will readily understand the mingled emotions that were in my heart. I was weary of war and of the long separation from my wife and children; my eyes yearned for a sight for the dear little boy who had been born in my absence and the thought of returning home to face no more the perils and hardships of a soldier's calling filled my soul with gratitude.... I was thankful too that [my] life had been spared and that a new career could be begun.... Yet, nevertheless, it was impossible to avoid a deep feeling of depression as memory bought back the high hope and courage with which we had entered the war and contrite also the brilliant successes that had marked the earlier stages of the conflict, with the ruin and desolation that had finally come down upon the South. The faces of many dear friends who had laid down their lives for the Cause, were present with me too.[89]

William Dixon of the same regiment wrote, "The Regiment was formed this morning and all the arms and accoutrement except six to a company was turned over to the ordnance officer and sent to Greensboro. I must confess I am yet in the dark as to the arrangement of this whole affair, but suppose if I follow the rest I will yet understand. I was called on a board of survey on flour, which was condemned."[90]

The 4th Tennessee Consolidated "moved slowly and sadly out into an open field where the officers sheathed their swords and the men silently stacked their trusty guns. Then the unarmed command moved out of sight."[91] The men of the 1st Tennessee Consolidated stacked their arms under a tree. Private George W. McDill took some branches of the tree home as a souvenir.[92] William Pollard from the same unit wrote that he received his parole at 4:30 P.M. on May 4, about a mile from Salisbury.[93]

Sumner Cunningham of the 3rd Tennessee Consolidated wrote, "The army was marched out and stacked their arms on what some said was, or at least very near, the old battle field of Guilford court-house. During all this time we had not seen a single Federal."[94] Sergeant Daniel Dantzler of the 2nd South Carolina Artillery (who had been converted to infantry) simply wrote, "We were lined up and stacked our guns in a field and left them there."[95]

Artilleryman Charles Jones of the Chatham Artillery (GA) recounted that how his battery ended its service. He notes that the men were particularly distressed to give up their guns, reflecting the fierce pride that artillerymen had in their cannons. His reference to Olustee refers to the largest battle fought in Florida, in which Confederate troops halted a Union invasion of the state:

> Its guns, and horses and equipments were turned in on the 2d. The guns were parked at Greensboro with the rest of the Confederate light artillery, and were not formally relieved by any Federal officer. The Battery surrendered consisted of four twelve-pounder Napoleon guns. Two of them had been manufactured at the Confederate arsenal in Macon, Georgia, and the other two were Federal guns which had been captured at the battle of Olustee and turned over to the company by the Battery during that memorable engagement. It was with feelings of peculiar regret that the company parted with these guns which their valor had won. At the time of the surrender, there were with the Battery about one hundred men present for duty. The battery animals were generally unfit for service, having suffered severely during late marches from fatigue and lack of forage. The sergeants were all dismounted, and some of the caissons were drawn by only four horses.[96]

William R. Talley of Havis' Battery (GA) described how his battery turned over their guns. The experience left an impression on him that never left him:

> Our Capt. one morning, I think it was the 27th of April, had the bugle to blow the assembly call as if we were to march. The cannoneers of each gun fell in just in front of the horses and the roll was called as usual. Then the Capt. stepped in front and read the order of surrender. Then he address[ed] us about like this "Men, at the sound of the bugle, I will give the usual order 'By piece from the fight forward march' but first 'Cannoneers to your post march' you cannoneers will take your positions at your guns and at the command of march you will get to the wheels and as usual help the horses to start and then stand to your position and let the guns go on to town." The command "to your post march" and we boys marched to our posts the last time. The command "By piece from the right forward march" I saw the 1st piece go and the cannoneers stand in their places. It looked terrible. The 2nd piece went, then the 3rd piece, then the 4th, my gun. We pushed and away the gun went and we stood in our places. That was the first time in three years that our gun had gone and I was not to go with it and as I watched that gun roll away I felt a loneliness and grief down in my heart and the tears streamed from my eyes. I was sad and sorrowed as if I had lost a loved one. We did love our guns. They had been our companions for three

years and we would have died in their defense. 'Twas a sad day in our camp that day.[97]

The 42nd Georgia was camped at this time near the railroad depot at High Point. A soldier in the regiment noted that their weapons "were stacked in the old field in front of us." Captain William Calhoun of the unit wrote, "After having our arms stacked out in the old field in front of us, which we turned over to the soldiers of Uncle Sam, I began to look around for transportation."[98] The regiment's colonel, Larack Thomas, wrote, "Our command moved on to High Point, a short distance from Greensboro, and there in an open field I had our regiment to stacked arms, about four hundred in number, and when that was done, amid a silence that could almost be felt, many a tear was shed by brave officers and brave men while standing there over those guns."[99] Hezekiah McCorkle of the 37th Georgia noted during his unit's stacking of arms that "we turn over four fifths of our arms to the U.S. Government, the remaining fifth we are allowed to keep." As the unit began its march for home a few days later, he noted, "The order to fall in was received by the troops with a deafening shout. Homeward bound once again after a three years toil in camp...."[100]

Daniel Dantzler of the 5th South Carolina Cavalry noted, "To day we were lined up and stacked our arms in a field and left them there." They had moved through Greensboro in the last few days and were camped below the town.[101] Sergeant I.W. Moore of the same unit noted, "Surrendered and stacked arms in the Public Road in High Point, N.C."[102] Tennessean William Pollard also noted that his unit surrendered all their arms, "retaining one fifth for self protection."[103] Salisbury had been the site of a large prison for captured Union troops, it being an ideal location along the railroad line. The Alabama and Virginia troops of General Pettus's Brigade camped at the site of the prison and stacked their arms there.[104]

To maintain a semblance of discipline, Johnston ordered that officers keep the paroles of the men while on the march and distribute them upon reaching home. As with everything else, chaos reigned, and some received them at Greensboro or on the journey home. The men of the 29th Georgia, for example, received their paroles at Thomasville, Georgia, when they reached home. But many units received them in their camps in Guilford County.[105] Captain William Dixon of the 1st Georgia Consolidated recalled when his unit got their paroles: "Today Col Olmstead went to High Point this morning and returned with the blanks for paroles signed. Each captain has to fill them out for his men. I filled out 39 for my company. The paroles will be held by Brigade commanders until the brigades are disbanded."[106] The paroles that the Confederates received read:

....has given his solemn obligation not to take up arms against the Government of the United States until properly released from this obligation; and is permitted to return to his home, not to be disturbed by the United States authorities so long as he observes this obligation and obeys the laws in force where he may reside.

Col. John Nethercutt told the men of his North Carolina unit that as they were detached from the Army of Northern Virginia, that technically they had already surrendered and were "at liberty" to go.[107]

On May 2 Johnston delivered his farewell to the troops who remained near his headquarters in downtown Greensboro. He gave his address in the yard of Ralph Gorrel's house on South Elm "under the green foliage of a spreading maple" tree. Today the site is near the railroad tracks in downtown Greensboro, indicated by historical markers. Similar in sentiment, Johnston's address is equally eloquent as that given by General Robert E. Lee at Appomattox. It read:

> Comrades—In terminating our official relations I earnestly exhort you to observe faithfully the terms of the pacification agreed upon, and to discharge the obligations of good and peaceful citizens, as well as you have performed the duties of thorough soldiers in the field. By such a course, you will best secure the comfort of your families and kindred and restore tranquility to your country.
>
> You will return to your homes with admiration of our people, won by the courage and noble devotion you have displayed in this long war. I shall always remember with pride the loyal support and generous confidence you have given me.
>
> I now part from you with deep regret—and bid you farewell with feelings of cordial friendship; and with earnest wishes that you may have hereafter all the prosperity and happiness in the world.[108]

Johnston delivered his address one mile away from the Edgeworth Female Seminary. It was just one day short of exactly five years from the date that the young ladies had presented an elaborate silk flag to the Guilford Grays, a local unit leaving for the war.[109] Reporter Theodore Wilson was on hand, and wrote, "The scene was an affecting one, and all who witnessed it regarded it in that light."[110]

Journalist David P. Conyngham of the *New York Herald* observed, "A large number of paroled officers and men were loitering about the depot. The women crowded out to see the Yankee troops, but the men made no display; even the band refrained from playing. Before night the rebels and ourselves were in best possible terms with each other. Rebel and Federal soldiers were camped together around the fires, trading coffee, whisky, meat, and tobacco. Some of these were fighting their battles over again."[111] (That same day, Schofield wrote, "The country is a good deal disturbed by the returned sol-

Gorrell house. In front of this home General Johnston addressed his troops (Greensboro Historical Museum Archives).

diers of Lee's and Johnston's armies.")[112] A soldier in the 17th North Carolina described events at their camp near Salem Church:

> About 2 o'clock the orderly sergeant was told to form his company (I suppose the same form was gone through with each company and regiment of the entire army, but I saw only my own company and regiment and am telling only what I saw and heard), the captain had something to say to them. The order to "fall in" was responded to promptly. Cap. Sam Johnston then told us that General Johnston desired every man to assemble around his headquarters when the drum beat, as he had something interesting to say to us. That was all, "break ranks."
>
> When the drum was beaten the men quickly gathered around headquarters, and General Johnston addressed them. I do not pretend to make a verbatim report of what he said but in substance he briefly reviewed the hardships and dangers they had shared and dared together; assured them of his appreciation of their faithfulness to the cause and to himself. Then he told them that General Lee had surrendered; that Richmond was in the hands of the Yankees; that in our front was the Yadkin River, so swollen that it was impassable; that if we crossed it Kautz's Cavalry awaited us on the other side; that Grant was on our right and Sherman in our rear and on our left, so we were completely surrounded. Then he told us that President Lincoln had been assassinated, was dead, and that the U.S. Government had asked for an armistice for ten days. "Now," said he, "most

of you are farmers; it is planting time; every day is important to you. I wish you would all go to your homes at once. I want to get home myself. But you have stood by me all these years, and I must stay with you now as long as there is a man in camp." He said he thought it was not necessary to wait for paroles or formal surrender; that there was considerable property to be looked after, horses, wagons, arms, etc., and as long as men remained in camp they would be required to do guard duty as usual; though he didn't think there would be any more fighting, as he considered the war over. Then he dismissed them. It was the last time he saw his whole army as their commander, and few of us ever saw him again. General Hoke and other officers spoke, but I have no idea what they said. By the time General Johnston had finished his speech, no one was in a mood to hear more. The men were excited and bewildered. Some laughed, some cried, some swore. The band played "Dixie" and many joined in singing it. What to do next was the question confronting us. Few realized fully the import of what General Johnston had said. Billy Williams, who lived near Williamston and realized the importance of getting his corn planted as soon as possible, was for starting at once for home, but was not quite sure he was right, came to me for advice. I advised him to take General Johnston at his word and go home right away. He started at once. It was then about 4 o'clock in the afternoon. About 6 o'clock Billy returned to camp looking sheepish. We at once began to ask questions. Had he been home and back in so short a time?–we'd all go right away — have breakfast at home. Come, tell us about it!

"Well," said Billy, "I'd gone a couple of miles down the road when I met Colonel Brown, of the 42nd. He asked me who I was, what regiment I belonged to, where I was going and so on. I told him my name and regiment and that I was going home. He wanted to know by what authority I was away from my regiment. I told him what General Johnston said. Then Colonel Brown ordered me to back to camp saying, 'We won't disband that way; we'll all go to Raleigh and surrender like soldiers.' So I thought it would be best to come back."

Later the soldier added, "Next morning early Billy again started homeward, met no further opposition, and had his corn planted when I reached home. Every day squads of men started home. They had to walk all the way and would have had to walk if they had waited for formal surrender and parole; for the railroads were all torn up, bridges were destroyed, rolling stock disabled, so that it would be weeks and perhaps months before traffic and transportation could be resumed."[113]

Soldiers were appropriating wagons and horse for transportation home, so much so that officers and generals were losing their mounts. On April 30 General Stephen D. Lee wrote to Union authorities: "They now lay claim to everything, and it is my belief that they will strip most of the generals of their wagons."[114]

William Worsham of the 3rd Tennessee Consolidated Regiment wrote of their start home: "We moved out in regular order for Salisbury. On our way we passed through Thomasville and the ladies (God bless them) waved the Confederate flag from the windows of the Academy, but they received only a faint response. We felt sad. We were but part of the funeral procession going home from the burial of the dead Confederacy."[115]

General Benjamin F. Cheatham's division of Tennessee, Georgia, and South Carolina troops marched from Greensboro to Salisbury, where he held a final review and inspection of his remaining men. In an emotional farewell, the general shook hands with the soldiers as he moved down the line, tears in his eyes. At this point Cheatham separated from his command, as he did not intend to immediately return to Tennessee. The Volunteer State soldiers moved west to cross over the mountains; the others marched straight down towards Charlotte. The Tennessee men knew they would be passing through the hostile pro-Union areas of western North Carolina and East Tennessee, but it was the fastest and most direct way to go.[116]

As he led his men of the Jeff Davis Cavalry (MS) toward home, Lieutenant Joseph Waring noted the countryside: "No grain is to be found in the country. The horses are starving. A few more days and Johnston's army would have starved out. It was perhaps wise, but it was certainly hard to give up after having struggled manfully for four years. The blue uniforms in Greensboro are certainly unpleasant to look at."[117] William Fletcher of the 8th Texas Cavalry witnessed firsthand the lawlessness and desperation gripping the region on his ride south:

> At one small town we passed, the town authorities opened quite a large store-room of army supplies of bolt cloth, and such like. The news of the opening for the soldiers soon spread and the citizens gathered in considerable number—the soldier went in, but got little of any use. The most of the boys cut off pants patterns. There was no attempt to close the doors after the soldiers came out, for by this time there was a jam of citizens who seemed to want all they could get while the opportunity offered; so they soon filled the house, which had a platform—and there were some amusing incidents seen, both men and women were in the grab; and when a fellow inside would shoulder up a bolt of goods, his rights would soon be contested; therefore, there would be a scuffle and unrolling of the bolt with a run for the streets and there was quite a piling up of those who retained their hold too near the edge of the platform. The whole street front was soon a struggling mass, with numbers of pocket knives being used to get a part of the bolt at least; and in some instances the cut was very small. It was all done in a good humored, noisy crowd, but the divide was not an equal one, by any means.[118]

Across the Department of the Carolinas, Georgia, and Florida, other Confederate troops learned about the surrender and began to lay down their arms. The 3rd Tennessee Mounted Infantry was moving towards Charlotte during the negotiations and ended up stacking its weapons there. William E. Sloan reported that they stacked arms "at what is known as Sugar Creek Church. No Federals were present, nor have we seen any Federals since we met them in battle on April 13th on our return from Raleigh."[119]

Through the last week of April and the first week of May, Johnston and his officers corresponded daily on issues such as security in the Greensboro-Salisbury-Charlotte corridor, the collection of weapons, the movement of supplies, and transportation for the troops. Perhaps the only thing as tedious and taxing as organizing an army is disbanding one. Although the fighting was over, there remained a great deal of administrative things to do.

Conyngham wrote of Johnston's camp that it was "a very plain one, scarcely as respectable as a division general's in the Union army. The tents were old, and scattered about without much regard to regularity. The General's tent was a plain wall tent, not much better than the rest. On the lid of a mess chest near them was the remains of a very plain frugal supper."[120] Of the general himself, he wrote, "He is evidently a man of great reflective power, schooled into the greatest subserviency, combined with untiring energy. His conversation is so natural, dignified and easy that you at once feel at your ease, though at the same time you are conscious that he is reading your thoughts like an open book. He possesses much of the refined ease and elegance of a gentleman with the penetration and firmness of a soldier."[121]

General William Hardee, Johnston's senior Corps commander, traveled to meet General John Schofield in Raleigh. Together they discussed the supplemental terms of the surrender, clarifying key points. Hardee breakfasted with General Judson Kilpatrick in Durham before returning to his command.[122] T.C. Wilson, another *Herald* correspondent, met with General Hardee on his return from meeting Union commanders in Raleigh. When asked if he thought real peace was possible, the general responded, "I do. I think the people of the South are anxious for it."[123]

On May 3 the 104th Ohio watched as Confederate troops stacked their weapons. It was nothing like the large formal ceremony held nearly a month earlier at Appomattox. Four hundred men of the 104th Ohio relieved General John Kennedy's men at 2 o'clock. These South Carolinians were the last troops of the Army of Tennessee to lay down their arms, and this was the only formal ceremony conducted during the surrender of this army.[124] A full division (of the Fifth Corps) of the Army of the Potomac had been on hand to oversee the surrender of Lee's army. Here a mere regiment represented the Union army at the Greensboro surrender. Private Joseph W. Gaskill of the 104th Ohio wrote of the turnover:

> A patrol guard of Union soldiers is placed on duty in the village to keep order while other detachments are sent to surrounding fields where rebel guards are

relieved from duty over supplies surrendered to our forces. Among these details I am sent with a squad of men to relieve rebel guards on duty in a field parked with artillery and ammunition wagons. Relieving this guard from duty over their own property is a new experience and some what embarrassing yet the change is made without friction and apparent regret on the part of the rebel guards we are relieving. The "Johnnies" knew what we are there for, so after receiving instructions from the sergeant of this guard we march along the line when the rebel guard takes proper position, instructs the "yank" who relieves him and drops in rear of the line until all are relieved. They are then formed in line by their sergeant and stack arms on which they hang a varied assortment of equipment, break ranks and their warfare is ended. A few of these boys seem to die hard, claiming they have been overpowered, overwhelmed and have worn themselves out "licking yanks" against great odds. They refer to General Lee who during the past eighteen months has "been whipping Yankees against great odds and worn themselves out on the job." Of course, we let the boys have their say for it's not hurting us a bit and seems consoling to them, yet ask them to point out any important battle they have won west of Virginia.

One of our "strategists" who happened to be in this squad of guard and always loaded with contention and indiscretion has to be smothered in order to prevent a scrap. To intimate to these rebs that they have been fairly defeated might make trouble for all are imbued with that southern spirit of "honah" that admits no defeat. A few of these rebs are sullen and snappy and have but little to say but we know by the way they are sizing us up they are doing considerable thinking and little effort is made to conceal their hatred of "yanks." Yet we have no ill feeling toward them and sincerely extend our sympathy for we know they will be paroled and sent away, many without homes, means or employment. All except the sergeant of the guard soon depart for the village. The sergeant is friendly and expresses sensible views of the situation. He thinks the war should have ended over a year ago thus saving the lives of thousands of men who have been sacrificed in order to gratify the ambition or perhaps to save the necks of a few men at the head of the conspiracy to destroy the Union. The sergeant says much credit is due their lives for a cause that seemed hopeless. Many of the rank and file in the Confederate army cannot read or write and by reason of this they have been made to believe their forces are gaining victories in other fields. Newspapers throughout the south are misleading in their accounts of the operation of their forces hoping to inspire soldiers and citizens to renewed effort to bolster up the "sacred cause" of disunion and human bondage. A newspaper issued a few days before the evacuation of Richmond informs its readers that Grant's army fronting Petersburg has been whipped and Sherman's army on its march from Savannah through the Carolinas is meeting disaster.[125]

Guarding a train of bacon was private George Bussey of the 7th South Carolina Consolidated Regiment. They had been permitted to give away any that was bad, and in fact gave away a lot to stragglers and civilians. He described the transfer ceremony:

It fell to my lot to be on post when the enemy came to relive us. Our regiment had gone out a few miles below town. A train load of Blue Coats rolled up beside our train of bacon. In a short time a detail was sent to relieve me. I simply gave the man direction as to what I was there for, and bade him adieu. They didn't take my gun or anything that I had. I walked leisurely alone down the railroad in the direction our regiment had gone, meditating upon what had happened and that the terrible fight was all over with, as it could not be helped and we had done all that a brave people could do, and felt relieved and glad that we were going home. I felt great pride in the fact that though we had been overcome, as a people we almost always whipped in the individual fight. I threw my rifle over into a briar patch by the railroad and walked up into the camp where we stayed a few days.[126]

In a large field on the east side of town sat 150 guns, 200 colors, 500 wagons, and 40,000 small arms. The rail yard downtown had 200 engines and 1,000 cars with supplies. Warehouses were full of ammunition and goods. Hundreds of weary horses and mules needed attention. It was a volatile and tense situation and one much too dangerous for one regiment to secure properly.[127]

As the Confederates left their camps, they retained some semblance of order. On May 5 the bulk of the army marched into Salisbury to get ten day's rations that awaited them there. Confederate guards would remain at this railroad town after the army passed through until Union troops arrived to relieve them.[128] As the Confederates broke camp and moved south, they were following the Great Wagon Road, a colonial road that ran from Philadelphia to Charlotte, then split, with one branch going to Augusta and the other across the upper part of South Carolina towards Atlanta. This was an ancient path, used by the prehistoric Indians, early European explorers, and colonial settlers. Today it is largely paralleled by Interstate 85 from Greensboro to Atlanta.

The Southerners followed predictable routes that funneled them through Salisbury, Charlotte, and York, or from Charlotte to Camden. For weeks village residents encountered a seemingly never-ending procession of former soldiers walking by their homes. William T. Ganaway observed the Confederate departure from Trinity College. He wrote, "Their arms were thrown in piles, their cannon abandoned, and all the paraphernalia of war left to be turned over to the enemy. On breaking camp, they formed a line in marching order, which reached for miles through town and country."[129] He later reflected, "The long procession of begrimed and scar-worn veterans presented a scene which rarely occurs, and one never to be forgotten. With its disappearance vanished my last vision of the ill-fated Confederacy."[130]

George Guild of the 4th Tennessee Cavalry wrote of their departure from Hillsborough that his regiment "would have been taken for a funeral procession."[131] Colonel John Black of the 1st South Carolina Cavalry noted, "When Johnston surrendered this Regiment fully armed & equipped, marched out of camp and was disbanded by companies in York County." Apparently the unit went home with all its weapons and gear, breaking up upon arrival in South Carolina.[132] Joseph MacKay of the 5th South Carolina Cavalry recalled that the men drew lots for their remaining mules for the trip home.[133] A Greensboro civilian recorded his impressions of the army's departure:

> When it was positively known that Johnston has surrendered, the soldiers from every State commenced their homeward journey, scattering and living upon the country. With only one dollar and five cents in silver in their pockets, these men turned their faces homeward. Some of them lived more than two thousand miles away in the remote regions of Texas, the swamps of Louisiana, or the prairies of Arkansas.
>
> A great rush was made by many of the demoralized and desperate men for horses and mules to carry them on their way, and nearly every citizen stood guard over his stables day and night.[134]

Another civilian, John Hiatt, who lived along the Salisbury Road about five miles from Greensboro, wrote of the army's' impact on him: "The Con's [Confederates] camped on my land 9 days ... all Johnsons army ... I had 160 acres in wheat & oats to the pasture ... all to the ground but 10 or 12 acres."[135] One Quaker woman, Mrs. Hockett, whose husband was fighting with the 21st North Carolina in Virginia, endured having hundreds of men camp near her home who also several times passed through her property. She was fortunate that their farm and animals were not looted, yet she was not spared the impact of the army.[136] A history of the area notes the following:

> Whilst the wagons and cattle of the army were passing, her own cattle got loose and started away with the army herds. The colored boy whom she employed went after them, and when the captain of the trains was told the circumstances, he ordered his men to help turn the straying cattle. A neighbor told the trusting wife that her horse was in too good condition; that the army was needing horses, and hers would surely be taken. The army was all day passing her house, and the excited horse was racing back and forth between the barn and the road in full view, but he was not taken. Although the neighborhood had been ransacked for miles around for horses, and scarcely one of any value had been left, this fine young horse, for which William Hockett had refused the five hundred dollars to purchase his freedom, had been spared.[137]

No doubt residents felt both relief and apprehension, for the army was leaving, but the men were bitter and more desperate than ever, and lawlessness was rampant. It must have seemed strange to look to their former enemies in blue as protectors. Private Gaskill of the 104th Ohio wrote of the tension during these days:

While on duty in Greensboro we treat these Confederate kindly and give but lit-tle heed to braggadocio, insults and insinuations occasionally heard. A few of our boys resent these windy attacks until both Union and Confederate officers take a hand in quieting the men. Rebel soldiers now feel under less restraining of military discipline and a few are found ready to make trouble if encouragement is given. Many of these man are believed to carry concealed weapons and enough might be found to dispose of about four hundred "Yanks" should these uncon-trolled "Johnnies" decide on another "killn." The first night on duty in the vil-lage the situation seeme[d] alarming at times. Drunken rebel soldiers are looking for more trouble, but we are patient, making due allowance for the frame of mind and condition of these men, are warned against entering into arguments with them, and are aided in keeping order by manly efforts of Confederate officers who give timely aid in keeping us out of trouble.

When it becomes known in the rebel ranks that their army has surrendered many leave at once without waiting parole, taking their horses and equipment with them declaring they intend to join other forces not yet surrendered and continue the war. We hear that these men have formed into squads and are mak-ing raids and robbing former friends in Georgia and the Carolinas. Helpless citi-zens are at the mercy of these raids until Union cavalry is brought into action who capture and turn them over to civil authorities for trial. An artillery ser-geant, who deserted Lee's army on the night of its surrender and joined John-ston's army, with a section of that battery, now appears where we are on guard to take a last look at the cannon he has been serving during the war. It will take many years to reconstruct this fellow.

A few hot headed fellows denounce their officers for that they say is a "cow-ardly surrender of the sacred cause." They know but little about the situation but, like our oracles, they have opinions though a large majority take a more sensible view of the matter and are pleased to know the strife is ended. These are the survivors of the rebel army we have been fighting during the past year, and who assaulted our works at Franklin, Tenn., where many of their companies and regiments were almost destroyed. They all seem to have an abundance of the Confederate scrip and poker playing is now their favorite pastime. Instead of counting this scrip they just reach in their hats or coat pockets and sometimes place a handful of these defunct shinplaster on a poor poker hand.[138]

Soon other troops joined the lone Ohio regiment. Gaskill noted, "On the morning of May 4, the 9th New Jersey regiment of infantry arrive and assist in this guard duty and within a few days the rem[a]inder of our division march in and camp near the village."[139]

On the afternoon of the 2nd, several companies of the 9th New Jersey boarded railroad cars in Raleigh for the trip to Greensboro. The next day the other half of the regiment departed. While passing through Company Shops, Company K was detached to maintain order, as the citizens complained of being unprotected. When the unit arrived in Greensboro they first set up camp near the depot, then moved to a site west of town on the McCullough plantation. This was about one mile west of the town (in the vicinity of today's UNC-Greensboro Peabody Park).[140] Describing their arrival in the city, Hermann Everts of the 9th New Jersey wrote, "Lumber was very scarce; the men set up their tents, each company putting up brush-houses, to be protected from the rays of the sun. Rations were very small, and poor: smaller than ever before, because we shared with the whole of Johnston's army; it was very noble to feed and clothe our enemies, but our men suffered much, because it lasted so long before proper arrangements were made to have plenty of supplies."[141]

General Johnston wrote to Schofield from Charlotte on May 8 that the Confederate archives were there and apparently were in danger of being looted. With an eye towards the future, he hoped that Union troops would quickly arrive to get them: "As they will furnish valuable materials for history, I am anxious for their preservation."[142]

On May 10, the 112th Illinois moved from Greensboro to Stokes County to organize a police force of loyal residents. The civilians would have to take the oath of allegiance and agree to obey military authorities. The troops then issued them captured arms and ammunition. It was a small step towards organizing law and order in the region.[143] This transition went fairly smoothly and without incident. Johnston noted that the Federal troops "treated the people around them as they would have done those of Ohio or New York if stationed among them, as their fellow-citizens."[144]

With the surrender complete, thousands of men made their way from Greensboro and Guilford and Randolph counties towards their homes. General Johnston did not consider it a surrender, insisting that his army had been given permission to disperse and return home. It was a technicality, but one he clung to tenaciously the rest of his life.[145]

The Army of Tennessee, an organization that had existed in some form since early 1862 (first as the Army of Mississippi) was no more. Many of these men had received their baptism of fire amid the confused, spring woods of Shiloh exactly four years earlier. They fought tenaciously through the cedar thickets and limestone outcroppings of Stones River, across the rolling hills of Kentucky, and the craggy, rocky ridges of northern Georgia. They endured the cold and the devastating combat at Franklin and Nashville. Now they had come to North Carolina, and now the army ceased to exist. The men went from being soldiers to instantly becoming citizens. It was an unreal transition for many of them.

As the former soldiers left for home, Johnston's work did not end, as he still had to oversee supplies, transportation, and security measures. He wrote they "had not other means of supplying the troops on their homeward march, than a stock of cotton yarn, and a little cloth, to be used as money." At this point he acknowledged the generosity of Sherman, for Johnston's own supplies were "entirely inadequate; and great suffering would have ensued, both of the troops and the people on their routes, if General Sherman ... had not given us two hundred and fifty thousand rations."[146] Captain Hampton J. Cheney of Nashville wrote, "The troops were permitted to retain one-fifth of their arms, with sufficient ammunition to protect them on their way, with a small wagon train carrying 'spun tuck' with which we were to trade for provisions ... on the march.... It was said that old women in the country would exchange anything they had for 'spun tuck' and we found it to be a fact, as we had no trouble to obtain enough food ... on the way."[147]

When he had some free time after the surrender proceedings, General Cox rode over with a group to see the site of the Revolutionary War battle of Guilford Court House. He recalled that the following of this battle:

> [It] ranks high in importance; for the check there given to the invading British army under Lord Cornwallis by the Continental forces under General Greene was the turning-point in a campaign.... [T]he "Old Court House" ... has disap-peared as a village, a few buildings almost unused being the only mark of the old town. Natural topography, however, does not change its material features easily, and in this case a clear field or two where the forest had formerly extended seemed to be the only change that had occurred in the past century. With Gen-eral Greene's official report of the battle in our hands, we could trace with com-plete accuracy every movement of the advancing enemy and his own disposition to receive the attack. We could see the reasons for the movements on both sides, and how undulations of surface and the cover of woods and fences were taken advantage of by either commander. Military principles being the same in all times, we found ourselves criticizing the movements as if they had occurred on one of our recent battlefields. It brought the older and the later war into almost startling nearness, and made us realize, as perhaps nothing else could have done, how the future visitor will trace the movements in which we had a part, and when we have been dust for centuries, will follow the path of our battalions from hill to hill, from stream to stream, from the border of a wood to the open ground where bloody conflict was hand to hand, and will comment upon the his-tory we have made.[148]

Private soldiers also journeyed out to this famous landmark. James Gaskill of the 104th Ohio recalled his visit:

> While encamped at Greensboro, accompanied by a comrade we walk a few miles out in the country to visit the old Revolutionary battlefield of Guilford Court-house where a battle was fought between Cornwallis and General Greene over eighty years prior. A trace of the old fortifications is found, and an aged oak tree with a portion of its top shot away at the battle shown us by a friendly Quaker living near by. After looking over the grounds a short time, where we are shown

other points of interest connected with this battle we are invited to the home of our new friend and without urging accept an invitation to remain for dinner — the first time we have heard or waited for an invitation of this kind for a long time. The people living in this vicinity are nearly all Quaker faith and with rare exceptions are both Union and anti-slavery in sentiment. We enjoy this visit and are interested while the family relate their experience within rebel lines during the war. By reason of this religious faith they have escaped persecution at the hands of Confederate soldiers and conscription officers but have been compelled to contribute liberally in support of the late C.S.A. We thank the family for their hospitality and return to camp late in the afternoon.[149]

Although the battlefield is described as "out in the country" and "a few miles" from Greensboro, the modern city has grown and overtaken the battle site. It is now completely within city limits.

Other activities took place in the Union camps, as related by Gaskill: "[A] convention of Ohio soldiers is held in a grove adjoining the village. At this convention General Jacob D. Cox, our division commander during the past year, is unanimously endorsed as a candidate for governor of Ohio. Delegates are elected to present the General's name at a convention to be held in the state and instructed to use their influence to secure his nomination for that office."[150] Cox would, in fact, be elected governor, in large measure due to his wartime record and popularity among the veterans.

As part of the surrender of Johnston's force, Confederate troops in Florida made arrangements on May 12, 1865, to comply with the terms. At Jacksonville the Confederates were to deposit weapons, ammunition, and any other public property. No mention was made of flags, and it is assumed any flags with the troops in Florida were either hidden or destroyed.[151]

On the 13th Morris C. Runyan of Company G, 9th New Jersey, wrote from Charlotte about their journey from Greensboro through Salisbury and Concord. The road was "filled with rebel soldiers, raids were made by mobs on stores [supplies] that had been left by the rebels. Drunkenness and disorder generally have been the order of the day."[152] In Salisbury he wrote, "[W]e came up with a division of Johnston's army moving South. We could hardly realize that these men, moving in broken, straggling groups and masses, all order and discipline abandoned, with sullen, downcast looks, ragged, dirty and footsore, with spirits broken, were the same soldiers who, with splendid discipline, had fought so bravely and gallantly on many hard contested battlefields."[153] He described one tense scene at Concord, just north of Charlotte. Some of the Union soldiers had found some liquor and were drunk. Former Confederates were drunk too, and tensions rose among the former enemies. "We were under two hundred Union soldiers, but fully armed and equipped." He continues: "Large numbers of the Confederates were surrounding us, many being armed and drunk, all desperate." A confrontation was avoided when Runyan quickly assembled his men and ordered them to march. The movement was twofold in purpose: to remove them from an escalating situation and to sober up his men.[154] Once in Charlotte, Runyan took charge of security in the town, stopped liquor sales, and placed guards over the medical stores and supplies he found there. Among other things, there were quantities of naval stores and machinery from the Confederate naval yard located in the center of the town.[155]

Runyan wrote of a remarkable discovery in Charlotte. A citizen had informed him of other stores hidden in the city. Finding a locked warehouse, Runyan wrote that they "effected a forcible entrance, when to my utmost astonishment, I saw in an open space near the main door, dozens of Federal colors, regimental, State and Union flags lying in the greatest disorder on the floor. Upon further investigation I found a very large number of boxes in the building." They were Union battle flags that had been captured during the war. He immediately stationed guards over the captured flags.[156] Hermann Everts of the regiment recalled, "A number of boxes, said to contain the records of the rebel War Department and all the archives of the so-called Southern Confederacy. Also, boxes, said to contain all the colors and battle-flags captured from the National forces since the beginning of the war."[157] He later noted, "Out of a large number of flags and trophies, taken from our forces during the whole of the war, Captain Runyon picked up the State-colors of the 33d New Jersey Reg't, intending to forward the same to the Adjutant-General of the State of New Jersey."[158] On May 17 General Schofield received the news that the Confederate War Department records had been seized at Charlotte. Among them were the captured Union regimental flags that had been taken during the war. Schofield ordered the contents sent to Washington. There were five boxes that had been filled with Union flags during the course of the war.[159]

7

Occupation

For the most part the Union occupation was a peaceful transition for the residents of Guilford and surrounding counties; for many it was a modest improvement over the chaos brought on by the straggling Confederates. One Greensboro citizen wrote, "Many of the Federal troops acted well and gentlemanly, among the most conspicuous for their fine appearance, excellent drill and good behavior was the 104th Ohio regiment."[1] General Johnston himself wrote,

> The United States troops that remained in the Southern States, on military duty, conducted themselves as if they thought that the object of the war had been the restoration of the Union. They treated the people around them as they would have done those of Ohio or New York if stationed amongst them, as their fellow-citizens. Those people supposed, not unnaturally, that if those who had fought against them were friendly, the great body of the Northern people, who had not fought, must be more so.[2]

Other incidents recorded by citizens showed harsher realities. Despite the relatively peaceful occupation, one wrote, "There were others, however, who behaved badly and would be a reproach to any service.... [There was] a Colonel ... who in his fanaticism put in arrest some ladies of the town ... because they chose to eat their dinner and a turkey on fast day appointed by the President of the United States!"[3] He continued with another example: "I saw six Federal soldiers attack one emanciated, drunken Confederate and beat his head against the ground.... [He] told them in response to a question that he killed many men in battle. This was in Main Street just opposite the Provost Marshall's office. When I remonstrated they informed me that if I took it up I wouldn't fare any better. Yet these men went unpunished."[4] Reverend Jacob H. Smith wrote that just a few days after their arrival "Federals on foot & on horseback moving [were] about in all directions, & in some places doing violence & pillages—one snapped a pistol in the face of Mrs. W.W. Wharton & did several other things ... robbed A. Cunningham of some silver, occupied Robt. M. McLean's house & premises & laid waste his yard & stable...."[5]

Union General Jacob D. Cox wrote extensively of his observations in Greensboro, and they are a wealth of information on the situation there at the time. After the paroles were issued, he noted, "All the Confederate officers from Johnston downward were very earnest in impressing upon us their confidence that the army gave up the struggle without bitterness, and that we could rely not only upon their keeping their parole in good faith, but in their anxiety to become again good citizens of the United States in every sense of the word."[6] Cox wrote of his early accommodations in the city:

> General Schofield and myself passed the night at the house of ex-Governor Morehead, who had urged us to do so. Our host had been one of the leading Whigs of North Carolina in the ante-bellum days.... We were frankly and cordially welcomed, and allowed to see the mixed feelings with which the reassembled family accepted the collapse of the Confederacy. Among the young people was a son of the governor who had been desperately wounded but had recovered. The rebellion had had their devoted support, but they said, "That is all past now." And seemed eagerly desirous to get into accord with the new order of things.[7]

He noted of the Confederate soldiers still lingering in the city:

> Whilst they [the Confederates] stayed they seemed never to tire of watching our men on duty and on the various parades. Our guard-mounting was particularly a show affair. From the moment the music struck up on the parade ground, and the detachments for the guard from the different companies began to file out and march into place, there was always a large concourse of the men in gray making a most interested body of spectators. The smart appearance of the men, the rapid inspection of arms, of haversacks and knapsacks, the march in review, the assignment to posts, the final marching off the field, all seemed to give them great enjoyment. They said they had not paid much attention to the formalities which so greatly relieve the drag and labor of military life even in the field, and they were ready with cordial and appreciative praise of the discipline and finish in drill which they saw.[8]

After most of the Southern soldiers had left, Cox brought the rest of the Twenty-third Army Corps into Greensboro. He sent one division down to Salisbury, and the cavalry under Kilpatrick still further south and west.[9]

Schofield, commanding the occupation of North Carolina, issued an order that summarized his goals:

> [V]isit all parts of the State, disperse or capture all bands of guerillas and marauders, and collect all military arms, other than side arms of paroled officers, which may be found in the State. The corps and district commanders will, as

Dunleath home site. The Union's General Cox established his headquarters on the grounds of the property.

soon as practicable, send to each county under their jurisdiction a discreet officer, with sufficient force to organize a small company of the most responsible loyal citizens to serve as a local police force until further orders. As far as necessary the companies so organized will be furnished with captured arms and ammunition, but will receive no compensation for their services. All the members will be required to take the oath of allegiance to the Government of the United States and an oath to preserve the peace, prevent crime, and arrest criminals, as far as practicable, within their county, and to obey all lawful orders of the U.S. military authorities. Criminals arrested by the police companies will be sent to the nearest military post for trial by military commission.[10]

General Cox wrote, "As soon as headquarters baggage could be brought up I established my camp in the northern edge of Greensborough, in a grove which was part of the grounds attached to the mansion of Mr. Dick, since that time judge of the United States District Court."[11] The home of Robert Dick, Dunleath, stood at 677 Church Street. The Swiss chalet style home was surrounded by 200 acres, encompassing an area bordered by modern Bessemer Street, Church Street, and Park Avenue. It was destroyed in 1969. Relic hunters have found Union minie balls in the vicinity, indicating an occupation camp.[12]

The Dunleath home (Greensboro Historical Museum Archives).

Letitia Walker wrote of Cox's arrival: "My father met them courteously and received them as guests, a fact which General Cox appreciated, and after placing his tent in the rear of Judge Dicks' house he rode up every afternoon to consult the Hon. J.A. Gilmer and my father on the conditions of the country. He was a most courteous and elegant man, and in delicate ways displayed his sympathy with us; no triumph of the conqueror in tone of voice and manner; spoke tenderly of the misfortunes of war, and in spite of ourselves won our heart's confidence."[13] Later, when General Cox's wife, Helen, joined him, Letitia went searching and "an old silk, dating back five years in style, came from the recesses of my trunk." She wore shoes and gloves obtained through the blockade. "As you may imagine," she wrote, "the discourse was on very general topics—the skies, the climate etc., of North Carolina-never an allusion to the events of the last four years!" Mrs. Gilmer, a friend of Letitia whose only son was maimed in battle, refused to go. Letitia observed, "These troops remained encamped for several weeks on the hills around the town, and at sunset each evening the practicing of the various bands of music would again open the floodgate of tears. But with the morning sun the avaricious desire for their 'greenbacks' seized the ladies of the town; pies, chicken and

The Walker-Scarborough home, one of the few wartime structures still standing in Greensboro.

fruit, beaten biscuit, cake and ice cream poured into camps."[14] Mary K.W. Smith of Greensboro wrote, "As we passed along, every street, store, doorway and corner was crowded with Federal troops, and the whole world looked blue in unison with our feelings that bitter morning."[15]

Mrs. Sloan of Greensboro noted that a Union officer stayed with them during the occupation. When he prepared to leave, "General Kilpatrick showed his appreciation of this hospitality to his subordinate officer by presenting my mother with a pair of valuable mules, a horse wagon and a generous supply of provisions."[16] Writing fifty years later, she recalled other people and events: "General Kilpatrick, as I remember, camped on the Eckel place on South Davie Street. His instructions to his men were to molest nothing." She also recalled that when their vegetable garden proved tempting to Union troops, their officers stopped them.

The Eckel home, an impressive Italianate mansion, stood on the corner of South Davie and East Washington streets. The home, located near the railroad tracks, burned after the war. Money had been hidden under a post in the yard of the home, and despite Federal troops camping on the property, they never discovered the hidden money.[17] Mrs. Nellie Rowe Jones noted,

"General Kilpatrick, cavalry commander in Sherman's army, occupied 'Rose Villa,' the Eckel's home, leaving only two rooms for the family, while on the ten-acre lawn the soldiers pitched their tents. The general made himself very agreeable, sending from his private table may delicacies to the family. On leaving he presented the young son of the family a colt of his beautiful thoroughbred saddler. After remaining several weeks, and just before leaving, he proceeded to have the grounds searched for hidden treasures; but the Confederate gold which lay buried under a vine-clad post in the yard was overlooked and remained undisturbed."

Mary Smith recalled, "Northern officers also had their quarters in the large oak grove of the Tate Place on Bellemeade Avenue." The famous North Carolina writer known as O. Henry (William S. Porter) grew up nearby, playing in the yard of the Tate house, which stood on Bellemeade Avenue at the current site of the city's baseball stadium.[18] In another instance, "General Beauregard camped directly across from our home on Asheboro Street, in the yard of Mr. Calvin McAdoo, and every morning we watched him ride off on his splendid charger." The McAdoo home was located on what is now Martin Luther King Boulevard, formerly Asheboro Street. Civil War relics have been found in the vicinity of the modern apartments and water tower that now occupy the site.[19]

With her own neighborhood occupied, the memories remained vivid for Mrs. Sloan:

> In our front yard Yankee soldiers were stay[t]ioned until regular camping quarters could be established on the outskirts of the town. Our front windows and door were kept closed, but no effort was made to molest us in any way, however, from our closed windows we could see beautiful silk quilts, silver cups and other handsome plate which told the story of raids made at other points before reaching Greensboro.
>
> In the rear of our home, on what is now Arlington Street, but then a stretch of woods partially cleared, and owned by Mrs. Martha Moderwell, a part of Johnston's army camped, and a young cousin made from one of the caissons left there a checker board...."
>
> It was the pleasant duty of the young women of Greensboro to visit our sick soldiers and carry them flowers and food. After the surrender, these visits were discontinued, because it was unsafe for a woman to appear on the street without the escort of a man, and for a few weeks until order was established, we stayed closely at home. This did not interfere with our receiving callers, and every Greensboro girl had her full share of suitors. Young Wade Hampton was a popular social figure during this time.[20]

Overall her impressions were favorable. She wrote, "There were refugees here, but as I recall, not a great number of these.... no depredations were committed here, and the northern officers in command of the town conducted themselves in a orderly and dignified manner, and treated those with whom they came in contact with courtesy and consideration." The checkerboard mentioned above is on display at the Greensboro Historical Museum.[21]

Letitia Walker wrote of the fear that gripped the city when it was learned that Union cavalry was nearby. "On their approach all stores of wines and liquors were destroyed, silverware and gold coins were buried, meats secreted in garrets at night, lest Yankee gold should tempt the faithful slaves to betray." Of the hundreds of wounded who arrived in the city she wrote, "[E]very available room was filled, and had been full all winter with the sick and dying. Never can I forget the farewell scene when the brave and grand Joseph E. Johnston called to set farewell, with the tears running down his brown cheeks. Not a word was spoken, but silent prayers went up for his preservation. The Salisbury road was filled with retreating troops—wretched, half clad starving and very many shoeless."[22] The chaos of her present and the uncertainty of the future are seen in her comments on their situation that spring: "We stood confronting new problems of life at every turn, and the solution of these problems seemed hopeless, with the flower of our youth and strong men slain on the battlefield! Property valueless, no money, and the former slaves made co-equal with his master and at the ballot-box to make laws."[23] Another resident, Mary Bogart, noted that refugees from New Bern, Wilmington, and even Virginia took up residence in the city. Confederate wounded from the war's last few weeks were eventually transferred to Edgeworth Female Seminary, where the downtown YMCA stands today.[24]

The physical occupation of Greensboro meant one more thing to a large segment of the population: enforcement of the Emancipation Proclamation. The city's slaves were freed upon the arrival of Union troops. Freedom of course, brought new challenges to a class of people who were largely illiterate and had few skills and no experience as citizens in society. Reverend Jacob Smith noted in his diary that he told his slave, "she and her children were free by the results of the war & the proclamation of Mr. Lincoln, but that she had better stay until she could look about and get a better situation. I told her I would help her too. She seemed very thankful and said she had no notion of leaving us."[25]

Union general Jacob D. Cox wrote his observations of Greensboro's civilians:

> We had opportunity to notice to what great straits the people had been reduced for two years in the matter of manufactured goods of all kinds. Factories of every sort were scarce in the South when the war began, and resources of every kind were so absorbed in the war that there was no chance for new ones to spring up. Carriages, wagons, and farm implements went to decay, or could only be rudely

patched up by the rough mechanics of the plantation. The stringent blockade shut out foreign goods, and the people were generally clothed in homespun. In many houses the floors were bare because the carpets had been cut up to make blankets for the soldiers. Ladies made their own shoes of such materials as they could find. They braided their own hats. They showed a wonderful ingenuity in supplying from native products the place of all the articles of use which had formerly been imported from foreign lands or from the North. A home-made straw hat ornamented with feathers of barnyard fowls and domestic birds was often as jaunty and pretty as any Parisian bonnet. Simple dyes were made to give to coarse cotton stuffs a lively contrast or harmony of pure colors as effective as the varied and elaborate fabrics from the European looms.[26]

William G. Bentley of the 104th Ohio wrote that citizens came into Greensboro "to see and talk with *live Yankees* who are a great curiosity. Some of them appear astounded to find us nearly human and like other people."[27] Of the Confederate soldiers who were vacating the area he said, "The rebel soldiers generally appear glad to get out of the army but a great many officers are very bitterly opposed to *giving up*."[28] In the village of Chapel Hill, Cornelia Spencer observed the interaction of Union occupiers and former Confederate soldiers:

> I am glad to say that wherever a Federal soldier met any of them, he was prompt to offer help and food, and express a kindly and soldierly cordiality. Grant's men, they all said, had been especially generous. There was something worth studying in the air and expression of these men, a something which had a beneficial and soothing effect on the observers. They were not unduly cast down, nor had any appearance of the humiliation that was burning into our souls. They were serious, calm, and self-possessed. They said they were satisfied that all had been done that could be done.[29]

James Gaskill of the 104th Ohio wrote of the calmer days of occupation duty in Greensboro once the Confederates had left:

> By the middle of May the paroled rebel prisoners have all departed for their homes where many will find desolation and poverty and the outlook is certainly gloomy for these misguided boys. Peace is now established, the Union is saved and the bondman can now enjoy the fruits of his labor.
>
> We now have only the arms and ammunition of war surrendered by our late enemy to guard and this is being loaded on cars and taken away. Our duties are light except the drill master and his awkward squad who are kept busy in order to punish the former and collect damages from the latter. June 16, we pass in review before Generals Schofield, Cox and Carter and on June 17, our regiment is mustered out of service and relieved from guard duty by Massachusetts troops. We scramble aboard freight cars and are soon homeward bound on a railroad of the old type construction with its wood stringers and strap iron railing and much out of repair. Over this road we slowly wend our way northward.[30]

Confederate monument, Green Hill Cemetery. Confederate dead from Bentonville, Avarysboro, and the Greensboro area campsites are buried here.

Private Edmund J. Cleveland of the 9th New Jersey recorded these days in his diary. On May 6 he wrote of the unit's arrival in Greensboro: "These people are strongly Unionist and frequently fed Yankee prisoners as they passed through on the cars. We climbed on the top of the box cars for our train ride. We reached camp, located in a field near the town, at noon. Cos. G, H, and I are absent. The first is in Charlotte, the second at Gen. Cox's headquarters and the third in Salisbury."[31] The next day he noted, "A quiet Sabbath in camp. More of Kilpatrick's Cavalry passed through en route to Charlotte." On May 8 he wrote, "Detailed guard supernumerary and afterwards as guard in front of the colonel's tent. Last night Nieman and I took a walk down town. Greensboro is a nice county seat but thinly settled. Two of the churches are now being used as Confederate hospitals. There are several other hospitals in town — all filled with sick and wounded."[32]

The dead from the city's makeshift hospitals were buried in Green Hill Cemetery. Today there is a mass grave with about 300 burials there, many from Bentonville.[33] The wounded who died in Greensboro's hospitals were initially buried in the old Methodist burying ground at Union Cemetery on South Elm Street. These graves were later moved to Green Hill.[34]

A reporter with the *Philadelphia Inquirer* visited Greensboro that summer and wrote his impressions of the war's aftermath:

Greensboro is abundantly supplied with all kinds of country produce, and at reasonable rates. The following is the list of the chief articles of consumption furnished here:

Flour, $12 per barrel; corn, $1.50 per bushel; bacon, 15 to 25 cents per pound; beef, mutton and veal, 10 cents per pound; chickens, 25 cents apiece; eggs, 25 cents per dozen; butter, 25 to 30 cents per pound; potatoes, $2 per bushel; apples of the best quality, $2 per bushel.

The stores appear to be doing a fair business, and would do much better did the country people possess the means of purchasing in production to their wants. As it is, trade is carried on chiefly through barter, the merchants accepting for their goods, provisions and tobacco in lieu of money. The presence here of six regiments of Union troops assist them in converting many of the articles so received into cash, without the trouble and delay of forwarding to distant markets.[35]

The transition to peace went smoothly, as Edmund Cleveland of the 9th New Jersey noted on May 12: "Citizens are to be organized into companies and given captured arms for the defence of the state against guerillas."[36] The Confederate artillery had not been moved from Greensboro yet. Cleveland wrote on May 13, "I went down and visited the artillery park near the depot. I counted 120 cannon surrendered by Johnston, parked wheel to wheel." He also passed by "a three story brick building, made into an arsenal for the surrendered infantry arms of Johnston's Army."[37] A week later he noted that eighty-two pieces of artillery had been added to the park at the depot, "several of them showing marks of being struck by shot and shell."[38]

As Union troops prepared to leave later that summer, William G. Bentley of the 104th Ohio noted, "The citizens of this place seem to be very sorry that we are going to leave soon."[39] General Cox insisted that regular church services resume in an attempt to return the city to normalcy. There were even dances held at the Britton Hotel to entertain the federal officers. Susan Dick Weir made costumes from curtains and drapes, no other materials being available.[40]

In those pockets of Unionism across the piedmont, the closing of the war was met with enthusiasm. In Winston, citizens organized a ceremony in which children raised the American flag at the courthouse, followed by a parade. The newspaper reported, "Thirteen little girls, between the ages of five and eleven, representing the original states, dressed in white, festooned with flowers and evergreens, and sashes of red, white and blue, wearing wreaths of roses and evergreens, and carrying small white flags, led the parade. Little boys presented flags to the officials."[41]

Resistance, if not by force then by mannerism, remained strong in other areas. Anna Maria Clewell wrote from Salem about the Union occupation there. The 10th Ohio Cavalry arrived and set a United States flag on a prominent house that was their headquarters. The flag was situated so that no one could pass the home without walking under the flag. Anna and a friend purposely walked around the flag so as to not pass under it, earning the scorn of the Union troops. A war of words ensued between officers and citizens regarding passing under the flag, causing tension but no violence.[42]

In the meantime, President Jefferson Davis and his remaining cabinet members and government officials had been making their journey south, hoping to reach the Mississippi and continue the war from the far west.[43] Davis and his party passed through Charlotte, then York, Union, and Abbeville, South Carolina. After crossing into Georgia they stopped at Washington, then moved cautiously, trying to avoid both unruly mobs of former Confederates who were plundering the countryside and Union cavalry looking for them.[44] Traveling in two separate parties were Davis and his wife, Varina, with the children. Davis felt that she would be safer away from him should his party run into trouble.[45]

On the evening of May 9, Davis and his entourage camped near Irwinville, in south-central Georgia. He left to visit Varina, and there the 4th Michigan Cavalry and 1st Wisconsin closed in on them. The Federal troops charged in early in the morning; the camp offered no resistance, but several Union soldiers were shot by friendly fire.[46]

8

Everything Is in Confusion

An observer in the piedmont counties of Guilford, Randolph, Rowan, and Davidson that spring of 1865 would have seen the roads crowded with thousands of men walking south. One Georgian began marching home May 3, and noted that roll call was taken periodically. Despite the best efforts of officers, straggling remained a problem and supply wagons had to be guarded at night to prevent stealing. He noted, "We had rice bread and pickle pork which Gen. Sherman issued to our army to march home on. Rice bread does very well when warm, but when cold would do to make solid shot out of. But we ought not to grumble as it will preserve us until we get home."[1] Private John Dooley, passing through the area on his way home to Virginia, wrote of what he saw in Greensboro:

> Everything is in confusion. An attack has just been made upon the Quartermaster's stores by stragglers, which was repulsed by a guard of Johnston's army. Great excitement prevails and the Quartermaster is out of shoes, etc. to those who ask for them.
>
> I walk around the town this morning and the relics of the departed Confederacy remind me of the abandoned remains of some large circus which sometimes when a child I used to move among when the tents had been struck, the horses gone, their gaudy trappings no longer visible, and feeling akin to sadness would creep into my young heart, as I looked upon the remnants of what had been its glories, now all, all departed.
>
> But now in the bitterness of an older and more disappointed heart I gaze on the ruins of a fallen Republic. Countless fragments of government papers, receipts, transportation papers, etc., etc. strew the ground in front, in hopeless confusion.[2]

Arthur P. Ford, a wounded South Carolinian, obtained permission to leave the makeshift hospital in the Guilford County courthouse and make his way home. He described his journey:

> The next day I struck out again, and after three or four more days walking

reached Salisbury, about thirty miles farther, where I again found another comrade in the hospital at that place. With the exception of the night I had spent at High Point, it was my habit, when night overtook me, to step aside into the bushes and sleep until morning. What food I got was only what I begged at the farmhouses on the way.

At the Yadkin River I found that the bridge had not been burned. It seems that the Federal General Stoneman had been raiding that section of country and had attempted to burn this bridge, but had been driven off by a Confederate force under General Pettus, and some cavalry. Just as I approached it, President Jefferson Davis, with quite a party, came riding by. He was sitting gracefully erect on his horse, and courteously returned our salutes. This was the one occasion on which I saw the President.

We were quite a large number of men along the roadside, and one of the President's party, a captain, rode up to my group and asked if we were willing to go on across the Mississippi and continue the war there? Many of us, I among them, volunteered to go, but we heard nothing more of it. It seems that this really was Mr. Davis's plan, and he was so much set on it, that as late as April 25 he suggested to General Johnston that instead of surrendering to General Sherman, he should disband his infantry, with instructions to them to rendezvous at some appointed place across the Mississippi, and to bring off his cavalry and all his horses and light pieces of artillery. As is well known, General Johnston fully realized the absolute hopelessness of the struggle and deliberately disobeyed his instructions, and surrendered to General Sherman the next day. When one looks back upon the condition of things then as they must have been known to the highest Confederate authorities, it seems almost incredible that such an impracticable idea as continuing the war across the Mississippi could have been entertained for a moment.[3]

George Washington Harper of the 58th North Carolina Consolidated Regiment wrote of the orderly and organized march home experienced by his unit:

In the march from Greensboro one-third or more of the men, by order, retained their arms and forty rounds in the cartridge boxes. A small wagon carried a chest of reserve ammunition, a few rations, and after caring for any who might be sick, the blankets of the men. No excesses or depredations were committed, and the men cheerfully responded to the orders of their officers, to whom, as we all knew, respect and obedience could no longer be enforced. The conduct of the rank and file of the regiment in the closing days of the war was in keeping with the fine soldierly qualities uniformly displayed by them throughout the long struggle, and reflects on all high credit and honor.[4]

At Boonhill, near Goldsboro, troops of the 128th New York noted that officers were "kept quite busy furnishing transportation to paroled men of Johnson's army, who were making their way home." Citizens were also receiv-

Guilford County Courthouse. An important landmark in downtown, the building swarmed with Confederate troops in April and May 1865 (Greensboro Historical Museum Archives).

ing relief rations at Goldsboro.[5] Artilleryman Clement Saussy of the Chatham Artillery (GA) wrote,

> When we had turned in our battery at the surrender at Greensboro, some of us got together to plan our homeward trip. Our commissary stores were exhausted. We had been promised rations from the Federals, but they were delayed. Some of

the fellows concluded to spare some of their scant clothing or whatever they had and trade for provisions to keep us going until the Yankee rations were issued. Some one suggested that we had better boil whatever clothing we could spare, so as to kill the graybacks with which every solder was more or less infected. One of our men said: "Well, boys the war is over and we have seen some tough times and been in some hard places, but up to this time I have never had a louse on me, not even when we were in the filthiest of places, Battery Wagner."

We of course doubted his word, but he was positive about it; and, being an expert at trading, we gave him what could be spared to trade to best advantage. Walker had a blue shirt to spare, and said: "Brother Champ, take this shirt and get as many eggs as you can for it, and we'll divide." Champ put the shirt under his arm, and with other article set off. When he got out of hearing, Walker said, "Well, if Champ has told the truth and has gone through all these years without having any lice on him, he will surely get his share now, for that old blue shirt is chock-full of them;" and sure enough when Champ returned with his goods in exchange for the clothing he was scratching like the rest of us.

While at Greensboro, N.C., awaiting our final discharge from bankruptcy, into which we had been forced with General Sherman as receiver, Jim Freeborn and I were walking in the town one morning when our attention was called to the strange actions of two Confederate soldiers. We asked them what was up. They told us to go back around the corner and keep quiet, and we would soon find out. This we did, and very soon a fellow came down the street with a bolt of cloth on his shoulder. The two soldiers stepped in front of him and said that they would relieve him of the pack. Being two to one, the fellow gave it up without any resistance and retraced his steps. We went over and asked what they were doing. They replied that a lot of miscellaneous stores belonging to the Confederate government were being taken away from the storehouse by men who intended to apply them to their own use. They believed they had as much right to them as anybody, and took the means of getting into the deal.

We determined to wait and see if we could get into the same game, and very soon another fellow came along with a bolt of sailcloth or duck on his shoulder. I stepped in front of him in a menacing manner, and demanded that he turn over his prize. At the same time Freeborn took hold of the cloth; and the man, being a noncombatant, concluded that it was wise to make no resistance. We took the cloth to a merchant and asked him what he would give us for it. He said that he had nothing but Confederate money, which we, of course, did not want. "I'll tell you what I will do," he said. "If you will accept it, I'll have my wife fix up as good a dinner as she can in exchange for the cloth." As eating was uppermost in our minds, we agreed to his proposition.

He sent us to his home, a negro boy taking a note to his wife. On reading it, she invited us in. We hesitated about going into a parlor in our ragged, dirty condition, and asked if she could not just put something to eat in a paper. "No sir," she said. "Confederate soldiers are more than welcome to anything that I have. Take a seat in the parlor until I can prepare for you the very best that my store room possesses." We waited for some time, amusing ourselves looking at books and pictures until she announced dinner. What a feast there was before us! Too many good things to enumerate, and we finished the course with ice cream and cake. Put yourself in the place of these two hungry Confederate soldiers, and you can partly imagine our feelings. And more than that, the dear, good old soul made up a bundle of what we could not eat and gave it to us to take away. The looters must have quit pilfering after having being relieved by our two Confederate boys and ourselves, for we failed to find any more stores so carelessly handled, though we made a diligent search.[6]

Not only the soldiers but the also officers were making their preparations for the journey home. Lieutenant A.R. Chisholm, and aide to General Beauregard, suggested to his commander that he procure a wagon and load it with stores to barter with for their journey back to Louisiana. Knowing that their Confederate money was worthless, Beauregard agreed and Chisholm gathered cloth and other supplies which served as their currency for the long trip south.[7]

A reporter with the *New York Herald* struck out on a mission to learn of events first-hand in North Carolina. Leaving the Union forces in Virginia, he journeyed from South Boston down towards Greensboro.[8] In the Tar Heel State he wrote, "I found the country literally alive with the officers and men belonging to Johnston's army. They were making their way homewards, unparoled. Some of them were carrying their arms and knapsacks with them. Almost every party I met stopped me and we had a brief talk. In all instances I passed off as one of General Lee's scouts, wounded and paroled. One party that I met in a dense woods evinced an intention to dismount me and take my horse away. Noting their intention, I dismounted, talked pleasantly with them, took some of the apple brandy which they offered me to drink, and before we parted made them friendly towards me."[9] With an optimistic eye on the future, he also noted that "North Carolina is not impoverished; that the planters are extensively cultivating their lands, that there is a vast amount of tobacco on hand, and that peace and quietness will be acceptable to the majority of those who have been in the army and those who have not. It will be some time before a few of the restless spirits can be subdued, but they too will come in when the popular sentiment of the State is directed back in the old channel of obedience to the laws of the United States."[10]

While events transpired in and around Greensboro, behind the Army of Tennessee other dramatic actions were taking place along the rail lines to the south and west. Foremost among these, and of interest to both sides, was the flight of President Davis and what remained of his cabinet. From Greensboro they moved on to Salisbury and then Charlotte. George Mitchell of the 9th Kentucky Cavalry (CSA) arrived in Salisbury and found that they were to be part of the escort for President Davis and the remaining cabinet members.

He recalled, "Gen. John C. Breckinridge and Judah P. Benjamin were at the head of the column as we rode into the town. We remained there until the next afternoon. We then marched southward to Washington, Ga." They eventually got $26 in gold and disbanded on May 9.[11]

From Charlotte, Davis' party moved south and crossed the Catawba River and entered South Carolina. They passed through the site of modern-day Rock Hill, along Eden Terrace Drive, and over to York. Spending the night at the Rose Hotel, Judah Benjamin gave an inspiring speech to civilians who had assembled to see their president. Next the entourage traveled southwest to Pinckneyville, now an abandoned site, and into the town of Union. Then it was on to Abbeville, where Davis met with his cabinet at the Burke-Stark mansion. Crossing into Georgia, they continued moving south, through Augusta and down towards Florida. Union cavalry surrounded and captured Davis and his party near Irwinville in south central Georgia on May 10. The Confederate government now ceased to exist, and remaining commands in the Carolinas either surrendered or simply broke up and went home.

In the meantime, monotony had set in for the Union troops occupying North Carolina. Many regarded their service as ended and longed to return home. Joseph Crowther with the 128th New York was stationed in Kinston. He wrote, "It is like all other evacuated Southern towns and cities about used up."[12] Between the lawlessness of the countryside, with paroled and fugitive soldiers, civilian refugees, wandering freedmen, bands of outlaws, and now the news of Lincoln's assassination, uncertainty was everywhere. Uncertainty was the common denominator for everyone in the postwar era: ex-Confederate soldiers, freed slaves, Southern civilians, Union soldiers, and former Confederate leaders.

Many Confederate units were either out of touch with General Johnston or simply left on their own. Piedmont North Carolina was full of armed men roaming the countryside, some going home, others looking to plunder. Across the eastern part of the state, scattered Confederate commands wandered, searching for news and trying to decide on a course of action. James M. Mullen of the 13th Battalion, North Carolina Artillery, recorded a diary during these days of uncertainty. In it he wrote the following:

> By sunrise on the 13th we resumed our march in a hard rain, and with the roads in a terrible condition. Not long after starting we began to meet stragglers making their way to our rear. Among the first to attract our attention was a weary-looking, foot-sore and jaded young fellow in the dirty and tattered uniform of a lieutenant of infantry, who told us he was going home; that Lee had surrendered, and that what was left of his army had been paroled. Up to this time we did not know that Petersburg had been abandoned, so completely were we isolated and cut off. Captain Webb, who was in command ... refused to believe him, and

ordered him and some others under guard to accompany the command until their story was verified. But it was not long before all were fully convinced of the truth of their statements, for the roads were soon filled with soldiers returning from Lee's army. I shall never forget the feeling that came over me when fully impressed with the fact that Lee had surrendered. Until then I had never permitted myself to doubt the ultimate successes of the Confederacy; and, as to the Army of Northern Virginia, I believed that, under "Marse Robert," it was simply invincible. I apprehended this feeling was shared by most of the Confederate soldiers; hence their endurance, courage and devotion under the sorest trials and in the darkest hours of the cause. With Lee's surrender, all hope fled, and thereafter obedience and discharge of duty were purely mechanical. Swift upon the heels of the news of this terrible disaster, and on the evening of the same day, came the rumor that Sherman was in possession of Raleigh, and that Johnston was retiring before him towards Greensboro. Madam Rumor was not a lying jade at that time. About night-fall, weary and hungry, depressed with the gloomy outlook, and after a hard day's work, we halted and went into camp near Warrenton Junction.... Captain Webb was in much doubt as to what course to pursue.[13]

The next day Mullen wrote,

About the time we were ready to move again a solitary horseman rode up to the depot, in whom I recognized General M.W. Ransom. He dismounted and hitched his horse, while I went forward to meet him. He confirmed the reports of Lee's surrender, having himself been there and witnessed it. I hardly knew what to do with the stores and men under my charge. He replied that he knew nothing of Sherman's' position, but hardly thought he was in Raleigh, and that, being a paroled soldier, he could not give me any advice.[14]

Back at Warrenton Junction, Mullen observed the following:

[There were] a considerable number of men in a state of disquietude and disorder amounting to almost total demoralization. They had broken into one of the cars containing supplies of food, were wantonly wasting the supplies, and were preparing to break open other cars. Springing from my horse and making my way to them, calling my bugler as I went, I had him sound the assembly, and bade them fall in with their several commands at once. The better and nobler instincts of good soldiers coming to their assistance, they soon quieted down and readily fell into line. I then addressed them as best I could; told them all the news I could learn ... that we had food enough for a week at least, and ... felt sure something would be done ... which would enable us either to continue or close our services as Confederate soldiers in an honorable way.[15]

Over the next few days Mullen and the other officers of his command debated their course of action. General Lawrence S. Baker, commander of the region, joined them and Mullen recorded what happened next:

On the 16th (Sunday), the general was urged by some of his officers to carry out at once the plan originally decided upon, to surrender; for they were satisfied they could not control their men longer. He promised to take the matter under consideration and announce his final decision at an assembly of all the forces that evening. The plan finally adopted was, to try and cut his way through to Johnston with all who would volunteer to follow him, the others to disband and go home as best they could. About fifty volunteered, of which nineteen were from our battery. These fifty were authorized to be mounted on government horses, and armed with Enfield rifles. This was done, and at mid night they took up their march.

The next morning, having been up all night, we presented anything but a martial appearance, and, if truth must be told, our enthusiasm was at a low ebb, for we were pretty well satisfied that ours was a "wild goose chase." Nothing but a sense of duty, and a reluctance to turn back as long as wee were called upon to go forward, carried us on. For two days we wandered on over the hills and through the woods of Franklin, Johnston and Wake counties. On one of these days we passed through Louisburg, worn out and hungry. The good citizens of the town received us enthusiastically, and treated us most hospitably. It must have been an amusing sight to see us straggling through the streets, with flowers in one hand and something to eat in the other. It made a deep impression on me at the time, and I shall never forget the scene.

About sundown on the 16th we reached Arpsboro and halted. There the general informed us he had reliable information that Johnston had surrendered, and he had determined to send in a flag of truce to Raleigh, tendering his surrender. On the next day, having recrossed the Tar river and countermarched several miles.[16]

Other scattered forces gradually surrendered or disbanded all across the region. The men of the 1st North Carolina Artillery surrendered to Union troops at Stantonsburg in lower Wilson County on the 25th. Their comrades in the 13th Artillery surrendered at Bunn's House in Nash County on April 20.[17]

To the southwest, George M. Norris of the 2nd South Carolina missed much of the confusion and chaos descending on piedmont North Carolina. He wrote, "From Greensboro ... our regiment, being State troops, were ordered back to Chester, South Carolina and from there to Spartanburg where we were disbanded, the war being over. When I came home in May, 1865, everything was in turmoil [and] the farm paid little that year."[18]

Also in South Carolina was Lieutenant Halcott P. Jones of the 13th Battalion North Carolina Artillery (in a different company from that of Mullens). His command reached Chester, where they were ordered to disband. He wrote, "[T]he Battery was disbanded by order of General Bragg and destroyed. It was a sad sight to see the old guns that I had been with so long laying battered about in the midst of a complete wreck of carriage ammunition and equip-

Center Meeting House site. Dating back to the late 1700s, the Center Meeting House was an important local landmark.

ment." Not satisfied the war was indeed over, Jones made his way towards the Trans-Mississippi to keep fighting.[19] Kirkland's Brigade of North Carolina Junior Reserves, young men under eighteen years of age who had "fought heroically" at Bentonville, disbanded at Center Meeting House in Randolph County. There were only 210 men left in the four units; the 1st Battalion numbered only 11.[20]

Henderson Deans of the 66th North Carolina was one of many who did not wait to be paroled. He recorded the following:

> I sat down By the side of a oak tree thinking what to doo for I Hade Sworen that the Yankees should not never take me Prison that I would die first. I Hade not Ben Setin thear Longe Before Captin Williams come to me and Sed Deans I have found man that Has Ben on the old Plank Road from Greensborough to Fayetteville and if I can Get to that Road wee can Get around Sherman armey and not one of us will Be taken Prisoner I was on my feet so quick I did not no whether I was Standin or Setin I went to the Stacke of Guns whears my was Stacked in and taken out my old Springfield Riful that I toted so meney Hundreds of miles & shot so meney Hundred of times and my cartridge Box goin to a fence.... By Rakin the Leaves a way from under the Bottom Rail I Put my gun and cartridge Box under thear Rakin the Leaves Backe good and nice — and if no one Has not found it — it is there until This day.[21]

He continues: "It was not Longe Before Captin Williams and 7 of his men was on the way to the Plank Road wee got to the Plank Road a Little Before Son Set Turned down it to Fayetteville — it is too much for me to ... write How wee got Home But will Say wee all got Home Safe...."[22]

Privates William A. Russell and Dave Walton of the Jeff Davis Legion Cavalry (MS) had a long odyssey while separated from their command. Skirmishing near Raleigh, Russell and Walton found themselves cut off from their regiment. They went through the woods, hoping to rejoin their unit.

Center Meeting House marker. The marker includes a carving of the meeting house.

They spent the next week wandering the back roads and piney woods of Wake County, trying to avoid Union cavalry, get enough food to keep going, and find their own command.[23] One day, Russell wrote, they were "aroused by the explosion of the ordnance supplies in the city. Looking across an open country southeast of the city, a half mile or so away we beheld a long blue line of infantry, with bayonets glistening in the rising sun, marching toward the old capital. We mounted at once and moved rapidly west."[24]

During their adventure the two encountered Union troops four separate times, in each instance managing to kill, capture, or evade their adversaries. In one encounter Russell was wounded. The two kept moving, Russell noting that "several times I thought I would fall from my horse from the loss of blood; but being encouraged by my comrade, I continued to go on."[25] Eventually they were cornered by another patrol, and this time their luck ran out. Walton drew his pistol and fired but was hit. Union troopers surrounded the two wounded men. Rather than finish them off or take them as prisoners, the Federals simply left, leaving a horse for Russell.[26] He sat by his friend's side, writing, "I laid him gently on his back, and he lay calmly breathing as though asleep for some time" before he expired. Russell then left his hiding place and met Union troops who paroled him. He learned for the first time that both Lee and Johnston had surrendered. He immediately began the journey home to Mississippi.[27]

Not all Southerners abided by the terms of the surrender. Colonel D.A. Dickert of the 3rd South Carolina Consolidated, camped along the Burlington Road outside of Greensboro, wrote of his actions in the third person:

> When it was learned that the army was to surrender near Greensboro, N.C., Dickert brought in his men.... But instead of surrendering, the night before the capitulation was to take place, Dickert, with his original company and his company of scouts, 150 men in all, with their rifles and each with 90 rounds of cartridges, left camp clandestinely and made their way westward. After getting beyond the confines of the Confederate army, they turned south, and passing through the Federal lines secretly at night, he brought all his men home with their arms and equipment intact.[28]

South Carolina artilleryman Robert Herriot noted that his command was sent to Charlotte for police duty from Greensboro. Along the way they passed through the devastation around Salisbury, where Union cavalry had raided: "There was much debris lying around—broken caissons and limbers, dismounted field pieces I noticed one piece that had been struck on the edge of the mouth and dismounted."[29] Upon reaching Charlotte, they learned that Davis and his party had moved on to Abbeville. Proceeding south to Columbia, he said, "Our force had been reduced to about twenty men and a lieutenant and sergeant. Having heard of the surrender of Johnston, every one realized that the war was over, and those of us present held an informal council of war, and it was suggested that the lieutenant give each man a thirty-day furlough, which would be evidence that we were not absent without leave, and at the end of the thirty days the war would be over. This was done."[30]

With his official duties finished, General Johnston headed to Charlotte to reunite with his wife and rebuild his personal affairs. One incident in particular illustrates Johnston's attention to detail and his concern with following the terms of the agreement. General Cox recorded the episode regarding a flag that had been hidden, and said that it was "striking proof of the scrupulous exactness he was determined to exercise in carrying out the terms of the surrender." Johnston had gone on to Charlotte to personally oversee the disbanding of units further down the line. Here he learned one cavalry unit had a silk guidon, a Union national flag, "scarce larger than a handkerchief." He immediately took possession of the flag and sent it back to Union authorities in Greensboro, noting the agreement that all captured Union flags held by the Confederates be turned over. He apologized and sent it with another he

First Presbyterian Church. Once a Confederate hospital site, it is now the home of the Greensboro Historical Museum.

discovered, noting that "they were not in my possession when we were in Greensborough, nor until I reached Charlotte."[31]

The ending of the war in North Carolina reveals early signs of the conciliatory attitudes that emerged later in the Reconstruction and postwar period. A hands-off approach and a spirit of cooperation among the Federal commanders resulted in their defeated enemies being regarded as equals, and they trusted them to turn over weapons, maintain their own discipline, and march home under their own power. In the years afterwards, as veterans of both sides looked back with nostalgia on the war, the causes and bitterness of the war were downplayed in favor of a sense of brotherhood and common valor.

In releasing the Confederates on light terms, allowing them to march home with weapons in hand and flags flying, the Greensboro surrender offers a glimpse of that feeling before the war formally ended. The generosity and spirit of cooperation is one similarity to Appomattox and is not unlike the armistice ending World War I, in which the German army marched home under its own power, weapons in hand.

Conclusion

In the end, any historical work must answer questions. Why is this important, and why will it always matter? This final, short chapter will analyze, probe, and speculate, but ultimately it will leave many issues unresolved. It is open ended, as history often is. The cataclysmal events that occurred around Greensboro, impacting thousands of lives, should not be forgotten. It was one of the largest events to ever take place in Guilford County.

One Confederate soldier wrote of the Army of Tennessee's end: "Some lie buried by Georgia streams, some on the hillsides of Alabama, some in the valleys of Tennessee, some on the bloody fields of Kentucky, some under the blue skies of Mississippi, some survived and struggled on until they reached the Carolinas."[1]

Two surrenders, only a little over one hundred miles and two weeks apart—one neat and orderly, the other chaotic. The Appomattox ending appeals to our sense of a formal closure to the war. It gives the violence a neat, tidy, and definite end. The reality was otherwise. Despite Appomattox's better known story and appeal, the events at Greensboro are more representative of the real ending of the war: massive chaos, wild rumors, deep uncertainty, and lingering hostility. The other surrenders, at Citronelle, Alabama; Galveston, Texas; Doaksville, Oklahoma; and Jacksonport, Arkansas, all share these similarities. Anxiety and insecurity characterized all of the other surrenders. In these other cases, as at Greensboro, many men simply went home rather than wait for a formal parole or surrender agreement. Appomattox was different; however, most likely any soldiers would have started to lose faith, given the circumstances at Greensboro.

General Kirby Smith, who reluctantly surrendered the Trans-Mississippi Department in Alabama at the urging of his subordinates, made his way to Mexico. He wrote of the events of the war's end:

[They] left me at liberty, and made it prudent if not my duty to place the Rio Grande between myself and harm until the excited feelings of the people at the north had calmed down, and the Government had settled upon some deiced course of policy toward the south. Partly through the kindness of friends I secured enough funds to take me out of the country and support me economically for some four months. After a most disagreeable journey through the desert wastes + cactus plains of Neuva Leon we arrived at Monterey, having ... passed through the lines of the Liberalisto's or Liberal Robbers into which they had degenerated. Here I found a crowd of some hundred or two Confederates, censorious, fault finding and dissatisfied, they disgusted me with their criminations and selfishness.[2]

All across North Carolina's piedmont, confusion, chaos, and uncertainty were the order of the day. For civilians—white and black—and for the soldiers going home, no one knew what the future held. The sites of the Army of Tennessee's campaigns are well known and well marked: Shiloh, Perryville, Stones River, Chickamauga, Chattanooga, Atlanta, Franklin, Nashville, and many others. Yet its ending point, and the story surrounding that end, remains relatively obscure in Civil War studies.

A drive through modern downtown Greensboro or the Guilford County countryside reveals very little of the important events that transpired there, or the thousands of men, famous and anonymous, who came through there. That Greensboro was the scene of weapons production, riots, and large campsites remains largely overlooked. The area it is a microcosm of the war itself: military production, logistics and mobilization, home front, civilian unrest, and military movements. Most of the Army of Tennessee's soldiers ended the war in various campsites scattered around the region, their last days as soldiers filled with tension and uncertainty.

If the armies left Appomattox largely with a sense of brotherhood and respect, it was less so at Greensboro. Thousands of Confederate soldiers deserted (it is impossible to estimate how many). These desertions were motivated by fear, uncertainty, bitterness, and a host of other reasons. The war did not end at Appomattox. The war did not end with a neat, final conclusion, with both sides coming together in mutual respect. Though events at Appomattox demonstrated that the country could move on and that both sides had the potential to end the war on a positive note, Greensboro illustrated that the larger war would not be so easy to end or move past. A study of Confederate desertions in the Civil War has found that over 20 percent of the desertions among all North Carolina troops occurred in the last two months of the war. In that time period over half of the state's artillery desertions for the entire war occurred.[3]

There is a clear pattern among the writings of the men of the Army of Tennessee. In general, accounts written at the time reveal great uncertainty, anxiety, tension, and frustration. Accounts recorded in later years, when many veterans reflected on their service and wrote memoirs in the 1880s, 1890s, and early 1900s, tend to be more romantic. These later testimonials often lack the gritty details of those written at the moment. The passage of time and subsequent reunification of the nation allowed many of these men to look back at the past with a sense of optimism and acceptance.

Over 30,000 Confederate soldiers camped in and around Greensboro in 1865. This work records just a few of the thousands of stories, and this small sampling sheds light on only some of these events. But how many are missing? For every enlightening and fascinating account, surely we are missing many more. History is haphazardly recorded and haphazardly preserved. What documentation comes to us is only a fraction of what occurred, just as what is marked on the landscape is only a fraction of what could be. Thousands of stories remain untold as they were simply not recorded. Moreover, the places of these events have also been randomly preserved, or not at all. Some historic sites, monuments, and markers exist, but the vast majority of these sites are forever lost.

It is hoped that this work sparks interest in not only researching the events of the spring of 1865 in North Carolina, but also in preserving some of these long-forgotten sites. Readers are urged to support North Carolina's state historic sites and the many locally run museums and historic sites throughout the Piedmont and Triad regions that interpret the Civil War. It is the past, and what remains of the past, that makes a region unique and gives it its character. By preserving the past we honor those who went before us and ensure that those who come after us will be able to appreciate their history and their region.

It is hoped this work will inspire more research and archaeology on this topic. There is a great deal that can be done if various organizations and individuals collectively work together to preserve and interpret these events. Much rich archaeological evidence still exists in the ground, and it is hoped that those who metal detect sites will consult with archaeologists about them. There once was a time when these two groups would have had no contact, but that is no longer the case. Recent collaboration on many sites in South Carolina shows the mutual benefits to both parties.[4]

Valuable information like the layout of campsites, the armament of units, and the style and amount of personal effects may be learned from careful archaeological investigations, including metal detecting. Features such as hut foundations, fire pits, latrines, trash dumps, and fortifications can also be delineated through proper surveying. Will the great divide between archaeologists and relic hunters continue to narrow?[5] Other lingering questions remain. Given the magnitude of the events that occurred in and around Greensboro, and the importance of those involved, why has its Civil War role

Confederate monuments, downtown Greensboro. These monuments commemorate the events of April and May 1865. They stand near the site of many of these important events.

in 1865 been largely forgotten? The surrender of a Confederate army would be nothing to celebrate in the postwar South. No monuments arose over the site of these camps as happened at the famous battlefields. The veterans preferred to commemorate the sites of deeds of valor. The nineteenth century saw monuments rise at many of the battle sites: Shiloh, Chickamauga, Gettysburg, Antietam, and others.

In many ways, the Army of Tennessee was not "Greensboro's army." The local units raised in Guilford and surrounding counties largely fought with General Robert E. Lee's Army of Northern Virginia. When the western army arrived at the city's doorstep in April 1865, citizens welcomed the troops, but few had direct connections to the army of General Johnston. In fact, only thirteen North Carolina infantry regiments were with the western army (along with other detachments and artillery units). Few residents had direct ties to the Army of Tennessee the way residents of Richmond or Petersburg had ties to the Army of Northern Virginia. Perhaps what is most important, the Appomattox surrender was quite simply more marketable. The most famous commanders, Lee and Grant, met at Appomattox. Their meeting and the resulting terms became the symbolic ending of the war. In addition, in North Carolina the forces were widely spread out — with Confederate troops in a half dozen locations. The surrender there was spread out over time and distance. There were few defining moments like the meeting in the parlor or the stacking of arms at Appomattox.

Greensboro's subsequent twentieth century history also affects how its Civil War history has been remembered. The city was the scene of sit-ins and violent racial unrest in the 1950s and 1960s. A large percentage of its residents had no interest in commemorating Confederate history. It is not insignificant that the monument to General Johnston's surrender in downtown Greensboro was erected at the end of the twentieth century, long after Confederate monuments rose across the rest of the South (including several at Appomattox).

Lastly, the Greensboro surrender does not fit nicely into the popular conception of the Civil War's end. The Appomattox scenario of a clean, neat finish simply does not apply to Greensboro and the other surrenders. Drunkenness, brawling, rioting, and desertion were the order of the day in the Gate City. Such harsh realities do not make for a neat and tidy history.

What will the sesquicentennial of the Civil War bring to Greensboro and piedmont North Carolina in 2015? How will the 150th anniversary of the war, and its end, be remembered? Unlike the commemorations of the war's 100th anniversary in the racially charged 1960s, the sesquicentennial commemoration in planning seems to be more inclusive, although not without its own controversies. A greater focus has been placed on relating personal experiences and including multiple viewpoints. Such an approach would serve the 1865 events of piedmont North Carolina well.

While much has been lost in Greensboro and Guilford County, much can still be saved. North Carolina historian Catherine Bisher sums this up well. She wrote that the state "will undergo overwhelming changes that will alter the whole landscape irretrievably in the next generation. Change is accelerating beyond my ability to imagine its impact.... [H]ow we are going to hang onto some vestiges of the hundreds of years of rural life that have passed, damned if I know. It will take powerful thought, and powerful effort."[6]

Appendices

I: Confederate Organizational Chart, March 31, 1865

ARMY OF THE SOUTH
GEN. J.E. JOHNSTON

Hardee's Corps: Gen. William Hardee

McLaws	Hoke	Taliaferro
Blanchard	Clingman	Elliott
Harrison	Colquitt	Rhett
Kennedy	Hagood	
Fiser	Kirkland	
Nethercutt		

ARMY OF TENNESSEE
GEN. ALEXANDER STEWART

Stewart's Corps: Gen. Edward C. Walthall

Loring-Jackson	Walthall/Johnston
Featherston/Oatis	Reynolds/Bunn
Adams/Harrison	Quarels/Jones
Scott/Dixon	

Lee's Corps: Gen. S.D. Lee

D.H. Hill	Stevenson	Clayton
Sharp	Cumming/Henderson	Stovall/Kellog
Brantley	Pettus/Bibb	Jackson/Kyle
Manigault/Carter	Palmer	Baker
Deas/Toulmin		

Cheatham's Corps: Gen. Benjamin Cheatham

Cleburne/J.A. Smith	Bate	Brown/Ripley
Govan/Green	Finley/Washburn	Gist/Field
Lowry/JF Smith	Tyler/Rice	Maney/McKinney
Granbury/Ryan	Strahl/Tillman	
Smith/Bonner	Vaughan/Bishop	

181

Cavalry: Gen. Wade Hampton

Butler
Logan
Young

Wheeler		
Allen	Holmes	Dibrell
Anderson	Ashby	Breck
Crews	Harrison	McLeane
Hagan		

Strength: 25,011[1]

II: Confederate Organizational Chart, April 26, 1865

ARMY OF TENNESSEE
J.E. JOHNSTON

Hardee's Corps: Gen. William Hardee

Brown	Hoke	Cheatham
Smith	Clingman	Palmer
Govan	Colquitt	Gist
Hagood		
Kirkland		
Armistead		

Stewart's Corps: Gen. Alexander P. Stewart

Loring	Anderson	Walthall
Featherston	Elliott	Harrison
Lowry	Rhett	Kennedy
Shelly		

Lee's Corps: Gen. S.D. Lee

D.H. Hill	Stevenson
Sharp	Henderson
Brantley	Pettus
McAllister	

Cavalry: Gen. Wade Hampton

Butler
Logan
Young

Wheeler		
Allen	Holmes	Dibrell
Anderson	Ashby	Breckinridge
Crews	Harrison	McLemore

Hagan
Estimated Strength: 40,000 men[1]

III: *Confederate Order of Battle, April 26, 1865*[1]

Army of Tennessee
General Joseph E. Johnston

Escort

Holloway's Cavalry Company (AL)
Gen. P.G.T. Beauregard

Escort

Jeff Davis Legion, Co. A (MS)
Hardee's Corps: Lt. Gen. William Hardee

Escort

Raum's Cavalry Co (MS)
Stono Scouts (SC)

Brown's Division: Maj. Gen. John. C. Brown
Smith's Brigade: Brig. Gen. James A. Smith[2]

1st FL Consolidated (1, 3, 4, 6, 7 FL, 1 FL Cavalry)
1st GA Consolidated (1, 57, 63 GA)
54th GA Consolidated (37, 54 GA, 4 Battalion GA Sharpshooters)

Govan's Brigade: Brig. Gen. David C. Govan

1st Arkansas Consolidated (1, 2, 5, 6, 7, 8, 13, 15, 19, 24 AR, 3 Confederate)
1st Texas Consolidated (6, 7, 10, 15 TX, 17, 18, 24, 25 TX Cavalry)

Hoke's Division: Maj. Gen. Robert F. Hoke
Clingman's Brigade: Brig. Gen. Thomas L. Clingman[3]

8th NC
31st NC
36th/40th NC
51st NC
61st NC

Colquitt's Brigade: Brig. Gen. Alfred H. Colquitt

6th GA
19th GA
23rd GA
27th GA
28th GA

Hagood's Brigade: Lt. Col. James Rion[4]
> 11th SC
> 21st SC
> 25th SC
> 27th SC
> 7th SC Battalion
> Kennedy Light Artillery (NC)

Kirkland's Brigade: Brig. Gen. William Kirkland[5]
> 17th NC
> 42nd NC
> 50th NC
> 66th/10th NC Battalion

Armistead's Brigade: Col. Frank S. Armistead[6]
> 1st NC Junior Reserves
> 2nd NC Junior Reserves
> 3rd NC Junior Reserves
> 1st NC Reserves Battalion

Cheatham's Division: Maj. Gen. Benjamin F. Cheatham
Maj. Gen William B. Bate
Palmer's Brigade: Brig. Gen. Joseph B. Palmer[7]

1st TN Consolidated (1, 6, 8, 9, 16, 27, 38, 34 TN, 24 TN Battalion)
2nd TN Consolidated (11, 12, 13, 29, 47, 50, 51, 52, 154 TN)
3rd TN Consolidated (4, 5, 19, 24, 31, 33, 35, 38, 41 TN)
4th TN Consolidated (2, 3, 10, 15, 18, 20, 26, 30, 32, 37, 45, 49 TN, 23 TN Battalion)

Gist's Brigade: Col. William Foster[8]
> 46th GA
> 65th GA Consolidated (65 GA, 8 GA Battalion)
> 16/24 SC Consolidated

Artillery: Col. Ambrossio Gonzales
> Artillery Battalion: Maj. Basil C. Manly
> Bridge's Battery (LA)
> Atkins's Battery (NC)
> Walter's Battery (SC)
> Zimmerman's Battery (SC)
> Paris's Battery (VA)

Reserve Artillery Battalion: Lt. Col. D. Kemper
> Guerard's Battery (GA)
> Lumpkin's Battery (GA)
> 1st MO Battery
> Charles' Battery (SC)
> DePass's Battery (SC)

C.E. Kanapaux's Battery (SC)
Shulz's Battery (Palmetto Lt Artillery, Co F) (SC)
Wagener's Battery (German Artillery, Cos A, C) (SC)
Huggins's Battery (TN)

Stewart's Corps: Lt. Gen. Alexander P. Stewart
Loring's Division: Maj. Gen. William W. Loring
Featherston's Brigade: Gen. William S. Featherston[9]

1st Arkansas Mounted Rifles Consolidated (4, 9, 25 AR, 1,2 AR Mounted Rifles)
3rd MS Consolidated (3, 31, 40 MS)
22nd (1, 22, 33 MS, 1 MS Battalion)
37th MS Battalion

Lowry's Brigade: Brig. Gen. Robert Lowry
29th AL
12th LA
14th MS Consolidated (5, 14, 43 MS)
15th (6, 15, 20, 23 MS)

Shelley's Brigade: Brig. Gen Charles M. Shelley[10]
1st AL Consolidated (1, 16, 26, 33, 45 AL)
17th AL
27th AL Consolidated (27, 35, 49, 55, 57 AL)
45th AL (2 Companies)

Anderson's Division: Maj. Gen. Patton Anderson
Elliott's Brigade: Lt. Col. J. Welsman Brown
22nd GA Battalion
27th GA Battalion
2nd South Carolina Artillery
Manigault's Battalion (SC)

Rhett's Brigade: Col. William Butler[11]
1st SC Regulars
1st SC Heavy Artillery
15th SC Battalion

Walthall's Division: Maj. Gen. Edward C. Walthall
Harrison's Brigade: Col. George P. Harrison
1st GA Regulars (includes old 47th GA)
5th GA Regulars
5th GA Reserves
32nd GA Reserves

Kennedy's Brigade: Brig. Gen. John Kennedy[12]
2nd SC Consolidated (2, 20 SC, Blanchard's Reserves)

3rd (3, 8 SC, 3 SC Battalion)
7th (7, 15 SC)

Artillery Battalion: Maj. A. Burnet Rhett

Brooks's Battery (GA)
Wheaton's Battery (GA)
LeGardeur's Battery (LA)
Parker's Battery (SC)
Stuart's Battery (SC)
Anderson's Battery (SC)

Lee's Corps: Lt. Gen. Stephen D. Lee
Escort
Ragland's Cavalry (GA)

Hill's Division: Maj. Gen. D.H. Hill
Sharp's Brigade: Brig. Gen. Jacob H. Sharp[13]

24th AL Consolidated (24, 28, 34 AL)
8th MS Consolidated Battalion (5, 8, 32 MS, 3 MS Battalion)
9th MS Consolidated (7, 9, 10, 41, 44 MS, 9 MS Battalion)
19th SC Battalion Consolidated (10, 19 SC)

Brantly's Brigade: Brig. Gen. William F. Brantly[14]

22nd AL Consolidated (22, 25, 39, 50 AL)
37th AL Consolidated (37, 42, 54 AL)
24th MS Consolidated (24, 27, 29, 30, 34 MS)
58th NC Consolidated (58, 60 NC)

Detachment, Army of Northern Virginia: Lt. Col. A.C. McAllister[15]

7th NC
15th NC
27th NC
32nd NC
43rd NC
45th NC
46th NC
55th NC

Stevenson's Division: Maj. Gen. Carter L. Stevenson
Henderson's Brigade: Brig. Gen. Robert J. Henderson[16]

1st Confederate Consolidated Battalion (1 Confederate, 25, 29, 30, 66 GA, 1 Battalion
   GA Sharpshooters)
39th GA Consolidated (34, 39, 52, 56 GA)
42nd (36, 42, 34, 56 GA)
40th (40, 41, 43 GA)

Pettus's Brigade: Brig. Gen. Edmund W. Pettus[17]
19th AL (19, 40, 46 AL)

20th   AL
23rd (23, 56 AL)
27th AL
54th VA Consolidated (54, 63 VA)

Artillery

J.T. Kanapaux's Battery (SC)

Naval Command

Naval Regiment: Flag Off. French Forest

Naval Brigade: Rear Adm. & Brig. Gen. Raphael Semmes

1st Regiment
2nd Regiment

Unattached Artillery

Palmer's Battalion: Maj. Joseph Palmer
Harris's Battery (GA)
Anderson's Battery (GA)
Yates's Battery (MS)
Moseley's Battery (NC)

Independent Artillery

Abell's Light Artillery (FL)
Swett's Battery (MS)

Artillery: Lt. Col. Joseph B. Starr

10th NC (1st Artillery)
   Darden's Battery
   Southernland's Battery
3rd NC Battalion
   Ellis's Battery
   Badham's Battery
   Sutton's Battery
13th NC Battalion
   Cumming's Battery
   Dickson's Battery
   Kelly's Battery (SC)

Cavalry Corps: Lt. Gen. Wade Hampton

Maj. Gen. Matthew C. Butler

Butler's Division: Brig. Gen. Evander M. Law
Logan's Brigade: Brig. Gen. Thomas M. Logan

1st SC Cavalry
4th SC Cavalry
5th SC Cavalry
6th SC Cavalry
19th SC Cavalry Battalion

Young's Brigade: Col. Gilbert Wright
Cobb's Legion Cavalry (GA)
Phillips Legion Cavalry (GA)
10th GA Cavalry
Jeff Davis Legion (MS)

Horse Artillery
Earle's Battery (SC)
Halsey's Battery (SC)

Wheeler's Contingent: Maj. Gen. Joseph Wheeler
Allen's Division: Brig. Col. Charles Crews
Anderson's Brigade: Brig. Gen. Robert H. Anderson[18]
3rd Confederate Cavalry (GA)
8th Confederate Cavalry (GA)
10th Confederate Cavalry (GA)
5th GA Cavalry

Crews' Brigade: Col. John. R. Hart
1st GA Cavalry
2nd GA Cavalry
3rd GA Cavalry
6th GA Cavalry
12th GA Cavalry

Hagan's Brigade: Col. David T. Blakey
1st AL Cavalry
3rd AL Cavalry
9th AL Cavalry
12th AL Cavalry
51st AL Cavalry

Hume's Division: Col. Henry M. Ashby
Harrsion's Brigade: Col. Baxter Smith[19]
3rd AR Cavalry
4th TN Cavalry
8th TX Cavalry
11th TX Cavalry

Ashby's Brigade: Col. James T. Wheeler
1st TN Cavalry
2nd TN Cavalry
5th TN Cavalry
9th TN Cavalry

Post of Greensboro: Brig. Gen. Alfred Iverson
Brig. Gen. John D. Kennedy[20]
2nd KY Mounted Infantry

4th KY Mounted Infantry
5th KY Mounted Infantry
6th KY Mounted Infantry
9th KY Mounted Infantry
2nd KY Cavalry Battalion
Tucker's Regiment (Pioneer Troops)
Invalid Corps

Post of Salisbury: Brig. Gen. Bradley T. Johnson

2 MD (detachment)
1 MD Cavalry (detachment)
Freeman's Battalion (NC)
Salisbury Prison Guard Co. A
Salisbury Prison Guard Co. B
Salisbury Prison Guard Co. C
1st Regiment Detailed Men (NC)

Post of Charlotte: Col. William J. Hoke

IV: An 1865 Time Line

March 15–16	Battle of Averaysboro, NC
March 19–21	Battle of Bentonville, NC
March 26	Army of Tennessee is reorganized at Smithfield, NC
March 31	Army of Tennessee's artillery arrives from Mississippi
April 1	Confederates driven from Five Forks near Petersburg, VA
April 2	Union forces break through Confederate defenses at Petersburg; Lee's army evacuates Richmond and Petersburg that night
April 3	Review is held for Governor Zebulon Vance at Smithfield, NC
	General Beauregard arrives in Greensboro, begins to organize defenses
	President Jefferson Davis and his cabinet arrive in Danville, VA
	Lee's army arrives at Amelia Court House, hoping to find supplies of food
April 4	Army of Tennessee reviewed at Smithfield, NC
	Army of Northern Virginia turns west towards Farmville, VA
April 5	Army of Tennessee reviewed at Smithfield, NC
April 6	Battle of Sailor's Creek, VA. Union forces capture one-fifth of Lee's army
April 8	Battle of Appomattox Station VA. Custer's Cavalry captures Confederate supply trains and artillery
April 9	Battle of Appomattox Court House VA, 7:00–10:00 a.m.
	Lee meets with Grant to surrender the Army of Northern Virginia, 1:30 p.m.
	Johnston reorganizes his forces at Smithfield, NC
April 10	Artillery of the Army of Northern Virginia is turned over at Appomattox, VA
	Union troops begin printing paroles for Lee's army

	Army of Tennessee leaves Smithfield, NC, marching west
	Union troops begin leaving Appomattox for Richmond and Washington
	Davis and Cabinet leave Danville, VA, for Greensboro, NC
April 11	Cavalry of the Army of Northern Virginia surrenders its weapons and equipment at Appomattox
	Davis and his cabinet arrive in Greensboro
	Johnston learns of Lee's surrender
	Army of Tennessee marches through Raleigh, NC
	Stoneman's raiders strike near Greensboro, NC
	Union troops enter Smithfield, NC
April 12	Infantry of the Army of Northern Virginia surrenders its weapons, flags, and equipment; men receive paroles
	General Lee leaves Appomattox for Richmond
	Army of Tennessee continues marching through Raleigh
	Davis, his cabinet, Beauregard, and Johnston meet
	Stoneman's raiders attack Salisbury
	Lee's surrender is announced to Sherman's troops
April 13	Soldiers from the Army of Northern Virginia begin the walk home
	Davis agrees to allow Johnston to meet with Sherman
	Army of Tennessee marches through Chapel Hill, NC, and Durham, NC
April 14	President Abraham Lincoln is shot at Ford's Theater, taken to a nearby house for treatment
	Last skirmishing between Union and Confederate forces in North Carolina occurs in Durham County
April 15	President Lincoln dies of wounds; Andrew Johnson becomes President
	Army of Tennessee marches through Burlington (Company Shops), NC
	Looting breaks out in Greensboro
	Davis and his party leave Greensboro
April 16	Army of Tennessee moves into camps in Guilford and Randolph counties, NC
(Easter)	Union scouts arrive in Chapel Hill, NC
	Mobs gather again in Greensboro but troops prevent looting
April 17	Johnston and Sherman meet at the Bennitt farmhouse
	Looting at storehouses in Graham and McLeansville, NC
April 18	Rumors of the surrender reach soldiers
	Surrendered men from Lee's army move through the region
	Sherman's soldiers hear news of Lincoln's assassination
April 19	Sherman's terms rejected by Congress
	Davis and his cabinet arrive in Charlotte
April 21	News of Lincoln's death spreads to other Union forces in North Carolina
	Sherman holds a review of his troops in Raleigh
April 23	General Grant arrives in Raleigh to confer with Sherman
April 24	With the truce over, Union and Confederate armies leave their camps and prepare for battle

April 25	Davis instructs Johnston to continue fighting and move the army south
April 26	Sherman and Johnston meet again at the Bennitt house, agree on final terms
	News of the terms reach southern camps; men begin to hide flags and discuss their journey home
	President Jefferson Davis learns of Johnston's final surrender to Sherman
	Davis and his party leave Charlotte for South Carolina; the attorney general, George Davis, leaves the group
April 27	Most of Sherman's troops begin marching north for Washington, DC
	Confederates start to park their artillery
April 28	Confederate infantry stack their weapons at their camps
	Governor Vance urges citizens to refrain from lawlessness
	Confederate troops are paid from the treasury
April 29	General Hartstuff arrives in Greensboro to print paroles
April 30	Paroles are printed and sent to officers for distribution
May 1	Generals Cox and Schofield and 104th Ohio arrive in Greensboro
	Paroles are distributed to the soldiers
May 2	Cox sends for more Union troops
	Paroles continue to be distributed
	Johnston delivers his farewell address at his headquarters
	Davis and his cabinet arrive in Abbeville, SC; the secretary of the navy, Stephen Mallory, resigns
May 3	South Carolina troops turn over weapons and supplies to the 104th Ohio in Greensboro
	Confederates begin to leave for home, most via Salisbury
	Davis and his party reach Washington, GA; the secretary of state, Judah Benjamin, leaves the group
May 4	The 9th New Jersey arrives in Greensboro to assist the 104th Ohio
	General Richard Taylor surrenders Confederate forces at Citronelle, AL
May 5	The 65th Illinois, 65th Indiana, 12th Kentucky (US), 16th Kentucky (US), 100th Ohio, 103rd Ohio, 177th Ohio, and 8th Tennessee (US) arrive in Greensboro
	Other Union troops are dispatched to Charlotte, NC and Danville, VA
May 8	Johnston arrives in Charlotte
May 9	Davis meets up with his wife, Varina, at Dublin, GA
	At Gainesville, AL, General Nathan B. Forrest disbands his cavalry
May 10	The 112th Illinois moves into Stokes County, NC, to maintain order
	Union cavalry captures Davis, his family, and his remaining escort at Irwinville, GA
May 12	Confederate forces in Jacksonville, FL, surrender to Union troops
May 13	The 9th New Jersey moves on to Charlotte; Confederate archives and documents are captured there

Confederate troops win in the last battle of the war at Palmetto Ranch, TX

June 2   General Edmund Kirby Smith surrenders Confederate forces in Texas at Galveston, TX. He had wanted to continue the war, but his officers arranged the surrender without his permission. Unable to stop it, he signed the documents of surrender.

June 8   John C. Breckinridge leaves Palm Beach, FL, for Cuba

June 23   Confederate general Stand Watie surrenders his command at Doaksville, OK, the last surrender of the war

November   The CSS Shenandoah arrives in Liverpool, England, and the crew breaks up, the last Confederate naval vessel in operation.

V: Governor Vance's Proclamation

State of North Carolina
Executive Department
Greensborough, April 28th, 1865
By the Governor of North Carolina
A Proclamation

Whereas, by the recent surrender of the principal armies of the Confederate States, further resistance to the forces of the United State has become vain, and would result in a useless waste of blood; and whereas all the natural disorders, attendant upon the disbanding of large armies are upon us, and the country is filled with numerous bands of citizens and soldiers disposed to do violence to persons and property:

Now, therefore, I, Zebulon B. Vance, Governor of the State of North Carolina, in the sincere hope of averting some of the many evils which threaten us, do issue this my Proclamation, commanding all such persons to abstain from any and all acts of lawlessness, to avoid assembling together in crowds in all towns and cities, or doing any thing whatsoever calculated to cause excitement; and earnestly appealing to all good citizens who are now at home to remain there, and to all soldiers of this State to retire quietly to their homes, and exert themselves in preserving order. Should it become necessary for the protection of citizens, I also appeal to the good and true soldiers of North Carolina, whether they have been surrendered and paroled or otherwise, to unite themselves together in sufficient numbers in the various counties of the State, under the superintendence of the civil magistrates thereof, to arrest or slay any bodies of lawless and unauthorized men who may be committing depredations upon the persons or property of peaceable citizens, assuring them that it will be no violation of their parole to do so. And I would assure my fellow-citizens generally that, under God, I will do all that may be in my power to settle the government of the State, to restore the civil authority in her borders and to further the great ends of peace, domestic tranquility and the general welfare of the people. Without their aid I am powerless to do anything.

Z.B. Vance[1]

VI: *Walking Tour*

While much of Civil War-era Greensboro has been lost, many of the sites are located in a compact area of downtown and are within easy walking distance. Ample parking and refreshments are also available in Old Greensborough, as the historic downtown is called.

Modern cities often have unique juxtapositions of old remnants side by side with modern structures. Downtown Greensboro is no different. Fortunately, the city's downtown grid pattern and location of railroad lines remain intact, allowing for comparisons with historic maps and permitting modern researchers to locate long-lost historic structures.

Only a handful of buildings in downtown Greensboro date back to the Civil War. Among them are the Walker-Scarborough house, Greensboro Historical Museum (once the Presbyterian church), and the Troy Bumpass house.

Begin your tour at the North Davie Street parking garage. Located adjacent to the main library, this is a good central location for your tour. Start by walking south on Davie Street to the intersection with Washington Street.

STOP 1: ECKEL HOUSE SITE

Here, where the parking lot sits in the southeast corner of the intersection, stood the Eckel home, known as Rose Villa. Perry Eckel was the mayor of the city at the time, and his home was an impressive structure. On this property money was hidden under a fence post during the Union occupation. General Judson Kilpatrick occupied the house during the summer, while some of his troopers spread out on the lawn surrounding the home.

Continue walking south on Davie Street, crossing under the railroad bridge and stopping at the intersection with Martin Luther King Jr. Drive. Turn to the north to face the empty lot. You will see the modern railroad yard in the distance.

STOP 2: GORRELL HOUSE SITE

Although it was one of the most important sites in Civil War Greensboro, there is nothing left of the house. Home to Ralph Gorrell and his family, it was General Johnston's headquarters upon his arrival in the city. Here he addressed the army for the last time.

In the distance you can see the railroad yard and modern station. At the time of the war there was a great deal of industrial activity here, including an arms manufacturing facility. When Union troops occupied the city, the rail yard was the center of their activity.

Beauregard, and later Davis and the cabinet, stayed in railroad cars in the yard here. During and after the surrender, supplies and ordnance were parked here, including hundreds of artillery guns.

Walk across the street to the small park and monument.

STOP 3: ARMY OF TENNESSEE MONUMENT

As you gaze back toward the Gorrell home site, remember that the railroad tracks ran flat on the ground; the current trestle and undercut highway are modern changes. A great deal of disturbance from modernization has occurred here.

This monument and the state marker call attention to the army's surrender

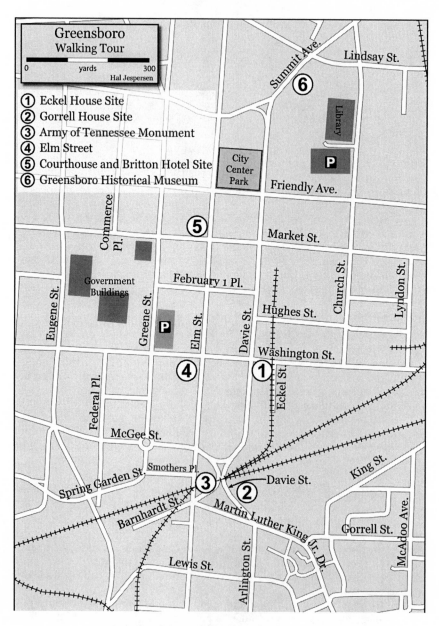

in Greensboro. The wartime railroad depot stood about where the current railroad bridge is located. Here, in leaky railroad cars, stayed Jefferson Davis and members of his cabinet. The depot and railroad line were the center of activity during April and May of 1865.

When the 104th Ohio arrived in the city, they relieved the South Carolina guards who were watching over the supply trains stationed here. This was the only semblance of a turnover of military supplies during the entire surrender. Continue west to Elm Street and turn right, going north up Elm.

Stop 4: Elm Street

While none of these structures along Elm Street date to the 1860s, they give you a feel for the scale of historic Greensboro. About halfway up the block between Megee Street and Washington Street is an empty lot. This is where the home that Wood rented and Davis stayed was located.

Elm Street was the site of looting in the days before Easter 1865. Continue to the intersection with Market Street. Along the way you will pass the Civil Rights Museum, scene of a Woolworth sit-in during the 1960s that started the desegregation of restaurants across the South. The intersection of Elm and Market was the exact center of Greensboro. Glance to the right, down East Market Street. Looting initially began in the area in front of you down Market Street. Violence between the mob and guards occurred on these streets. At Market Street turn left, to the west.

Stop 5: Britton Hotel and Courthouse Site

Directly across the street, where the massive Jefferson Standard Building now stands, was the Guilford County Courthouse. It stood at the very center of town, and nearly in the center of the county.

Along the side where you stand, somewhere in the middle of the block, was the site of the Britton Hotel. This was another important landmark during the war. It was here that Union officers oversaw the distribution of paroles to the Confederates.

From here return back across Elm Street and continue east on Market to the intersection of Davie Street and turn left, going north. As you walk along Market Street, note that there was looting in this area as well. Turn right onto Summit Avenue, and you will see the Greensboro Historical Museum in the old Presbyterian church.

Stop 6: Greensboro Historical Museum

The museum covers Greensboro's two hundred years of history and occupies the old church, which was used as a military hospital in 1865. Jacob H. Smith was the minister at the time; his and his wife's (Mary) letters were quoted in the preceding chapters. The museum also has one of the best collection of Confederate weapons in the nation.

From here you may return to your vehicle or explore other attractions in downtown. There are many other Civil War points of interest in the area that are outside the scope of this study; the museum and city visitor center can assist with information on them.

VII: Captured Confederate War Matériel

Artillery

12-Pound Howitzers	30
6-Pound Guns	17

10-Pound Smoothbore Guns	6
12-Pound Mountain Howitzers	16
12-Pound Heavy Guns	3
12-Pound Napoleons	13
Wiard Guns	2
3-Inch Rodmans	5
3-Inch Rifle Guns	2
12-Pound Guns	68
10-Pound Parrot Rifles	8
3-Inch rifles	3
20-Pound Parrot Rifles	3
Brooke Rifle	1
10-Pound Whitworth	2
Blakely Guns	2
Dahlgren Howitzer	1

ARTILLERY AMMUNITION

12-Pounder Shells	144
12-Pounder Shot	136
12-Pounder Canister	32
20-Pounder Shells	16
Cannon Powder	600 Pounds

SMALL ARMS

Springfield Rifles	2,342
Enfield Rifles	4,526
Austrian Rifles	319
Harpers Ferry Rifles	392
U.S. .69 Muskets	300
Sharps Carbines	2
Burnside Carbines	3

ACCOUTREMENTS

Sets (cartridge box, belt, cap box)	980
Cartridge Boxes	988
Cavalry Cartridge Boxes	11
Bayonet Scabbards	1,086
Cap Boxes	798

SMALL ARMS AMMUNITION

.58 Cartridges	341,500
.54 Cartridges	12,000
.69 Cartridges (buck and ball)	4,000
Sharps .52 Cartridges	6,000
Percussion Caps	500,000

MISCELLANEOUS

Sabers	130

Artillery Harnesses	980 sets
Saddles	112
Bridles	12
Sulphur	12,500 pounds*
Saltpeter	37,000 pounds*

The list is a testament not only to how well armed the Army of Tennessee was in the spring of 1865, but also to the extraordinary efforts of the limited Southern industrial base to produce and transport military ordnance.[1]

*Used in manufacturing gunpowder

Chapter Notes

INTRODUCTION

1. "The Last Roll," *Confederate Veteran* 12, no. 12 (December 1904), 598; John H. Lynn, "Re-enlistment in the Western Army," *Confederate Veteran* 10, no. 6 (June 1902), 259; "The Last Roll," *Confederate Veteran* 15, no. 9 (September 1907), 516.

2. Fred Hughes, *Guilford County, NC: A Map Supplement* (Jamestown, NC: Custom House, 1988), 62.

CHAPTER 1

1. Craig Symonds, *Joseph E. Johnston* (New York: W.W. Norton, 1992), 29–30, 59, 69.

2. Ezra Warner, *Generals in Gray* (Baton Rouge: Louisiana State University Press, 1987), 183.

3. *Ibid.*, 124.

4. *Ibid.*

5. *Ibid.*, 293–4.

6. *Ibid.*, XLVII.

7. *Ibid.*, 12203.

8. Symonds, 235; Warner, 332–3; Mark Bradley, *Last Stand in the Carolinas: The Battle of Bentonville* (Campbell, CA: Savas, 1996), 83.

9. Mark A. Moore, *The Wilmington Campaign and the Battle for Fort Fisher* (Mason City, IA: Savas, 1999), 3, 5; Jacob D. Cox, *Sherman's March to the Sea* (New York: Da Capo, 1994), 178.

10. *Ibid.*

11. William T. Sherman Papers, Library of Congress, Washington, DC.

12. Louis Bringier Papers, Louisiana State University.

13. Robert C. Black, *The Railroads of the Confederacy* (Chapel Hill: University of North Carolina Press, 1952), 273.

14. *Ibid.*

15. *Ibid.*, 274.

16. *Ibid.*, 174.

17. Hughes, 61.

18. Mary Massey, *Ersatz in the Confederacy* (Columbia: University of South Carolina Press, 1952), 29.

19. Black, 274–6.

20. Moore, 3, 5; Cox, 183; Stephanie McCurry, *Confederate Reckoning* (Cambridge, MA: Harvard University Press, 2010), 292, 419. As Confederate control of southeastern North Carolina crumbled, slaves plotted an uprising. The armies swept through the region before violence erupted.

21. Moore, 15.

22. Bradley, 115, 125.

23. *Ibid.*, 132.

24. Moore, 16.

25. Walter C. Clark, *North Carolina Regiments*, vol. 2 (Wendell, NC: Broadfoot, 1982), 754–64.

26. Bradley, 320.

27. *Ibid.*, 203–8.

28. Henderson Deans Reminiscences, Chapel Hill, NC, Southern Historical Collection, University of North Carolina

29. Black, 277.

CHAPTER 2

1. Irving Buck, *Cleburne and His Command* (Jackson, TN: McCowat-Mercer, 1959), 302; Glenn Dedmondt, *The Flags of Civil War Alabama* (Gretna, LA: Pelican, 2001), 78, 71; *Official Records of the War of the Rebellion*, vol. 59 (Washington, DC: War Department, 1895), 696 (hereafter referred to as *Official Records*); *Annals of an American Family: A Chronicle of the Lives and Times of Successive Generations from Merging Pioneer Lines of the Richardson and Smith Families* (Greensboro, NC, 1953), 177.

2. *Official Records*, vol. 47, p. 715; vol. 41, pp. 696, 701, 704, 716.

3. *Ibid.*, vol. 47, pp. 711, 694, 715.

4. Charles Inglesby, *Historical Sketch of the*

1st South Carolina Artillery (Walker, Evans, and Cogswell), 15.

5. Daniel Barefoot, *Robert F. Hoke: Lee's Modest Warrior* (Winston-Salem, NC: John F. Blair, 1996), 304.

6. Joseph E. Johnston, *Narrative of Military Operations* (New York: D. Appleton, 1874), 394.

7. John Simpson, *Reminiscences of the 41st Tennessee* (Shippensburg, PA: White Mane, 2001), 129.

8. D.E. Huger Smith, *A Charlestonian's Recollections* (Charleston, SC: Carolina Art Association, 1950), 104.

9. Barefoot, 305.

10. James Clary, *A History of the 15th South Carolina Volunteer Infantry Regiment* (Columbia: South Carolina Department of Archives and History, 2007), 285.

11. Barefoot, 305.

12. Richard M. McMurry, ed., *Footprints of a Regiment* (Atlanta: Longstreet, 1992), 177.

13. Wheeler Family Papers, Alabama Department of Archives and History, Montgomery.

14. B.L. Ridley, "Last Battle of the War," *Confederate Veteran* 3, no. 1 (January 1895), 36.

15. D.A. Dickert, *History of Kershaw's Brigade* (Dayton, OH: Morningside Books, 1988), 526.

16. Barefoot, 305.

17. Devereaux Cannon, *The Flags of the Confederacy* (Memphis, TN: St. Luke's, 1988), 57; National Register Nomination, Stevens House, Salem, NC, North Carolina State Historic Preservation Office.

18. William L. Calhoun, *History of the 42nd Georgia* (Amberg, 2008), 51.

19. W.J. McMurry, *History of the 20th Tennessee Regiment* (Nashville, TN: Elder's Bookstore, 1976), 177.

20. W.H. Andrews, *Diary of W.H. Andrews* (Atlanta, GA: 1891).

21. James Brown Diary, Georgia Department of Archives and History, Atlanta.

22. *Ibid.*, 37; Grimsley, Mark, "Learning to Say 'Enough,'" in *The Collapse of the Confederacy*, ed. Mark Grimsley and Brooks D. Simpson Lincoln (Lincoln: University of Nebraska Press, 2001), 61.

23. John Johnson Diary, Duke University, Durham, NC.

24. *Official Records*, vol. 47, part 3, pp. 757–758.

25. Weymouth Jordan, *North Carolina Troops*, vol. 15 (Raleigh, NC: Department of Archives and History, 2003), 310.

26. David T. Copeland Papers, Southern Historical Collection, University of North Carolina, Chapel Hill.

27. Roger Durham, ed., *The Blues in Gray: Journal of William D. Dixon* (Knoxville: University of Tennessee Press, 2000), 274; Letitia Walker, "The Surrender at Greensboro," 334,

Civil War File, Greensboro Public Library, Greensboro, NC.

28. Alfred Tyler Fielder Diary, vol. 4, Tennessee State Library and Archives, Nashville.

29. National Register Nomination, Stevens House, Salem, NC, North Carolina State Historic Preservation Office; "Last Review," North Carolina Civil War Trails Marker, Johnston County.

30. *Official Records*, vol. 47, part 3, 772.

31. *Ibid.*, 773; Grimsley, 61.

32. Henderson, 42.

33. *Official Records*, vol. 47, part 3, p. 781; John C. Oeffinger, ed., *A Soldier's General: The Civil War Letters of Major General Lafayette McLaws* (Chapel Hill: University of North Carolina Press, 2002), 273; McMurry, 177.

34. Charles C. Jones, *Historical Sketches of the Chatham Artillery During the Confederate Struggle for Independence* (Albany, NY: Joe Munsell, 1867), 215.

35. Henderson, 43.

36. Michael Hardy, *The Fifty-Eighth North Carolina Troops* (Jefferson, NC: McFarland, 2010), 161.

37. Joseph E. Johnston, *Narrative of Military Operations* (New York: D. Appleton, 1874), 395.

38. *Official Records*, vol. 47, part 3, pp. 773–774, 770.

39. W.M. Ives, "History of the 4th Florida Regiment," *Confederate Veteran* 3, no. 4 (April 1895), 103; Grimsley, 60.

40. Gerald Prokopowicz, *All For the Regiment* (Chapel Hill: University of North Carolina Press, 2001), 5–6.

41. Sumner A. Cunnigham, *Reminiscences of the 41st Tennessee Regiment* (nd, np), 54; John Simpson, *Reminiscences of the 41st Tennessee* (Shippensburg, PA: White Mane, 2001), 130.

42. Durham, 274.

43. Thomas L. Sullivan, Account Book, Tennessee State Library and Archives, Nashville.

44. Henderson, 43.

45. James Clary, *A History of the 15th South Carolina Volunteer Infantry Regiment* (Columbia: South Carolina Department of Archives and History, 2007), 286; D.A. Dickert, *History of Kershaw's Brigade* (Dayton, OH: Morningside, 1988), 527; McMurry, 358.

46. Ibid; Stan Harley, "Flag of the 6th Arkansas—Cleburne's Flag," *Confederate Veteran* 5, no. 10 (October 1897), 518; Larry Daniel, *Soldier in the Army of Tennessee* (Chapel Hill: University of North Carolina Press, 1991), 132.

47. Larry Daniel, *Cannoneers in Gray* (Huntsville: University of Alabama Press, 1984), 184.

48. John Croxton, "Second Palmetto Regiment," in *Recollections and Reminiscences*, vol. 9 (South Carolina United Daughters of the Confederacy, 1998), 272.

49. George Guild, *A Brief Narrative of the 4th Tennessee Cavalry Regiment* (Nashville: 1913), 137.

50. Lilley M. Hawes, ed., "Memoirs of Charles Olmstead," *Georgia Historical Society Quarterly* 45 (June 1961), 153.

51. Durham, 274–5.

52. John Simpson, 130.

53. Sarah Chapman, ed., *Bright and Glory Days* (Knoxville: University of Tennessee Press, 2003), 170, 172.

54. Grady Howell, *Going to Meet the Yankees: A History of the Sixth Regiment, Mississippi Infantry* (Jackson, MS: Chickasaw Bayou, 1981), 264, 288.

55. McMurry, 177–78.

56. Michael Hardy, *The Fifty-Eighth North Carolina Troops* (Jefferson, NC: McFarland, 2010), 161. There were other regiments from the Old North State with the army, such as the North Carolina Junior Reserves and troops from the Army of Northern Virginia. Yet these two regiments had been with the Army of Tennessee for years, while the others were recent additions that spring.

57. Johnson Hagood, *Memories of the War of Secession from the Original Manuscripts of Johnson Hagood* (Columbia, SC: State Company, 1910), 364.

58. *Ibid.*

59. Dickert, 527.

60. Durham, 275.

61. Howard Madus, *The Battle Flags of the Confederate Army of Tennessee* (Milwaukee: Milwaukee Public Museum, 1976), 70.

62. Walker, 344.

63. *Ibid.*, 345.

64. Oeffinger, 272.

65. Charles Woodward Hutson Papers, Southern Historical Collection, University of North Carolina, Chapel Hill.

66. Alfred Roman, *The Military Operations of General Beauregard in the War Between the States, 1861 to 1865: Including a Brief Personal Sketch and a Narrative of His Services in the War with Mexico, 1846–8* (New York: Da Capo, 1994), 387, 90. No firsthand accounts of building the fortifications have been found.

67. Irving Buck, *Cleburne and His Command* (Jackson, TN: McCowat-Mercer, 1959), 306; *Official Records*, vol. 47, part 3, p. 774.

68. Robert C. Black, *The Railroads of the Confederacy* (Chapel Hill: University of North Carolina Press, 1952), 277.

69. Johnston, 396; Rachel Susan Cheves Papers, Duke University, Durham, NC.

70. Cunningham, 55.

71. Fielder Diary.

72. *Ibid.*

73. Eleanor D. McSwain, *Crumbling Defenses* (Macon, GA: 1960), 118.

74. *Ibid.*

75. George W. Bussey, "Memoirs of Reverend G.W. Bussey," in *Recollections and Reminiscences*, vol. 11 (South Carolina United Daughters of the Confederacy, 2001), 422.

76. Cheves Papers.

77. Hutson Papers.

78. Jones, *Chatham Artillery*, 215–220.

79. McMurry, 178.

80. Hutson Papers.

81. William J. Worsham, *The Old Nineteenth Tennessee Regiment* (Knoxville, TN: Paragon, 1902), 175.

82. D.E. Huger Smith, *A Charlestonian's Recollections* (Charleston, SC: Carolina Art Association, 1950), 104–5.

83. *Ibid.*

84. Hawes, 153.

85. Durham.

86. Walter Clark, *History of the Several Regiments and Battalions from North Carolina in the Great War, 1861–1865*, vol. 4 (Goldsboro, NC: Nash Brothers, 1901), 60.

87. "Johnston Moves West," North Carolina Civil War Trails Marker, Alamance County.

88. *Ibid.*

89. James Brown Diary, Georgia Department of Archives and History, Atlanta, 10.

90. Alester G. Holmes, *Diary of Henry M. Holmes, Army of Tennessee Assistant Surgeon, Florida Troops* (State College of Mississippi, 1968).

91. McMurry, 178.

92. Durham, 276.

93. *Ibid.*

94. Lovie P. Thomas Papers, Atlanta History Center, Atlanta.

95. Joseph Frederick Waring Diary, Southern Historical Collection, University of North Carolina, Chapel Hill.

96. Sidney Wilkinson, "These Confederates Never Surrendered," Undesignated Newspaper Article, North Carolina State Archives, Raleigh.

97. W.W. Gordon Diary, Southern Historical Collection, University of North Carolina, Chapel Hill.

98. J.W. Evans, "With Hampton's Scouts," *Confederate Veteran* 32 (1924), 470.

99. Hagood, 368.

100. Norman D. Brown, ed., *One of Cleburne's Command* (Austin: University of Texas Press, 1980), 163–4.

101. Jacob H. Smith Diary, Southern Historical Collection, University of North Carolina, Chapel Hill.

102. D.E. Huger Smith, 105–6.

103. Barefoot, 307.

104. Charles Beatty Mallett Papers, Southern Historical Collection, University of North Carolina, Chapel Hill.

105. Joseph W. Crowther Diary, Virginia Military Institute Archives, Lexington.
106. Don Wharton, *Smithfield as Seen by Sherman's Soldiers* (Smithfield, NC: Smithfield Herald, 1917), 4.
107. Hagood, 368.
108. Daniel D. Dantzler, *A Brief Diary of Events During the Last Months of the Civil War* (Greensboro, NC: Greensboro Historical Museum, Greensboro), 12–13.
109. *Ibid.*
110. Robert Alexander Jenkins, "Reminiscences of Robert Alexander Jenkins," Duke University, Durham, NC.
111. Pamela J. Bennett, ed., "Curtis R. Burke's Civil War Journal," *Indiana Magazine of History* 47, no. 2 (June, 1971), 153.
112. Stephen Mallory, "The Last Days of the Confederate Government," *McClure's*, issue 7 (December 1900), 59–60.
113. Bradley R. Foley and Adrian L. Whicker, *The Civil War Ends: Greensboro, April 1865* (Greensboro, NC: Guilford County Genealogical Society, 2008), 14–15.
114. Robert L. Phillips, *History of the Hospitals in Greensboro* (Greensboro, NC: Printworks, 1996), 4.
115. John Taylor Wood Papers, Southern Historical Collection, University of North Carolina, Chapel Hill, 2; William B. Trotter, *Silk Flags and Cold Steel* (Winston Salem, NC: John F. Blair, 1998), 326.
116. Wood.
117. Trotter, 326.
118. *Ibid.*, 324–5.
119. Mallory, 61.
120. *Official Records*, vol. 47, part 3, p. 787.
121. G.G. Dickson, "Trailing the Treasure of the Confederacy," *Raleigh (NC) News and Observer*, April 29, 1928.
122. Richard Yates, "Governor Vance and the End of the War in North Carolina," *North Carolina Historical Review* 18, no. 4 (October 1941), 328.
123. Henderson, 90.
124. Barefoot, 311–12.
125. Joseph B. Cummings, "How I Knew That the War Was Over," *Confederate Veteran* 9, no. 1 (January 1901), 18.
126. Grimsley, 62; Henderson, 92.
127. Cummings, 18–19.
128. Henderson, 93.
129. Albert Q. Porter Collection, Library of Congress, Washington, DC.
130. Josepth T. Glatthaar, *The March to the Sea and Beyond* (New York: New York University Press, 1986), 176.
131. Herman Everts, *A Complete and Comprehensive History of the Ninth Regiment, New Jersey Volunteers* (Newark, NJ: A. Stephen Holbrook, 1865), 173.

132. Crowther.
133. Jack K. Bauer, *Soldiering* (New York: Berkley Books, 1977), 240.
134. Glatthaar, 177.
135. Norman D. Brown, 163.
136. *Ibid.*, 165–67.
137. *Ibid.*, 165.
138. Cunningham, 55.
139. John Simpson, 131.
140. Johnston, 396; Gilbert Govan and James Livingood, *A Different Valor* (Indianapolis: Bobbs Merrill, 1956), 360.
141. Trotter, 329; Johnston 396.
142. Johnston, 397.
143. *Ibid.*
144. *Ibid.*, 397–8.
145. *Ibid.*, 398–9; Craig Symonds, *Joseph E. Johnston* (New York: W.W. Norton, 1992), 354.
146. Mallory, 625.
147. *Ibid.*, 399–400; Foley and Whicker, 42.
148. Trotter, 332.
149. *Ibid.*, 333.
150. *Ibid.*; Johnston, 400–401.
151. Heyward-Ferguson Papers, "Memoirs of S.W. Ferguson," Southern Historical Collection, University of North Carolina, Chapel Hill.
152. Henderson, 95.
153. Buck, 306; *Official Records*, vol. 47, part 3, p. 774; Johnston, 400–401; Bradley, 151.
154. Barefoot, 307–8.
155. *Ibid.*
156. *Ibid.*, 311.
157. *Ibid.*
158. *Ibid.*
159. Brenda C. McKean, *Blood and War at My Doorstep*, vol. 2 (Xlibris, 2011), 1041.
160. Henderson, 97; Guild, 143.
161. Bromfield Ridley, *Battles and Sketches of the Army of Tennessee* (Dayton, OH: Morningside, 1976), 457.
162. Durham, 276–77.
163. Calhoun, 51.
164. Guild, 144.
165. John Lindsley, *Military Annals of Tennessee* (Wilmington, NC: Broadfoot, 1996), 896.
166. Donald Hopkins, *The Little Jeff* (Shippensburg, PA: White Mane, 1999), 278–79.
167. Henry _____ Letter, Duke University, Durham, NC.
168. C.A. DeSaussure, "War Experiences at Haw River," in *Recollections and Reminiscences*, vol. 7 (South Carolina United Daughters of the Confederacy, 1997), 299.
169. *Ibid.*, 299–300.
170. Clark, 60; Barefoot, 313. The unit was recruited in Wake, Granville, Nash, Chatham, and Randolph counties.
171. Clark, 60, 32.
172. *Ibid.*, 61.
173. Barefoot, 312.
174. *Ibid.*, 313.

175. Clark, 60.
176. Stanley Hoole, "Admiral on Horseback: The Diary of Brigadier-General Raphael Semmes, February-May, 1865," *Alabama Review* 28, no. 2 (April 1975), 140.
177. *Ibid.*, 141.
178. M.M. Buford, "Surrender of Johnston's Army," *Confederate Veteran* 27, no. 5 (May 1920), 170.
179. Gordon Diary.
180. Henderson, 126.
181. *Ibid.*, 127.
182. Charles Kirk, *History of the 15th Pennsylvania Cavalry* (Philadelphia: 1906), 493
183. Daniel, 184; *Official Records*, vol. 29, p. 334.
184. *Official Records*, vol. 49, p. 333.
185. *Ibid.*
186. Kirk, 503; Johnston, 409.
187. McKean, 972–3.
188. *Ibid.*, 1028.
189. *Official Records*, vol. 49, pp. 555–56.
190. Kirk, 501.
191. Henderson, 129.
192. Nicholas Schenck Diary, University of North Carolina-Wilmington.
193. Kirk, 502.
194. *Ibid.*, 542.
195. *Ibid.*
196. *Ibid.*, 543.
197. *Ibid.*, 555; Fred Hughes, *Guilford County, NC: A Map Supplement* (Jamestown, NC: Custom House, 1988), 97–98, http://jamestownnews.womacknewspapers.com/articles/2011/11/09/news/features/features61.txt.
198. Henderson, 130.
199. Mrs. J.S. Welborne, "A Wayside Hospital," *Confederate Veteran* 38, no. 3 (March 1930), 95.
200. Ibid; Mary L. Joyce, ed., *Clark's Collection of Historic Remembrances* (High Point, NC: 1950), 104; Paula S. Jordan and Kathy W. Manning, *Women of Guilford* (Greensboro, NC: 1979), 54.
201. Welborne; Joyce, 104; Jordan and Manning, 54–55.
202. Sheldon B. Thorpe, *The History of the Fifteenth Connecticut Volunteers in the War for the Defense of the Union, 1861–1865* (New Haven, CT: Price, Lee, and Adkins, 1893), 253–5.
203. *Ibid.*, 96.
204. Johnston, *Narrative*, 409.
205. Kirk, 504.
206. *Ibid.*, 505.
207. *Ibid.*, 505, 564.
208. Margaret Stanly Beckwith Reminiscences, Virginia Historical Society, Richmond.
209. "Johnston Moves West," North Carolina Civil War Trails Marker, Alamance County, NC.
210. Charles Beatty Mallett Papers, Southern Historical Collection, University of North Carolina, Chapel Hill.
211. George Washington Harper, "G.W.F. Harper's Diary," Caldwell Heritage Museum, Lenoir, NC, p. 80.

CHAPTER 3

1. Hughes, 96.
2. Foley and Whicker, 9–11.
3. Chris Fonvielle, *The Wilmington Campaign* (El Dorado Hills, CA: Savas Beattie, 1996), 446; Ed and Sue Curtis to author, e-mail, 5 May 2011.
4. Blackwell Robinson and Alexander Stoesen, *History of Guilford County, North Carolina* (Greensboro, NC: Guilford Bicentennial Commission, 1971), 96.
5. Robert Herriot, "At Greensboro, N.C., in April, 1865," *Confederate Veteran* 30, no. 3 (March 1922), 102.
6. Dantzler, 13.
7. Henderson, 186.
8. *Philadelphia Inquirer*, "Special Correspondence of the Inquirer, Greensboro, N.C., July 6, 1865," July 18, 1865.
9. Henderson, 186.
10. Mary E. Massey, *Ersatz in the Confederacy* (Columbia: University of South Carolina Press, 1952), 83.
11. *Ibid.*, 83–89.
12. Letitia Walker, "The Surrender in Greensboro," Civil War File, Greensboro Public Library, Greensboro, NC.
13. *Ibid.*
14. James R. Cole, "Athos Recounts the Civil War's End in Greensboro," *Guilford Genealogist* 34, no.1 (Spring 2007), 2.
15. Mary Kelly Watson Smith, *The Women of Greensboro, N.C., 1861–1865: A Paper* (Little Rock, AR: Democrat P & L, 1919), 4.
16. *Ibid.*
17. *Ibid.*, 6–7.
18. Robert L. Phillips, *History of the Hospitals in Greensboro* (Greensboro, NC: Printworks, 1996), 1.
19. *Ibid.*, 2–3.
20. Arthur P. Ford, *Life in the Confederate Army: Being Personal Experiences of a Private Soldier in the Confederate Army by Arthur P. Ford and Some Experiences and Sketches of Southern Life* (New York: Neale, 1905), 63.
21. Foley and Whicker, 11.
22. James R. Cole, "Greensboro in April 1865," *Greensboro Patriot*, March 29, 1866, p. 2.
23. George W. Bussey, "Memoirs of Reverend G.W. Bussey," in *Recollections and Reminiscences*, vol. 11 (South Carolina United Daughters of the Confederacy, 2001), 422.
24. *Ibid.*
25. Heriott, 101.

26. C.A. DeSaussure, "War Experiences at Haw River," in *Recollections and Reminiscences*, vol. 7 (South Carolina United Daughters of the Confederacy, 1997), 212.

27. Hutson Papers.

28. George Mitchell, "Memories of Surrender and Journey Home," *Confederate Veteran* 17, no. 4 (April 1909), 172.

29. McMurry, 179.

30. Weymouth Jordan, *North Carolina Troops*, vol. 14 (Raleigh, NC: Department of Archives and History, 1998), 500.

31. Crowther.

32. Isaac G. Bradwell, "Gambling in the Army," *Confederate Veteran* 31 (1932), 475.

33. Foley and Whicker, 26.

34. *Official Records*, vol. 47, part 3, p. 800.

35. *Ibid.*

36. James W. Albright, *Greensboro, 1808–1904* (Greensboro, NC: Joseph Stone, 1904), 298.

37. Copeland.

38. *Official Records*, vol. 47, part 3, p. 799.

39. Albert Ferry Letter, April 19, 1865, Greensboro Historical Museum, Greensboro, NC.

40. Harrison, 42.

41. *Ibid.*

42. "Last Shots," North Carolina Civil War Trails Marker, Durham County.

43. William Vatavuk, *Dawn of Peace* (Bennett Place Support Fund, 1989), 10.

44. *Official Records*, vol. 47, part 3, p. 800.

45. John Simpson, 132.

46. McMurry, 180.

47. *Ibid.*

48. *Ibid.*

49. Albright, 298.

50. *Ibid.*, 299.

51. Norman D. Brown, ed., *One of Cleburne's Command* (Austin: University of Texas Press, 1980), 164.

52. Schenck Diary.

53. Dantzler, 14.

54. Jones, *Chatham Artillery*, 216.

55. Robert M. Collins, *Chapters from the Unwritten History of the War Between the States* (St. Louis: Nixon Jones, 1893), 294–98.

56. Cathy Wright to author, e-mail, 1 June 2009; http://www.historynet.com/an-eyewitness-account-of-the-evacuation-of-richmond-during-the-american-civil-war.htm/3.

57. Foley and Whicker, 26.

58. *Ibid.*, 28.

59. *Ibid.*

60. *Ibid.*

61. Mallory, 60.

62. Harrison, 132.

63. John Taylor Wood Papers, Southern Historical Collection, University of North Carolina, Chapel Hill.

64. Harrison, 132–3.

65. Foley and Whicker, 37–8.

66. Mallory, 61–2.

67. Herriot, 101–2.

68. James R. Cole, "The Home Guards," in *History of the Several Regiments and Battalions from North Carolina in the Great War*, vol. 5, ed. Walter Clark (Goldsboro, NC: Nash Brothers, 1901), 50–2.

69. *Ibid.*, 2.

70. *Ibid.*

71. Burton N. Harrison, "The Capture of Jefferson Davis," *The Century* 27 (November 1883), 134.

72. Mallory, 65.

73. Chris Bingham, "From New Berne to Bennett Place with Cooke's Foot Cavalry," master's thesis, East Carolina University, 2007, p. 460; Foley and Whicker, 32.

74. Bingham, 459.

75. *Ibid.*, 29.

76. James Harris, *Historical Sketches of the 7th Regiment, North Carolina State Troops* (Mooresville, NC: Mooresville Printing), 61.

77. *Ibid.*

78. J.M. Mullen, "Last Days of Johnston's Army," *Southern Historical Society Papers* 18 (January 1890), 97–113.

79. John Lindsley, *Military Annals of Tennessee* (Wilmington, NC: Broadfoot, 1996), 676.

80. Bingham, 32–3.

81. Robert Amos Jarman Papers, Mississippi Department of Archives and History, Jackson.

82. Hezekiah McCorkle Diary, Georgia Department of Archives and History, Atlanta.

83. *Ibid.*; Cole, 14.

84. Cole, 33.

85. *Ibid.*, 34; *Official Records*, vol. 47, part 3, p. 815.

86. William B. Trotter, *Silk Flags and Cold Steel* (Winston Salem, NC: John F. Blair, 1998), 336.

87. Cornelia Phillips Spencer, *The Last Ninety Days of the War in North Carolina* (New York: Watchman, 1866), 169.

88. Trotter, 337; Bradley, 148.

89. *Ibid.*

90. *Ibid.*

91. Charles Beatty Mallett Papers, Southern Historical Collection, University of North Carolina, Chapel Hill.

92. *Ibid.*

93. Foley and Whicker, 42; Bradley, 145.

94. Wilson Angley, Jerry L. Cross, and Michael Hill, *Sherman's March Through North Carolina* (Raleigh, NC: Division of Archives and History, 1995), 81; Trotter, 321; James Clary, *A History of the 15th South Carolina Volunteer Infantry Regiment* (Columbia: South Carolina Department of Archives and History, 2007), 291; site visit led by Timothy Thompson and Boyd Lamberth.

95. Buck, 306; *Official Records*, vol. 47, part 3, p. 774; Weymouth Jordan, *North Carolina Troops*, vol. 8 (Raleigh, NC: Department of Archives and History, 1981), 428; Weymouth Jordan, *North Carolina Troops*, vol. 9 (Raleigh, NC: Department of Archives and History, 1985), 190;Weymouth Jordan, *North Carolina Troops*, vol. 14 (Raleigh, NC: Department of Archives and History, 1998), 271.

96. Abbie Rogers, "Confederates and Quakers: The Shared Wartime Experience," *Quaker History* 99, no. 2 (Fall 2010), 5.

97. Mary A Browning, *Remembering Old Jamestown* (Charleston, SC: History, 2008), 116.

98. Yvonne B. Thomas, *Roads to Jamestown* (Fredericksburg, VA: Book Crafters, 1997), 20.

99. Victoria E. Bynum, *The Long Shadow of the Civil War* (Chapel Hill: University of North Carolina Press, 2010), 48–50; Rogers, 5; William Pegg, Jr., *Something of the Story of Deep River* (Greensboro, NC: Guilford County Genealogical Society, 1999), 27–8. The region's Quakers offered food and shelter to anyone in need. Although they opposed the war, they did not participate in any of the more active and vocal protests.

100. Bynum, 48–50; Pegg, 27–8; L.B. Mills, Jr., *Randolph County: A Brief History* (Raleigh: North Carolina Department of Archives and History, 2008), 60–1.

101. Seth B. Hinshaw and Mary Edith Hinshaw, eds., *Carolina Quakers* (Greensboro, NC: North Carolina Yearly Meeting, 1972), 32.

102. *Ibid.*, 34; Seth B. Hinshaw, *Friends at Holy Spring* (Greensboro, NC: North Carolina Yearly Meeting, 1982), 54–5.

103. J.G. Hamilton, *History of North Carolina*, vol. 2 (Chicago: Lewis, 1919), 47.

104. Mana D. Foust Letter, Greensboro Historical Museum, Greensboro, NC.

105. James S. Brawley, *The Rowan Story* (Salisbury, NC: Rowan Printing, 1953), 192–3.

106. Mills, 58–60; Pegg, 64.

107. Hinshaw, *Friends*, 54–5.

108. *Ibid.*, 57; Mills, 35.

109. Tillinghast Family Papers, Duke University, Durham, NC.

110. Hinshaw, *Carolina Quakers*, 35.

111. Bynum, 48–50; Pegg, 27–8.

112. Hinshaw, *Carolina Quakers*, 34; Mills, 60.

113. Brenda C. McKean, *Blood and War at My Doorstep*, vol. 2 (Xlibris, 2011), 977.

114. *Randolph County, 1779–1979* (Winston-Salem, NC: Randolph County Historical Society, 1980), 89.

115. Mills, 60–1.

116. Bynum, 48–50; Pegg, 27–8.

117. Pegg, 60, 64; Betty L. Brown, *Hugh Leach of Randolph County, North Carolina, and Some of His Descendents and Neighbors* (Archdale, NC: 1999), 41.

118. Hardy, 165.

119. J.Q. Holland, "Historical Sketch of Co. C, 71st Regiment," North Carolina Department of Archives and History, Raleigh, NC; Randolph County, 86; site visit with Boyd Lamberth and Timothy Thompson.

120. Fielder Diary.

121. Clark, *North Carolina Regiments*, vol. 4, p. 61.

122. Ibid; Mary Breckinridge,"The Flag of the 20th Tennessee," *Confederate Veteran* 2, no. 4 (April 1894), 118–9.

123. Henderson, 120; Hughes, 296; Jerome Dowd, *The Life of Braxton Craven* (Durham, NC: Duke University Press, 1939), 100.

124. Dowd, 100.

125. Mills, 58.

126. William T. Ganaway, *The Trinity Archive* 6, no. 8 (May 1893), 328; Andrews, 30.

127. Christopher M. Watford, *Civil War Roster of Davidson County, NC* (Jefferson, NC: McFarland, 2001), 14.

128. Helen P. Sockwell, *Life, Lore, and Legend of McLeansville* (Kernersville, NC: Sockwell, 2009), 39; site visit with Boyd Lamberth and Timothy Thompson.

129. Lovie P. Thomas Papers, Atlanta Historical Society, Atlanta, GA; Sockwell, 39.

130. Site visit with Boyd Lamberth and Timothy Thompson; Sockwell, 39.

131. Robert H. Dacus, *Reminiscences of Company H, 1st Arkansas Mounted Rifles* (Dayton, OH: Morningside, 1972); Gary R.Goodson, *Georgia Confederate 7,000* (Shawnee, CO: Goodson Enterprises, 1995), 79.

132. Harper.

133. Clark, *North Carolina Regiments* 4, p. 61.

134. James H. McCallum, *Martin County During the Civil War* (Enterprise, 1971), 72.

135. Carol Moore, *Images of Greensboro's Confederate Soldiers* (Charleston, SC: Arcadia, 2008), 108.

136. George Pepper, *Personal Recollections of Sherman's Campaigns in Georgia and the Carolinas* (Zanesville, OH: Hugh Dunne, 1866), 428.

137. Mac Wykoff, *History of the 3rd South Carolina Regiment* (Wilmington, NC: Broadfoot, 2008), 342.

138. Worsham, 176.

139. Norman Brown, 164–5.

140. Archer Anderson Collection, Eleanor S. Brockenbrough Library, Museum of the Confederacy, Richmond, VA.

141. William A. Fletcher, *Rebel Private, Front and Rear* (Austin: University of Texas Press, 1954), 146.

142. Henry _____ Letter, Duke University, Durham, NC.

143. *Ibid.*

144. *Ibid.*

145. Louis H. Manarin, *North Carolina Troops*, vol. 1 (Raleigh: Department of Archives and History, 1966), 568.
146. Thomas Papers.
147. Henderson, 144.
148. Jones, *Chatham Artillery*, 215–221.
149. John Curry, *History of Company B, 40th Alabama, C.S.A* (Colonial, 1963), 89.
150. Walter Clark, *Under the Stars and Bars* (Augusta, GA: Augusta Chronicle, 1900), 198.
151. George William Brent Papers, Duke University, Durham, NC.
152. *Ibid.*

CHAPTER 4

1. Johnston, *Narrative*, 400.
2. *Ibid.*, 400, 402.
3. Johnson Hagood, *Memories of the War of Secession from the Original Manuscripts of Johnson Hagood* (Columbia, SC: State, 1910), 369.
4. Henderson, 137.
5. Roger Durham, ed., *The Blues in Gray: Journal of William D. Dixon* (Knoxville: University of Tennessee Press, 2000), 277.
6. *Official Records*, vol. 47, part 3, p. 809.
7. William C. Stevens Correspondence, University of Michigan, Ann Arbor; Bradley, 186.
8. *Ibid.*; Barbara B. Smith and Nina B. Baker, eds., *Burning Rails as We Please* (Jefferson, NC: McFarland, 2004), 152.
9. N.A. Pinney, *History of the 104th Regiment, Ohio Volunteer Infantry, from 1862 to 1865* (Akron, OH: Werner and Lohmann, 1886), 83.
10. Bradley, 159–60.
11. Jack Fryar, ed., *Blue Tide Rising* (Wilmington, NC: Dram Tree Books, 2007), 77–8; Bradley, 160–1; Johnston, *Narrative*, 402.
12. Johnston, *Narrative*, 402–3; Bradley, 160–1.
13. Bradley, 165–6.
14. *Ibid.*, 170–1.
15. Fryar, 80; Johnston, *Narrative*, 403.
16. *Official Records*, vol. 47, part 3, p. 809.
17. Fletcher, 194.
18. W.H. Andrews Diary.
19. Hutson Papers.
20. *Ibid.*
21. Rachel Susan Cheves Papers, Duke University, Durham, NC.
22. Dickert, 529.
23. Cunningham, 56; John Simpson, 132.
24. Hagood, 370.
25. Taylor Beatty Papers, Southern Historical Collection, University of North Carolina, Chapel Hill.
26. Johnston, *Narrative*, 410.
27. Edwin Rennolds, *History of Henry County Commands* (Jacksonville, FL: Sun, 1904), 116.

28. James Brown, 165; Ridley, *Battles*, 459; Weymouth Jordan, *North Carolina Troops*, vol. 14, p. 271; Angley et al., 88.
29. Hagood, 369.
30. Larack P. Thomas, "Reminiscences of the Forty-Second Georgia," *Confederate Veteran* 12 (1904), 14–5.
31. Colleen M. Elliott and Louise A. Moxley, *Tennessee Veterans Questionnaire* (Easley, SC: Southern Historical Press, 1985), 1745.
32. Hutson; Henderson 140.
33. Albert Q. Porter Collection, Library of Congress, Washington, DC.
34. Durham, 278.
35. Ridley, *Battles*, 45–59.
36. Elliot and Moxley, vol. 5, p. 2219.
37. Brown Diary, 11.
38. Johnston, *Narrative*, 410.
39. Halcott P. Jones Diary, Eleanor S. Brockenbrough Library, Museum of the Confederacy, Richmond, VA.
40. *Ibid.*
41. Fielder Diary.
42. Johnston, *Narrative*, 408; Roman, 396.
43. Johnston, *Narrative*, 410.
44. *Official Records*, vol. 47, part 3, p. 815.
45. *Ibid.*
46. *Ibid.*, 811; Angley et al., 82.
47. Eugene Jones Jr., *Enlisted for the War* (Hightstown, NJ: Longstreet, 1997), 252; Hagood, 370.
48. Jacob H. Smith.
49. *Ibid.*
50. Norman D. Brown, 166.
51. Cheves Papers.
52. Harris, 62.
53. Darrell Taylor, "THer Uncovers Unknown Civil War Camp," *Treasure*, 16–18.
54. *Ibid.*
55. *Ibid.*
56. Joyce, 104, 105, 31.
57. *Ibid.*, 102.
58. Durham, 278.
59. Hagood, 369; Norman D. Brown, 165.
60. Porter.
61. Crowther.
62. Civil War Diary of Col. David G. McIntosh, p. 12, Virginia Historical Society, Richmond, VA.
63. Fryar, 100; Angley et al., 92.
64. Fryar, 88; Bradley, 213–14; Johnston, *Narrative*, 412; *Official Records*, vol. 47, part 3, p. 835.
65. Durham, 279.
66. *Ibid.*
67. *Ibid.*, 279–80.
68. McMurry, 181.
69. Cunningham, 56–7.
70. Durham, 279.
71. W.H. Andrews.
72. Hagood, 370.
73. Archer Anderson.

74. D.E. Huger Smith, *A Charlestonian's Recollections* (Charleston, SC: Carolina Art Association, 1950), 106.

75. Hagood, 370–71.

76. Dantzler, 15.

77. *Ibid.*

78. Waring.

79. Jones, *Chatham Artillery*, 215–221.

80. Norman D. Brown, 166.

81. James R. Cole, "Athos Recounts the Civil War's End in Greensboro," *Guilford Genealogist* 34, no. 1 (Spring 2007), 11.

82. William T. Sherman, *Memoirs of William T. Sherman* (New York: D. Appleton, 1875), 370.

83. *Ibid.*

84. Fryar, 91.

85. Kirk, 595.

86. Angley et al., 94; Sherman, 370; Fryar, 112; *Official Records*, vol. 47, part 3, p. 866.

87. Johnston, *Narrative*, 418; *Official Records*, vol. 47, part 3, p. 320.

88. Archer Anderson.

89. Francis T. Hawks Papers, Southern Historical Collection, University of North Carolina, Chapel Hill.

90. Bradley, 222.

91. Charles P. Hansell, "Surrender of Cobb's Legion," *Confederate Veteran* 10, no. 25 (October 1917), 463.

92. John S. Wise, *The End of an Era* (Boston: Houghton Mifflin, 1899), 453–54.

93. *Ibid.*

94. *Ibid.*

95. Evans, 470.

96. Guild, 145–46.

97. *Ibid.*

98. Henry B. Ragan, *A Warrior and His Wife* (1962), 49.

99. "Johnston's Last Volley," *Southern Historical Society Papers* 30 (1902), 175–76.

100. *Ibid.*

101. Ridley, *Battles*, 464.

102. *Ibid.*, 147.

103. Fielder Diary.

104. George P. Wilson, "The Last Shot," in *Camp Fires of the Confederacy*, ed. Ben Labree.

105. Vatavuk, 19.

106. Bradley, 217; Grimsley, 64.

107. Vatavuk, 19.

108. *Official Records*, vol. 47, part 3, p. 835.

109. *Ibid.*, 814.

110. Angley et al., 92.

111. *Official Records*, vol. 49, no. 345.

112. *Ibid.*, 336.

113. Fryar, 111.

114. Bradley, 203.

115. Henderson, 143.

116. Buford, 170–1.

117. Archer Anderson.

118. Vatavuk, 21.

119. Sam Watkins, *Co. Aytch* (New York: Collier, 1962), 243; McMurry, 359.

120. Jordan, *North Carolina Troops*, vol. 14, pp. 271, 646, 500, vol. 15, p. 311.

121. Norman D. Brown, 173.

122. Hagood, 372; Glenn Dedmondt, *The Flags of Civil War South Carolina* (Gretna, LA: Pelican, 2000), 100.

123. Charles Inglesby, *Historical Sketch of the 1st South Carolina Artillery* (Walker, Evans, and Cogswell), 19.

124. Rennolds, 116.

125. Ed Gleeson, *Illinois Rebels* (Carmel, IN: Guild, 1996), 82.

CHAPTER 5

1. Bradley, 169.

2. Frank Tursi, *Winston-Salem: A History* (Winston-Salem, NC: J.F. Blair, 1994), 101.

3. Clary, 293.

4. George Brewer, *History of the 46th Alabama Regiment Volunteer Infantry.* (Montgomery, AL: 1902), 40–41.

5. Alester G. Holmes, *Diary of Henry M. Holmes, Army of Tennessee Assistant Surgeon, Florida Troops* (State College of Mississippi, 1968).

6. Carroll Henderson, Memoir, Tennessee State Library and Archives, Nashville, TN; Christopher Lossen, *Tennessee's Forgotten Warriors* (Knoxville: University of Tennessee Press, 1989), 247–48.

7. Lossen, 248.

8. James Fleming, *The Confederate 9th Tennessee Infantry* (Gretna, LA: Pelican, 1906), 31.

9. Fielder Diary.

10. Jarman.

11. *Ibid.*

12. W.A. Betts, ed., *Experiences of a Confederate Chaplain* (Greenville, SC, 1865), 77–78.

13. Hawes, 153.

14. Durham, 280.

15.. Harris, *7th North Carolina*, 62.

16. D.E. Huger Smith, 108.

17. Duncan McLaurin, *Recollections and Reminiscences*, vol. 8 (South Carolina United Daughters of the Confederacy, 1998), 462.

18. Edna V. Funderburk, "The Life of Mr. E.B.C. Funderburk," in *Recollections and Reminiscences*, vol. 9 (South Carolina United Daughters of the Confederacy, 1998), 587.

19. Eugene Jones, 249.

20. Barry Benson, "How General Sedgwick Was Killed," *Confederate Veteran* 22 (March 1919), 115.

21. Robert Womack, *Call Forth the Mighty Men* (Bessemer, AL: Colonial, 1987), 508.

22. Ridley, *Battles*, 465.

23. Norman D. Brown, 173.

24. Hagood, 372.
25. *Ibid.*
26. *Ibid.*
27. Womack, 510.
28. DeSaussure, 212.
29. Jeffrey C. Weaver, *63rd Virginia* (Lynchburg, VA: H.E. Howard, 1991), 80.
30. George L. Sherwood and Jeffrey C. Weaver, *54th Virginia* (Lynchburg, VA: H.E. Howard, 1993), 156.
31. Fryar, 110.
32. Norman D. Brown, 170.
33. Bussey, 423.
34. McMurry, 184.
35. Norman D. Brown, 173.
36. Betty L. Brown, *Hugh Leach of Randolph County, North Carolina, and Some of His Descendents and Neighbors* (Archdale, NC, 1999), 31.
37. William R. Talley, *Autobiography of Reverend William R. Talley* (Kennesaw, GA: Kennesaw Mountain National Battlefield), 47.
38. James J. Hawthorne, "Active Service with the 3rd Alabama Cavalry," *Confederate Veteran* 34, no. 9 (September 1926), 336.
39. *New York Herald*, May 9, 1865.
40. Glenn Dedmondt, *The Flags of Civil War Alabama* (Gretna, LA: Pelican, 2001), 71.
41. *Ibid.*, 89.
42. *Ibid.*, 90; Howard Madaus, *The Battle Flags of the Confederate Army of Tennessee* (Milwaukee: Milwaukee Public Museum, 1976), 108.
43. Dedmondt, *Alabama*, 92.
44. *Ibid.*, 95.
45. *Ibid.*, 101.
46. Rebecca Rose, *Colours of the Gray* (Richmond: Museum of the Confederacy, 1998), 10.
47. *Confederate Military History*, vol. 11 (Atlanta: Confederate, 1899), 187; Robert Graetz to author, e-mail, 4 2009 August.
48. Madus, 112; Hawes, 154.
49. Hawes, 154.
50. Cathy Wright, Museum Visit, 3 December 2009
51. *Confederate Flags in the Georgia State Capitol Collection* (Atlanta: Georgia Office of Secretary of State, 1994), 26; Calhoun, 51.
52. Rose, 11; Cathy Wright, Museum Visit, 3 December 2009
53. *Charleston (SC) Daily News*, April 4, 1915, Charleston, SC.
54. *Ibid.*, July 15, 1915.
55. Hugh R. Simmons, "The Story of the 12th Louisiana Infantry in the Final Campaign in North Carolina with the Confederate Army of Tennessee," 1992, p. 32; Madus, 98.
56. Weymouth Jordan, *North Carolina Troops*, vol. 4 (Raleigh, NC: Department of Archives and History, 1973), 405, 407; Jennifer Burns to author, e-mail, 22 September 2009.
57. Glenn Dedmondt, *The Flags of Civil War North Carolina* (Gretna, LA: Pelican, 2003), 102.

58. Hardy, 165.
59. Dedmondt, *South Carolina*, 62; "The Last Roll," *Confederate Veteran* 10, no. 6 (June 1902), 274.
60. William S. Hoole, ed., *Pee Dee Light Artillery* (Dayton, OH: Morningside, 1983), 34; Mattie Brunson, "The Flag of the Pee Dee Artillery," *Confederate Veteran* 34, no. 3 (March 1926), 94.
61. Dedmondt, *South Carolina*, 73; O.G. Thompson, "3rd Regimental Flag," in *Recollections and Reminiscences*, vol. 8 (South Carolina United Daughters of the Confederacy, 1998), 65.
62. Hagood, 369.
63. Dedmondt, *South Carolina*, 113.
64. *Ibid.*, 90.
65. *Ibid.*, 98; Irvine C. Walker, "Sketch of the Career of the 10th and 19th South Carolina Regiments in the Service of the Southern Confederacy During the War with the United States," in *Recollections and Reminiscences*, vol. 12 (South Carolina United Daughters of the Confederacy, 2002), 135.
66. Dedmondt, *South Carolina*, 111, 120.
67. *Ibid.*, 137.
68. John Motte Papers, South Carolina Historical Society, Columbia, SC; D.E. Huger Smith, 108.
69. Watkins, 244.
70. Candace Adelson, e-mail to author, 27 May 27 2009, from information in the 3rd Tennessee Flag File, Tennessee State Museum, Nashville.
71. W.B. Stewart, "Battle Flag of the 6th and 9th Tennessee," *Confederate Veteran*, no. 9 (September 1901), 404.
72. "Flag of the Twentieth Tennessee." *Confederate Veteran* 19, no. 11 (November 1911), 544; Greg Biggs to author, e-mail, 13 November 2010.
73. www.geocities.com/bsdunagan/31st.htm.
74. Bradley, 242; Guild, 129.
75. Cathy Wright, Museum Visit, 3 December 2009.
76. Hutson Papers.
77. *Ibid.*
78. Darrell Taylor, "Research Leads to Glory Hole," *Treasure Search*, 61.
79. *Ibid.*

CHAPTER 6

1. Vatavuk, 19.
2. Archer Anderson.
3. Roman, 407.
4. *Official Records*, vol. 47, part 3, p. 843.
5. *Ibid.*, 336. 320, 850; Vatatuk, 19; Fryar, 106.
6. *Official Records*, vol. 47, part 3, p. 843, 851; Clary, 293.
7. *Official Records*, vol. 47, part 3, p. 851.
8. Stevenson Collection, Eleanor S. Brock-

enbrough Library, Museum of the Confederacy, Richmond, VA.

9. Charles C. Jones, 220.
10. Vatatuk, 21; Frank Moore, ed., *Rebellion Record*, vol. 11 (New York: D. Van Nostrand, 1868), 632.
11. Frank Moore, 633.
12. *Ibid.*
13. Vatatuk, 29.
14. *New York Herald,* May 2, 1865.
15. John C. Arbuckle, *Civil War Experiences of a Foot Soldier Who Marched with Sherman* (Columbus, OH: 1930), 153–54.
16. Smith and Baker, 148.
17. *Ibid.*
18. Clary, 294.
19. J. K. Blackburn, *Reminiscences of the Terry Rangers* (University of Texas: 1919), 68–69.
20. *Ibid.*, 69.
21. C.C. Jeffries, *Terry's Rangers* (New York: Vantage, 1961), 129.
22. Bussey, 422.
23. Angley et al., 96; Fryar, 109.
24. Foley and Whicker, 57; Vatatuk, 21; McMurry, 182, 359; Simmons, 32; Sherwood and Weaver, 81.
25. Bert Barnett, *A Certificate of Honor* (2004), 2; *Official Records*, vol. 47, part 3, pp. 801, 850; Clary, 291.
26. Herriot, 102; Clary, 291; Eugene Jones, 253.
27. Harper, 444–45.
28. R.H. Flemming, "The Confederate Treasury," *Confederate Veteran* 12, no. 4 (April 1904), 170.
29. Bussey, 442–43.
30. Hagood, 372.
31. Norman D. Brown, 168.
32. "Reminiscences," *Southern Bivouac* 1, no. 4 (December 1882), 172–3.
33. Lossen, 248.
34. Cole, "Athos," 10.
35. *Official Records*, vol. 47, part 3, p. 349; McMurry, 183.
36. Ridley, "Last Battle."
37. *New York Herald,* May 9, 1865.
38. William Moore, Interview, April 22, 2011.
39. Roman, 410.
40. *Ibid.*, 409.
41. Sam Elliott, *Soldier of Tennessee: General A.P. Stewart* (Baton Rouge: Louisiana State University Press, 1999), 272.
42. *Official Records*, vol. 47, part 3, p. 854.
43. Johnston, *Narrative*, 418.
44. Lovie P. Thomas Papers.
45. Fryar, 113.
46. Sockwell, 47; Albright, *Greensboro*, 79.
47. Albright, *Greensboro*, 83.
48. *Ibid.*, 300.

49. Ethel Stephens Arnett, *Confederate Guns Were Stacked at Greensboro, North Carolina* (Greensboro, NC: Piedmont, 1965), 108.
50. Fryar, 112; *Official Records*, vol. 47, part 3, p. 866.
51. Fryar, 113; Hughes, 296.
52. *New York Herald,* May 9, 1865.
53. James W. Gaskill, *Footprints Through Dixie* (Alliance, OH: Bradshaw, 1919), 179.
54. Pinney, 85.
55. *Ibid.*, 85–86.
56. Smith and Baker, 152.
57. Henderson, 207.
58. Smith and Baker, 152; Pinney, 87.
59. Angley et al., 95; Henderson, 207.
60. Fryar, 105.
61. *Official Records*, Vol. 47, Part 3, 354.
62. William Miller, "My Experience as a Soldier in the Confederate Army," in *Recollections and Reminiscences*, vol. 5 (South Carolina United Daughters of the Confederacy, 1994), 224–225.
63. *Official Records*, vol. 47, part 3, p. 483.
64. *Philadelphia Inquirer*, "Special Correspondence of the Inquirer, Greensboro, N.C., July 6, 1865," July 18, 1865.
65. Foley and Whicker, 57.
66. Hoole, 147; Raphael Semmes, *Memories of Service Afloat During the War Between the States* (Baltimore: Kelly Piet, 1869), 822.
67. Foley and Whicker, 57, Albright.
68. *Official Records*, vol. 47, part 3, p. 483.
69. Pinney, 86.
70. Schenck Diary.
71. *Official Records*, vol. 47, part 3, p. 862.
72. *Ibid.*, 859.
73. *Ibid.*, 856.
74. Pepper, 426–27.
75. *Official Records*, vol. 47, part 3, p. 482.
76. *New York Herald,* May 9, 1865.
77. Buck, 306, 392.
78. Henderson, 151.
79. Weaver, 130, 136.
80. Hardy, 167.
81. Jack Perdue, "Part of Confederate Treasure Paid Out to Paroled Troops in Greensboro-Jamestown-High Point-Archdale Area," in *Lt. F.C. Frazier Camp 668 SCV Newsletter*, October 1996.
82. Bert Barnett, 4.
83. Barefoot, 319–20.
84. Sherman, 370.
85. *Ibid.*; Fryar, 107; *Official Records*, vol. 47, part 3, p. 867; Archer Anderson. Anderson's papers indicate 29,533 men were present on April 26.
86. Hutson.
87. Barefoot, 321.
88. Collins, 300–301.
89. Hawes, 154.
90. Durham, 281–82.

91. Henderson, 155.
92. Flemming, 186, 176.
93. Elliot and Moxley, vol. 4, p. 1742.
94. Cunningham, 57.
95. Trotter, 362.
96. Jones, *Chatham Artillery*, 221.
97. Talley, 47.
98. Henderson, 51; Calhoun, 51; Joyce, 31.
99. Larack P. Thomas, 15.
100. McCorkle.
101. Dantzler, 16.
102. I.V. Moore Diary, Georgia Department of Archives and History, Atlanta.
103. William Pollard Diary, Tennessee State Library and Archives, Nashville.
104. Brewer, 40.
105. Army of Tennessee Collection, Stevenson's Division, Box 1, Eleanor S. Brockenbrough Library, Museum of the Confederacy, Richmond, VA.
106. Durham, 282.
107. Weymouth Jordan, *North Carolina Troops*, vol. 14, p. 311.
108. Foley and Whicker, 59.
109. *Ibid.*, 5.
110. Vatavuk, 21.
111. *New York Herald*, May 9, 1865.
112. *Official Records*, vol. 47, part 3, p. 394.
113. Bingham, 71–72.
114. *Official Records*, vol. 47, part 3, p. 857.
115. Worsham, 177.
116. Lossen, 248; Bradley, 242; John C. Oeffinger, ed., *A Soldier's General: The Civil War Letters of Major General Lafayette McLaws* (Chapel Hill: University of North Carolina Press, 2002), 170.
117. Waring.
118. Fletcher, 196.
119. William E. Sloan Diary, Tennessee State Library and Archives, Nashville.
120. *New York Herald*, May 9, 1865.
121. *Ibid.*
122. Bradley, 238.
123. *New York Herald*, May 9, 1865.
124. Clary, 294.
125. Gaskill, 179–83.
126. Bussey, 422.
127. Gaskill, 179–83.
128. McMurry, 359; Hugh R. Simmons, 32; *Official Records*, vol. 47, part 3, p. 868.
129. Ganaway, 329.
130. *Ibid.*, 330.
131. Guild, 147.
132. McSwain, 119.
133. Joseph MacKay, "Some Recollections of My Four Years in the Confederate Army from Fort Sumter to Bentonville," in *Recollections and Reminiscences*, vol. 13 (South Carolina United Daughters of the Confederacy), 33.
134. Cole, "Athos," 11.
135. "Letter from John Hiatt to His Sons Philander and Thomas Hiatt," *Guilford Genealogist* 8, no. 2 (Winter 1981), 28.
136. Fernando G. Cartland, *Southern Heroes; or, The Friends in War Time* (Poughkeepsie, NY: Fernando G. Cartland, 1897), 251.
137. *Ibid.*, 251–52.
138. Gaskill, 179–83.
139. *Ibid.*
140. Everts, 175–76; James M. Drake, *History of the Ninth New Jersey Volunteers* (Elizabeth, NJ: Printing House, 1889), 299.
141. Everts, 176; Drake, 299. Brush huts were commonly made by soldiers in the field, who used sticks or logs to build a framework, upon which were placed branches with leaves. The shelter provided shade from the sun.
142. *Official Records*, vol. 47, part 3, p. 443.
143. *Ibid.*, 460.
144. Johnston, *Narrative*, 419.
145. Bradley, 223.
146. Johnston, *Narrative*, 418.
147. Frederick H. Dyer, *A Compendium of the War of the Rebellion*, vol. 2 (Des Moines: Dyer, 1908), 497–98 ;Oeffinger, 170.
148. Fryar, 118–19.
149. Gaskill, 179–83.
150. *Ibid.*
151. *Official Records*, vol. 47, part 3, p. 485.
152. *Ibid.*, 490.
153. Morris Runyan, *Eight Days with the Confederates* (Princeton, NJ: Zapf, 1896), 12.
154. *Ibid.*, 16–18.
155. *Ibid.*
156. *Ibid.*, 28.
157. Everts, 178.
158. *Ibid.*, 179.
159. *Official Records*, vol. 47, part 3, pp. 520, 600.

Chapter 7

1. Cole, "Athos," 12.
2. Angley et al., 106.
3. Cole, "Athos," 12.
4. *Ibid.*
5. Henderson, 231.
6. Fryar, 107.
7. *Ibid.*, 109.
8. *Ibid.*, 110–11.
9. *Ibid.*, 111.
10. Henderson, 220.
11. *Ibid.*, 113.
12. Robinson and Stoesen. 102.
13. Walker.
14. *Ibid.*
15. Mary K.W. Smith.
16. Mrs. Thomas Sloan, "Reminiscences" September 26, 1918," Civil War File, Greensboro Public Library, Greensboro, NC.
17. Dickson.
18. Carol Moore, 4–22.

19. Tim Thompson, April 22, 2011.
20. Mrs. Thomas Sloan.
21. *Ibid.*
22. Walker.
23. *Ibid.*
24. Jacob H. Smith Diary.
25. Jacob D. Cox, *Sherman's March to the Sea* (New York: Da Capo, 1994), 117.
26. Smith and Baker, 153.
27. *Ibid.*
28. Spencer, 189.
29. Gaskill, 183.
30. Edmund J Cleveland Diary, 61, Southern Historical Collection, University of North Carolina, Chapel Hill.
31. *Ibid.*, 61–70.
32. Jim Schlosser, *The Beat Goes On* (Greensboro, NC: Greensboro Bicentennial Commission, 2008), 120.
33. William Moore; "Methodist Church," Marker on South Elm Street, Greensboro, NC.
34. *Philadelphia Inquirer*, "Special Correspondence of the Inquirer, Greensboro, N.C., July 6, 1865," July 18, 1865.
35. Cleveland, 61–70.
36. Mary Bogart, "Refugees in Greensboro During the Sixties." Civil War File, Greensboro Public Library.
37. Cleveland, 61–70.
38. *Ibid.*
39. Smith and Baker, 154.
40. Paula S. Jordan and Kathy W. Manning, *Women of Guilford* (Greensboro, NC: 1979), 58.
41. *Winston (NC) People's Press*, May 20, 1865.
42. Melinda Ray Diary, North Carolina Department of Archives and History, Raleigh.
43. James C. Clark, *Last Train South* (Jefferson, NC: McFarland, 1984), 83.
44. *Ibid.*, 83, 87.
45. *Ibid.*, 94.
46. *Ibid.*, 95.

Chapter 8

1. McMurry, 184.
2. John Dooley, *John Dooley, Confederate Soldier: His War Journal* (Ithaca, NY: Georgetown University Press, 1945), 203–4.
3. Arthur Ford, 64–65.
4. Harper, 445–55.
5. D. H. Hanabaugh, *History of the One Hundred and Twenty Eighth Regiment New York Volunteers in the Late Civil War* (Pokeepsie [*sic*], NY: 1894), 205; Crowther.
6. Clement Saussy, "With Wheaton's Battery in the War," *Confederate Veteran* 14, no. 5 (May 1906), 212.
7. Roman, 411.
8. *New York Herald*, May 8, 1865.
9. *Ibid.*

10. *Ibid.*
11. George Mitchell, "Memories of Surrender and Journey Home," *Confederate Veteran* 17, no. 4 (April 1909), 172.
12. Crowther.
13. Mullen, 105.
14. *Ibid.*, 106.
15. *Ibid.*, 106–7.
16. *Ibid.*, 108–9.
17. Manarin, 39, 551.
18. George M. Norris, *Recollections and Reminiscences*, vol. 10 (South Carolina United Daughters of the Confederacy), 18.
19. Halcott P. Jones.
20. Charles G. Elliott, "Kirkland's Brigade, Hoke's Division," *Southern Historical Society Papers* 23 (November 1895), 174; Matthew Brown and Michael Coffey, *North Carolina Troops*, vol. 17 (Raleigh: Office of Archives and History, 2009), 118.
21. Dean.
22. *Ibid.*
23. W.A. Russell, "Tragic Adventures as the War Closed," *Confederate Veteran* 22, no. 2 (February 1914), 401.
24. *Ibid.*
25. *Ibid.*, 402.
26. *Ibid.*
27. *Ibid.*, 403.
28. Dickert, 397.
29. Heriott, 102.
30. *Ibid.*
31. Fryar, 108–9; Govan and Livingood, 375.

Conclusion

1. *Confederate Military History*, 167.
2. Kirby Smith Papers, Southern Historical Collection, University of North Carolina, Chapel Hill.
3. Richard Reid, "A Test Case of the 'Crying Evil': Desertion Among North Carolina Troops During the Civil War," *North Carolina Historical Review*, no. 58 (Summer 1981), 245, 261.
4. Steven D. Smith and James B. Legg, *The Best Ever Occupied: Archaeological Investigations of a Civil War Encampment on Folly Island, South Carolina* (Columbia, SC: South Carolina Institute for Archaeology and Anthropology, 1989), 129–131; Steven D. Smith, James B. Legg, Tamara S. Wilson, and Jonathan Leader, "*Obstinate and Strong*": The History and Archaeology of the Siege of Fort Motte (Columbia: South Carolina Institute for Archaeology and Anthropology, 2007); Steven D. Smith, James B. Legg, and Tamara S. Wilson, *Understanding Camden: The Revolutionary War Battle of Camden as Revealed Through Historical, Archaeological, and Private Collections Analysis* (Columbia: South Carolina Institute for Archaeology and Anthropology, 2005); Steven D. Smith, James B. Legg, and

Tamara S. Wilson, *The Archaeology of the Camden Battlefield: History, Private Collections, and Field Investigations* (Columbia: South Carolina Institute for Archaeology and Anthropology, 2009).

5. *Ibid.*

6. Samuel Stokes et al., *Saving America's Countryside* (Baltimore: Johns Hopkins University Press, 1989), 1.

APPENDIX I

1. *Official Records*, vol. 47, part 3, p. 715.

APPENDIX II

1. Bradley, 290–300.

APPENDIX III

1. *Ibid.* The Order of Battle dramatically reveals the Confederacy's greater commitment to the Army of Northern Virginia. Units in the Army of Tennessee were consolidated throughout the war and faced a final, sweeping reorganization in North Carolina in the spring of 1865. The Virginia army never endured such a dramatic overhaul.

2. Ives, 103; *Official Records*, vol. 47, part 3, p. 770. The 4th Florida had 103 men, the 37th Georgia 150 men.

3. Frances Casstevens, *Clingman's Brigade* (Jefferson, NC: McFarland, 2002), 105; Clark, *North Carolina Regiments*, vol. 2, p. 764; Jordan, *North Carolina Troops*, vol. 14, p. 646. The 8th North Carolina had 150 men, the 40th 100, and the 61st only 14.

4. Barefoot, 321. The 11th regiment had 16 men, the 25th had 5, and the 27th had 7.

5. Gerald H. Starnes, "Tom Dooley and the 42nd North Carolina," *Confederate Veteran* (January-February 1994), 20; Jordan, *North Carolina Troops*, vol. 14, p. 311. The 42nd Georgia had 300 men, the 66th only 33.

6. Brown and Coffey, 118. The 1st Junior Reserves had 48 men, the 2nd had 109, the 3rd counted 32, and the 1st Reserve Battalion had only 11 men.

7. Fleming, 15; Lynn; Alfred J. Vaughan, *Personal Record of the 13th Regiment Tennessee Infantry* (Memphis, TN: S.C. Toof, 1897), 35; Rennolds, 116; Stanley Horn, *Army of Tennessee* (Wilmington, NC: Broadfoot, 1987), 427; Cunningham, 54; McMurry, 359; James Van Eldik, *From the Flame of Battle to the Fiery Cross* (Las Cruces, NM: Yucca Tree, 2001), 276. These were the regimental strengths at the surrender: 1st TN, 65 men; 9th, 40 men; 154th, 18 men; 13th,

under 50 men; 5th, 30 men; 19th, 64 men; 41st, 45 men; 24th, 34 men; 20th, 34 men; 3rd, 29 men.

8. Eugene Jones, 253. The 24th SC had 180 men.

9. Dacus; Phillip Chew, "Reunion of the 22nd Mississippi," *Confederate Veteran* 6, no. 9 (September 1899), 387. The 1st Arkansas Mounted Rifles had 84 men, the 22nd Mississippi 218.

10. H.A. Killen, "Six Brothers' Confederate Summers," *Confederate Veteran* 10, no. 3 (March 1902), 114; Crute, 15. The 27th AL had only 7 men left; the 16th had 50 men.

11. Inglesby, 19. The 1st Regulars had 137 men.

12. Wykoff, 345; O.G. Thompson, 65. The 3rd SC had 169 men.

13. Joseph H. Crute, Jr., *Confederate Staff Officers* (Powhatan, VA: Derwent, 1982). The 10th SC had 55 men.

14. Jordan, *North Carolina Troops*, vol. 14, pp. 500–501; Crute, 26, 181. The 58th NC had 116 men, and the 60th had only 3. The 39th AL had 90 men, and the 37th had 75. The 24th MS had 25 men.

15. Clark, 665; Crute, 217. The 7th NC had 152 men. Nineteen men of the unit surrendered at Appomattox.

16. Crute, *Units of the Confederate States Army* (Midlothian, VA: Derwent, 1987), 108. The 42nd GA had 131 men at the surrender.

17. Brewer, 38; Crute, 29, 17, 19, 22. The 46th AL had 75 men, the 19th had 76, the 20th had 165, the 23rd had 75.

18. Crute, 71. The 10th Cavalry had about 300 men at the surrender.

19. *Official Records*, vol. 47, part 3, p. 818; "Terry's Texas Rangers," *Confederate Veteran* 15, no. 11 (November 1907), 499. The 8th TX had 78 men.

20. Crute, 135. Some of the 9th Kentucky escorted President Davis and his party as they continued south into Georgia. Only a handful of men remained with the Kentucky units by the time of the final surrender.

APPENDIX V

1. Buck W. Yearns and John G. Barrett, eds., *North Carolina Civil War Documentary* (Chapel Hill: University of North Carolina Press, 1980), 340–1.

APPENDIX VII

1. *Official Records*, vol. M, p. 1066.

Bibliography

Primary Sources

Adamson, A.P. *A Brief History of the 30th Georgia.* Jonesboro, GA: Freedom Hill, 1987.

———. "Flag of the 30th Georgia Regiment." *Confederate Veteran* 20, no. 3 (March 1912), 118.

Albright, James W. *Greensboro, 1808–1904.* Greensboro, NC: Joseph Stone, 1904.

Anderson, Mrs. John H. "North Carolina Boy Soldiers at the Battle of Bentonville." *Confederate Veteran* 5, no. 5 (May 1927), 174–6.

Andrews, Fran. *Trinity, North Carolina.* Trinity, NC: 2009.

Andrews, W.H. *Diary of W.H. Andrews.* Atlanta, GA: 1891.

———. "First Georgia Regulars at Johnston's Surrender." *Atlanta Journal,* November 15, 1902.

Arbuckle, John C. *Civil War Experiences of a Foot Soldier Who Marched with Sherman.* Columbus, OH, 1930.

Babin, L.U. "An Old Confederate Flag." *Confederate Veteran* 40, no. 3 (March 1932), 115.

Barnett, W.R. "The Flags of the Confederacy." *Confederate Veteran* 36, no. 4 (April 1928), 139–40.

Bauer, Jack K. *Soldiering.* New York: Berkley Books, 1977.

Bennett, Pamela J., ed. "Curtis R. Burke's Civil War Journal." *Indiana Magazine of History* 47, no. 2 (June 1971), 129–170.

Benson, Barry. "How General Sedgwick Was Killed." *Confederate Veteran* 22, (March 1919), 115.

Betts, W.A., ed. *Experiences of a Confederate Chaplain.* Greenville, SC, 1865.

Bishop, Carter. "The Bonnie Blue Flag and Others." *Confederate Veteran* 30, no. 10 (October 1922), 394.

Blackburn, J.K. *Reminiscences of the Terry Rangers.* University of Texas, 1919.

Bomar, Joe Lee. "The Audarain County Flag." *Confederate Veteran* 36, no. 4 (March 1928), 98–99.

Boyce, Joseph. "Missourians in the Battle of Franklin." *Confederate Veteran* 24, no. 3 (March 1916), 101–3.

Bradwell, Isaac G. "Gambling in the Army." *Confederate Veteran* 31 (1932), 475.

Breckinridge, Mary. "The Flag of the 20th Tennessee." *Confederate Veteran* 2, no. 4 (April 1894), 118–9.

Brunson, Mattie. "The Flag of the Pee Dee Artillery." *Confederate Veteran* 34, no. 3 (March 1926), 94–5.

Buford, M. "Surrender of Johnston's Army." *Confederate Veteran* 27, no. 5 (May 1920), 170–1.

Bussey, George W. "Memoirs of Reverend G.W. Bussey." In *Recollections and Reminiscences.* Vol. 11. South Carolina United Daughters of the Confederacy, 2001.

Cabell, W.L. "Vivid History of Our Battle Flag." *Confederate Veteran* 8, no. 5 (May 1900), 238–9.

Castleberry, L.B. "Flag of the 3rd Kentucky Regiment." *Confederate Veteran,* no. 5 (May 1913), 220.

Chapman, Sarah, ed. *Bright and Glory Days.* Knoxville: University of Tennessee Press, 2003.

Charleston (SC) Daily News, April 4, 1915 and July 18, 1924.

Chenery, William H. *14th Regiment Rhode Island Heavy Artillery (Colored).* New York: Negro Universities Press, 1998.

Chew, Phillip. "Reunion of the 22nd Mississippi." *Confederate Veteran* 6, no. 9 (September 1899), 387.

Cole, James R. "Athos Recounts the Civil War's End in Greensboro." *Guilford Genealogist* 34, no.1 (Spring 2007), 4–12.

_____. "Greensboro in April 1865." *Greensboro Patriot*, March 29, 1866.

_____. "The Home Guards." In *History of the Several Regiments and Battalions from North Carolina in the Great War*. Vol 5. Edited by Walter Clark. Goldsboro, NC: Nash Brothers, 1901.

_____. *Miscellany*. Dallas, TX: Ewing B. Bedford, 1897.

Coleman, W.N. "Concerning Flag of Twenty-fourth Alabama Infantry." *Confederate Veteran* 17, no. 2 (February 1910).

Collins, Robert M. *Chapters from the Unwritten History of the War Between the States*. St. Louis: Nixon Jones, 1893.

Confederate Flags in the Georgia State Capitol Collection. Atlanta, GA: Georgia Office of Secretary of State, 1994.

Confederate Military History. Vol. 11. Atlanta: Confederate, 1899.

Confederate Veteran 1, no. 5 (May 1893). "Captured Battle Flags," 211.

Confederate Veteran 1, no. 5 (May 1893). "Presentation of the Flag in May, 1861," 139.

Confederate Veteran 2, no. 2 (January 1894), 68. No title.

Confederate Veteran 2, no. 4 (April 1894). "The Flag of the 1st Regiment South Carolina Regular Artillery," 126.

Confederate Veteran 3, no. 3 (March 1895). "The Flag of the Florida Battery," 73.

Confederate Veteran 4, no. 7 (July 1896), 241. No title.

Confederate Veteran 7, no. 11 (November 1899). "Flag Preserved by Ladies of Franklin," 484.

Confederate Veteran 7, no. 12 (December 1899). "Flag of Terry's Texas Rangers," 545–6.

Confederate Veteran 8, no. 5 (May 1900). "Flag to Be Returned," 393.

Confederate Veteran 9, no. 9 (September 1901). "Flag of the Grenada Rifles," 400.

Confederate Veteran 9, no. 11 (November 1901). "Flag Presentation at Fayetteville, Arkansas," 493–4.

Confederate Veteran 10, no. 6 (June 1902). "The Last Roll," 269–75.

Confederate Veteran 10, no. 9 (September 1902). "Decline to Return the Flags," 388.

Confederate Veteran 12, no. 2 (February 1904). "The Last Roll," 86–7.

Confederate Veteran 12, no. 10 (October 1904). "Color Bearer and Guard at Perryville, Kentucky," 475.

Confederate Veteran 12, no. 12 (December 1904). "The Last Roll," 596–99.

Confederate Veteran 14, no. 2 (February 1906). "Confederate Flag on the Rio Grande," 64.

Confederate Veteran 14, no. 9 (September 1907). "The Last Roll," 420–3.

Confederate Veteran 15, no. 9 (September 1907). "The Last Roll," 510–20.

Confederate Veteran 15, no. 10 (October 1907). "Flag in Washington Artillery Army Hall," 468.

Confederate Veteran 15, no. 11 (November 1907). "Terry's Texas Rangers," 498–99.

Confederate Veteran 17, no. 11 (October 1910). "Captured Thirtieth Illinois Regimental Flag," 458.

Confederate Veteran 19, no. 2 (February 1911). "Death Under Flag of Eighth Tennessee," 55.

Confederate Veteran 19, no. 4 (April 1911). "Confederate Flags in the Ohio Capitol," 166.

Confederate Veteran 19, no. 11 (November 1911). "Flag of the Twentieth Tennessee," 544.

Confederate Veteran 22, no. 6 (June 1914). "Flag of the 76th Ohio Regiment," 255–56.

Confederate Veteran 23, no. 10 (October 1915). "The Oldest Flag," 436.

Confederate Veteran 32, no. 6 (June 1924). "Flags of the Confederacy," 205.

Confederate Veteran 32, no. 12 (December 1924). "Flag of the Eighteenth Tennessee," 484.

Coulter, Della Richards. "Three Flags Presented to the Wade Hampton Chapter in 1923." In *Recollections and Reminiscences*. Vol. 5. South Carolina United Daughters of the Confederacy, 1994.

Cox, Jacob D. *Sherman's March to the Sea*. New York: Da Capo, 1994.

Croxton, John. "Second Palmetto Regiment." In *Recollections and Reminiscences*. Vol. 9. South Carolina United Daughters of the Confederacy, 1998.

Cummings, Joseph B. "How I Knew That the War Was Over." *Confederate Veteran* 9, no. 1 (January 1901), 18–19.

Dawes, Ephriam C. "My First Day Under

Fire at Shiloh." In *Military Order of the Loyal Legion of the United States* (MOL-LUS). Vol. 4. 1896.

DeSaussure, C.A. "War Experiences at Haw River." In *Recollections and Reminiscences*. Vol. 7. South Carolina United Daughters of the Confederacy, 1997.

Dickert, D.A. *History of Kershaw's Brigade*. Dayton, OH: Morningside, 1988.

_____. "Sketch of the Life and Adventure of Col. D.A. Dickert." In *Recollections and Reminiscences*. Vol. 12. South Carolina United Daughters of the Confederacy, 2002.

Dickson, G.G. "Trailing the Treasure of the Confederacy." *Raleigh News and Observer*, April 29, 1928.

Dooley, John. *John Dooley, Confederate Soldier: His War Journal*. Washington, D.C.: Georgetown University Press, 1945.

Durham, Roger, ed. *The Blues in Gray: Journal of William D. Dixon*. Knoxville: University of Tennessee Press, 2000.

Eckel, Alexander. "Captured Flags Sought." *Confederate Veteran* 24, no. 6 (June 1916), 285.

Elliott, Charles G. "Kirkland's Brigade, Hoke's Division." *Southern Historical Society Papers* 23 (November 1895), 165–74.

Elliott, Colleen M., and Louise A. Moxley. *Tennessee Veterans Questionnaire*. Easley, SC: Southern Historical Press, 1985.

Emond, John. "Flag of the 28th Alabama Regiment." *Confederate Veteran* 27, no. 8 (August 1919), 311.

Evans, J.W. "With Hampton's Scouts." *Confederate Veteran* 32 (December 1924), 470.

Flemming, R.H. "The Confederate Treasury." *Confederate Veteran* 12, no. 4 (April 1904), 170–1.

Fletcher, William A. *Rebel Private, Front and Rear*. Austin: University of Texas Press, 1954.

Ford, Arthur P. *Life in the Confederate Army, Being Personal Experiences of a Private Soldier in the Confederate Army by Arthur P. Ford and Some Experiences and Sketches of Southern Life*. New York: Neale, 1905.

Fryar, Jack, ed. *Blue Tide Rising*. Wilmington, NC: Dram Tree Books, 2007.

Funderburk, Edna V. "The Life of Mr. E.B.C. Funderburk." In *Recollections and Reminiscences*. Vol. 9. South Carolina United Daughters of the Confederacy, 1998.

Ganaway, William T. *The Trinity Archive* 6, no. 8 (May 1893), 324–330.

Gaskill, J.W. *Footprints Through Dixie*. Alliance, OH: Bradshaw, 1919.

"General Butler at New Orleans." In *Recollections and Reminiscences*. Vol. 10. South Carolina United Daughters of the Confederacy (1997).

"General Shelby's Flag." In *Recollections and Reminiscences*. Vol. 7. South Carolina United Daughters of the Confederacy (1997).

Hagood, Johnson. *Memories of the War of Secession from the Original Manuscripts of Johnson Hagood*. Columbia, SC: State, 1910.

Hanifred, D.H. "Reminiscences of D.H. Hanifred." In *Recollections and Reminiscences*. Vol. 7. South Carolina United Daughters of the Confederacy, 1997.

Hansell, Charles P. "Surrender of Cobb's Legion." *Confederate Veteran* 25, no. 10 (October 1917), 463–4.

Harley, Stan. "Flag of the 6th Arkansas: Cleburne's Flag." *Confederate Veteran* 5, no. 10 (October 1897), 518.

Harper, George Washington. "Fifty-Eighth Regiment." In *Histories of the Several Regiments and Battalions from North Carolina in the Great War*. Vol. 5. Edited by Walter Clark. Goldsboro, NC: Nash, 1901).

_____. "G.W.F. Harper's Diary." Caldwell Heritage Museum, Lenoir, NC.

Harris, James. *Historical Sketches of the 7th Regiment, North Carolina State Troops*. Mooresville, NC: Mooresville Printing.

Harris, O.P. "We Kept Fighting and Falling Back." *Civil War Times Illustrated* 8, no. 8 (December 1968), 37–42.

Harrison, Burton N. "The Capture of Jefferson Davis." *Century* 27 (November 1883), 130–45.

Hawes, Lilley M, ed. "Memoirs of Charles Olmstead." *Georgia Historical Society Quarterly* 45 (June 1961), 137–55.

Hawthorne, James J. "Active Service with the 3rd Alabama Cavalry." *Confederate Veteran* 34, no. 9 (September 1926), 334–6.

Herriot, Robert. "At Greensboro, N.C., in April, 1865." *Confederate Veteran* 30, no. 3 (March 1922), 101–2.

Holmes, Alester G. *Diary of Henry M. Holmes, Army of Tennessee Assistant Surgeon, Florida Troops*. State College of Mississippi, 1968.

Hoole, Stanley. "Admiral on Horseback: The Diary of Brigadier-General Raphael Semmes, February-May, 1865." *Alabama Review* 28, no. 2 (April 1975), 129–50.

Hubbard, John Milton. "Memoir of John Milton Hubbard." In *Notes of a Private*. Memphis, TN: E.H. Clarke & Brother, 1909.

Hutchins, Morris, "The Battle of Franklin, Tennessee." In *Military Order of the Loyal Legion of the United States* (MOLLUS). Vol. 5.

Hyde, Anne B. "Furled Banners of the South." *Confederate Veteran* 21, no. 7 (July 1913), 362–3.

Inglesby, Charles. *Historical Sketch of the 1st South Carolina Artillery*. Charleston, SC: Walker, Evans, and Cogswell, 1896.

Inzer, W. "Flag of Alabama Regiment Not Captured." *Confederate Veteran* 12, no. 11 (November 1904), 451.

Ives, W.M. "History of the 4th Florida Regiment." *Confederate Veteran* 3, no. 4 (April 1895), 102–3.

Johnston, Joseph E. *Narrative of Military Operations*. New York: D. Appleton, 1874.

Jones, Charles C. *Historical Sketches of the Chatham Artillery During the Confederate Struggle for Independence*. Albany, NY: Joe Munsell, 1867.

Jones, Frank. "Personal Recollections and Experiences of a Soldier During the War of the Rebellion." In *Military Order of the Loyal Legion of the United States* (MOLLUS). Vol. 6. 1908.

Jordan, M.C. "Flag of the 20th Tennessee Infantry." *Confederate Veteran* 19, no. 11 (November 1911), 544.

Kellie, E.I. "The Flag of Whitfield's Legion." *Confederate Veteran* 14, no. 4 (April 1906), 192.

Killen, H.A. "Six Brothers' Confederate Summers." *Confederate Veteran* 10, no. 3 (March 1902), 114.

"Kirby Smith." In *Recollections and Reminiscences*. Vol. 10. South Carolina United Daughters of the Confederacy, 2000.

"Letter from John Hiatt to His Sons Philander and Thomas Hiatt." *Guilford Genealogist* 8, no. 2 (Winter 1981), 28.

Lowe, Richard, ed. *A Texas Cavalry Officer's Civil War*. Baton Rouge: Louisiana State University Press, 1999.

Lozedon, John E. "Flag of 9th Texas Infantry." *Confederate Veteran* 17, no. 9, (September 1909), 455.

Lynn, John H. "Re-enlistment in the Western Army." *Confederate Veteran* 10, no. 6 (June 1902), 259.

MacKay, Joseph. "Some Recollections of My Four Years in the Confederate Army from Fort Sumter to Bentonville." In *Recollections and Reminiscences*. Vol. 13. United Daughters of the Confederacy, 34–85.

Mallory, Stephen. "The Last Days of the Confederate Government." *McClure's*, issue 7 (December 1900), 99–107, 239–48.

McCallum, James H. *Martin County During the Civil War*. Enterprise, 1971.

McDonald, James A. "The Flag of the Hamilton Guards." *Confederate Veteran* 33, no. 10 (October 1925), 363–4.

McKinstry, J.A. "With Colonel Rogers When He Fell." *Confederate Veteran* 4, no. 7 (July 1896), 220–222.

McLaurin, Duncan. In *Recollections and Reminiscences*. Vol. 8. South Carolina United Daughters of the Confederacy, 1998.

McSwain, Eleanor D. *Crumbling Defenses*. Macon, GA: 1960.

Merrifield, J.K. "Col. Hugh Garland: Captured Flags." *Confederate Veteran* 24, no. 12 (December 1916), 551–55.

Miller, William. "My Experience as a Soldier in the Confederate Army." In *Recollections and Reminiscences*. Vol. 5. South Carolina United Daughters of the Confederacy, 1994, 216–225.

Mitchell, George. "Memories of Surrender and Journey Home." *Confederate Veteran* 17, no. 4 (April 1909), 172.

Moore, Frank, ed. *Rebellion Record*. Vol. 11. New York: D. Van Nostrand, 1868.

Morgan, William. *Personal Reminiscences of the War of 1861–5*. Freeport, NY: Books for Libraries Press, 1971.

Mullen, J.M. "Last Days of Johnston's Army." *Southern Historical Society Papers* 18 (January 1890), 97–113.

New York Herald, May 2, 1865 and May 9, 1865.

New York Times, "Mexican War Survivor Dead," October 11, 1900.

New York Times, "Tattered War Flags Put in Army's Care," November 18, 1907.

Norris, George M. In *Recollections and Reminiscences*. Vol. 10. South Carolina United Daughters of the Confederacy.

Oeffinger, John C., ed. *A Soldier's General: The Civil War Letters of Major General Lafayette McLaws*. Chapel Hill: University of North Carolina Press, 2002.

Official Records of the War of the Rebellion. Washington, DC: War Department, 1895.

Owen, William M. *In Camp and Battle with the Washington Artillery*. Baton Rouge: Louisiana State University Press, 1885.

Winston (NC) People's Press, May 20, 1865.

Pepper, George. *Personal Recollections of Sherman's Campaigns in Georgia and the Carolinas*. Zanesville, OH: Hugh Dunne, 1866.

Philadelphia Inquirer, July 18, 1865.

Philadelphia Inquirer, "Special Correspondence of the Inquirer, Greensboro, N.C., July 6, 1865," July 18, 1865.

Posey, Mrs. Samuel. "The Crimson Battle Flag." *Confederate Veteran* 31, no. 3 (March 1923), 98–100.

Power, J.L. "The Tennessee Army in 1865." *Confederate Veteran* 5, no. 1 (January 1897), 24–5.

Preston, W.E. "Facts About the Cleburne Flag." *Confederate Veteran* 19, no. 7 (July 1909), 348.

Puckett, Nettie. "The First State Flag of Alabama." *Confederate Veteran* 40, no. 7 (July 1932), 247.

Rennolds, Edwin. *History of Henry County Commands*. Jacksonville, FL: Sun, 1904.

Rice, C.S.O. "Incidents of the Vicksburg Siege." *Confederate Veteran* 12, no. 2 (February 1904), 77–78.

Ridley, B.L. *Battles and Sketches of the Army of Tennessee*. Mexico, MO: Missouri Printing, 1906.

_____. "Coming Home from Greensboro, NC." *Confederate Veteran* 3, no. 7 (July 1895), 203–4.

_____. "Last Battle of the War." *Confederate Veteran* 3, no. 1 (January 1895), 36–7.

Rountree, Maude M. "The Texas Rangers' Flag." *Confederate Veteran* 9, no. 4 (April 1902), 159.

Roziene, F.A. "Flag of the 72nd Illinois." *Confederate Veteran* 21, no. 3 (March 1913), 120.

Runyan, Morris. *Eight Days with the Confederates*. Princeton, NJ: Zapf, 1896.

Russell, W.A. "Tragic Adventures as the War Closed." *Confederate Veteran* 22, no. 2 (February 1914), 401–3.

Saussy, Clement. "With Wheaton's Battery in the War." *Confederate Veteran* 14, no. 5 (May 1906), 209–13.

Semmes, Raphael. *Memories of Service Afloat During the War Between the States*. Baltimore: Kelly Piet, 1869.

Sherman, William T. *Memoirs of William T. Sherman*. New York: D. Appleton, 1875.

Simmons, J.W. "Heroic Mississippians." *Confederate Veteran* 5, no. 2 (February 1897), 73.

Smith, Austin. "Service with the 4th Louisiana Battalion." *Confederate Veteran* 19 (November 1911), 542–3.

Smith, Barbara B., and Nina B. Baker, ed. *Burning Rails as We Please*. Jefferson, NC: McFarland, 2004.

Smith, D.E. Huger. *A Charlestonian's Recollections*. Charleston, SC: Carolina Art Association, 1950.

Smith, Mary Kelly Watson. *The Women of Greensboro, N.C., 1861–1865: A Paper*. Little Rock, AR: Democrat P & L, 1919.

Southern Bivouac 1, no. 4 (December 1882). "Reminiscences," 172–3.

Southern Historical Society Papers 19 (1891). "Return of a Confederate Flag to Its Original Owner," 263–6.

Southern Historical Society Papers 44: 167.

Southern Historical Society Papers 30. "Johnston's Last Volley." Richmond, VA: Southern Historical Society, 1902.

Southern Historical Society Papers 39: 97–8.

Southern Historical Society Papers 32: 196.

Southern Historical Society Papers 12 (1884). "Flag Presentation to the Washington Artillery," 28–32.

Spencer, Cornelia Phillips. *The Last Ninety Days of the War in North Carolina*. New York: Watchman, 1866. Stewart, W.B. "Battle Flag of the 6th and 9th Tennessee." *Confederate Veteran* 9, no. 9 (September 1901), 404.

Stiles, John C. "The Private Soldier." *Confederate Veteran* 29, no. 4 (April 1921), 135–6.

Thomas, Larack P. "Reminiscences of the Forty-Second Georgia." *Confederate Veteran* 12 (1904), 14–5.

Thompson, O.G. "3rd Regimental Flag." In *Recollections and Reminiscences*. Vol. 8. South Carolina United Daughters of the Confederacy, 1998.

Turpin, James A. "Breckinridge Flag to the 20th Tennessee." *Confederate Veteran* 19, no. 4 (April 1911), 156.

Vaughan, Alfred J. *Personal Record of the 13th Regiment Tennessee Infantry*. Memphis, TN: S.C. Toof, 1897.

Waddell, A.B. "Original Flag of 24th Mississippi Regiment." *Confederate Veteran* 15, no. 5 (May 1907), 203.

Walker, C. Irvine. "Sketch of the Career of the 10th and 19th South Carolina Regiments in the Service of the Southern Confederacy During the War with the United States." In *Recollections and Reminiscences*. Vol. 12. South Carolina United Daughters of the Confederacy, 2002.

Watkins, Sam. *Co. Aytch*. New York: Collier, 1962.

Welborne, Mrs. J.S. "A Wayside Hospital." *Confederate Veteran* 38, no. 3 (March 1930), 95–6.

Wilkinson, Sidney. "These Confederates Never Surrendered." Article from Unnamed Newspaper, North Carolina State Archives, Raleigh, NC.

Wilson, George P. "The Last Shot." In *Camp Fires of the Confederacy*. Edited by Ben Labree. Louisville, KY, 1898.

Winston, Salem, and Greensboro, North Carolina, Directory. Chas Emerson, 1879–80.

Wise, John S. *The End of an Era*. Boston: Houghton Mifflin, 1899.

REGIMENTAL HISTORIES

Brewer, George. *History of the 46th Alabama Regiment Volunteer Infantry*. Montgomery, AL, 1902.

Calhoun, William L. *History of the 42nd Georgia*. Amberg Press, 2008.

Chance, Joseph. *The Second Texas Infantry*. Austin, TX: Eakin Press, 1984.

Clark, Walter. *History of the Several Regiments and Battalions from North Carolina in the Great War, 1861–1865*. Vol. 4. Goldsboro, NC: Nash Brothers, 1901.

_____. *Under the Stars and Bars*. Augusta, GA: Augusta Chronicle, 1900.

Clary, James. *A History of the 15th South Carolina Volunteer Infantry Regiment*. Columbia: South Carolina Department of Archives and History, 2007.

Cunningham, Sumner A. *Reminiscences of the 41st Tennessee Regiment*. Np. Nd.

Curry, John. *History of Company B, 40th Alabama, C.S.A.* Colonial, 1963.

Dacus, Robert H. *Reminiscences of Company H, 1st Arkansas Mounted Rifles*. Dayton, OH: Morningside, 1972.

Drake, James M. *History of the Ninth New Jersey Volunteers*. Elizabeth, NJ: Printing House, 1889.

Everts, Hermann. *A Complete and Comprehensive History of the Ninth Regiment, New Jersey Volunteers*. Newark, NJ: A. Stephen Holbrook, 1865.

Fleming, James. *The Confederate 9th Tennessee Infantry*. Gretna, LA: Pelican, 1906.

Fowler, John D. *Mountaineers in Gray*. Knoxville: University of Tennessee Press, 2004.

Guild, George. *A Brief Narrative of the 4th Tennessee Cavalry Regiment*. Nashville, 1913.

Hale, Douglass. *The 3rd Texas Cavalry in the Civil War*. Norman: University of Oklahoma Press, 1993.

Hall, Winchester. *The Story of the 26th Louisiana Infantry*. Gaithersburg, MD: Butternut, 1984.

Hanabaugh, D.H. *History of the One Hundred and Twenty Eighth Regiment New York Volunteers in the Late Civil War*. Pokeepsie [*sic*], NY, 1894.

Hardy, Michael. *The Fifty-Eighth North Carolina Troops*. Jefferson, NC: McFarland, 2010.

Hoole, William S., ed. *Pee Dee Light Artillery*. Dayton, OH: Morningside, 1983.

Hopkins, Donald. *The Little Jeff*. Shippensburg, PA: White Mane, 1999.

Howell, Grady. *Going to Meet the Yankees: A History of the Sixth Regiment, Mississippi Infantry*. Jackson, MS: Chickasaw Bayou, 1981.

Irvine, Walker. *Rolls and Historical Sketch of the 10th Regiment, South Carolina Volunteers*. Charleston, SC: Walker, Evans, and Cogswell, 1881.

Jeffries, C.C. *Terry's Rangers*. New York: Vantage, 1961.

Jones, Charles Colcock. *Historical Sketch of the Chatham Artillery During the Confederate Struggle*. Albany, NY: Joel Munsel, 1867.

Jones, Eugene Jr. *Enlisted for the War*. Hightstown, NJ: Longstreet, 1997.

Kirk, Charles. *History of the 15th Pennsylvania Cavalry*. Philadelphia, 1906.

Lee, E.T. *Sketch of the 41st Illinois Volunteer Infantry*. 1885.

McMurray, W.J. *History of the 20th Tennessee Regiment*. Nashville, TN: Elder's Bookstore, 1976.

McMurry, Richard M., ed. *Footprints of a Regiment*. Atlanta: Longstreet, 1992.

Pinney, N.A. *History of the 104th Regiment, Ohio Volunteer Infantry, from 1862 to 1865*. Akron, OH: Werner and Lohmann, 1886.

Sherwood, George L., and Jeffrey C. Weaver. *54th Virginia*. Lynchburg, VA: H.E. Howard, 1993.

Simmons, Hugh R. "The Story of the 12th Louisiana Infantry in the Final Campaign in North Carolina with the Confederate Army of Tennessee." 1992.

Simpson, John. *Reminiscences of the 41st Tennessee*. Shippensburg, PA: White Mane, 2001.

Thorpe, Sheldon B. *The History of the Fifteenth Connecticut Volunteers in the War for the Defense of the Union, 1861–1865.* New Haven, CT: Price, Lee, and Adkins, 1893.

Van Eldik, James. *From the Flame of Battle to the Fiery Cross*. Las Cruces, NM: Yucca Tree, 2001.

Vaughan, A.J. *Personal Record of the 13th Regiment Tennessee Infantry*. Memphis, TN: S.C. Torf, 1897.

Weaver, Jeffrey C. *5th and 7th Battalions North Carolina Cavalry and 6th North Carolina Cavalry (65th North Carolina State Troops)*. Lynchburg, VA: H.E. Howard, 1995.

_____. *63rd Virginia*. Lynchburg, VA: H.E. Howard, 1991.

Worsham, William J. *The Old Nineteenth Tennessee Regiment*. Knoxville, TN: Paragon, 1902.

Wykoff, Mac. *History of the 3rd South Carolina Regiment*. Wilmington, NC: Broadfoot, 2008.

Young, J.P. *The Seventh Tennessee Cavalry*. Dayton, OH: Morningside, 1976.

SECONDARY WORKS

Alford, Kenneth D. *Civil War Museum Treasures*. Jefferson, NC: McFarland, 2008.

Angley, Wilson, Jerry L. Cross, and Michael Hill. *Sherman's March Through North Carolina*. Raleigh, NC: Division of Archives and History, 1995.

Arnett, Ethel Stephens. *Confederate Guns Were Stacked at Greensboro, North Carolina*. Greensboro, NC: Piedmont Press, 1965.

_____. *Greensboro, North Carolina*. Chapel Hill: University of North Carolina Press, 1955.

Arnold, James R. *Grant Wins the War*. New York: John Wiley, 1997.

Barefoot, Daniel. *Robert F. Hoke: Lee's Modest Warrior*. Winston-Salem, NC: John F. Blair, 1996.

Barnett, Bert. *A Certificate of Honor*. 2004.

Bingham, Chris. "From New Berne to Bennett Place with Cooke's Foot Cavalry." Master's thesis, East Carolina University, 2007.

Black, Robert C. *The Railroads of the Confederacy*. Chapel Hill: University of North Carolina Press, 1952.

Bradley, Mark. *Last Stand in the Carolinas: The Battle of Bentonville*. Campbell, CA: Savas, 1996.

_____. *This Astounding Close: The Road to Bennett Place*. Chapel Hill: University of North Carolina Press, 2000.

Brawley, James S. *The Rowan Story*. Salisbury, NC: Rowan Printing, 1953.

Brown, Betty L. *Hugh Leach of Randolph County, North Carolina and Some of His Descendents and Neighbors*. Archdale, NC, 1999.

Brown, Matthew, and Michael Coffey. *North Carolina Troops*. Vol. 17. Raleigh: Office of Archives and History, 2009.

Brown, Norman D., ed. *One of Cleburne's Command*. Austin: University of Texas Press, 1980.

Browning, Mary A. *Remembering Old Jamestown*. Charleston, SC: History Press, 2008.

Buck, Irving. *Cleburne and His Command*. Jackson, TN: McCowat-Mercer, 1959.

Bynum, Victoria E. *The Long Shadow of the Civil War*. Chapel Hill: University of North Carolina Press, 2010.

Cannon, Devereaux. *The Flags of the Confederacy*. Memphis, TN: St. Luke's, 1988.

Cannon, Doris. "Restored House Near Selma Had Prominent Role at Civil War's End." *Smithfield (NC) Herald*, October 28, 1989.

Carter, Samuel. *The Final Fortress*. New York: St. Martin's, 1980.

Cartland, Fernando G. *Southern Heroes, or, The Friends in War Time*. Poughkeepsie, NY: Fernando G. Cartland, 1897.

Casstevens, Frances. *Clingman's Brigade*. Jefferson, NC: McFarland, 2002.

Clark, James C. *Last Train South*. Jefferson, NC: McFarland, 1984.

Clark, Walter, ed. *Histories of the Several Regiments and Battalions from North Carolina in the Great War, 1861–1865*. Goldsboro, NC: Nash Brothers, 1901.

_____. *North Carolina Regiments*. Vols. 2, 5, 6. Wendell, NC: Broadfoot, 1982.

Crute, Joseph H., Jr. *Confederate Staff Officers*. Powhatan, VA: Derwent, 1982.

_____. *Units of the Confederate States Army.* Midlothian, VA: Derwent, 1987.

Daniel, Larry. *Cannoneers in Gray.* Huntsville: University of Alabama Press, 1984.

_____. *Soldier in the Army of Tennessee.* Chapel Hill: University of North Carolina Press, 1991.

Dedmondt, Glenn. *The Flags of Civil War Alabama.* Gretna, LA: Pelican, 2001.

_____. *The Flags of Civil War North Carolina.* Gretna, LA: Pelican, 2003.

_____. *The Flags of Civil War South Carolina.* Gretna, LA: Pelican, 2000.

Dickert, D. Augustus. *History of Kershaw's Brigade.* Dayton, OH: Morningside, 1976.

Dowd, Jerome. *The Life of Braxton Craven.* Durham, NC: Duke University Press, 1939.

Dyer, Frederick H. *A Compendium of the War of the Rebellion.* Vol. 2. Des Moines: Dyer, 1908.

Elliott, Sam. *Soldier of Tennessee: General A.P. Stewart.* Baton Rouge: Louisiana State University Press, 1999.

Foley, Bradley R., and Adrian L. Whicker. *The Civil War Ends: Greensboro, April 1865.* Greensboro, NC: Guilford County Genealogical Society, 2008.

Fonvielle, Chris E., Jr. *The Wilmington Campaign.* El Dorado Hills, CA: Savas Beattie, 1996.

Glatthaar, Joseph T. *The March to the Sea and Beyond.* New York: New York University Press, 1986.

Gleeson, Ed. *Illinois Rebels.* Carmel, IN: Guild, 1996.

Goodson, Gary R. *Georgia Confederate 7,000.* Shawnee, CO: Goodson, 1995.

Govan, Gilbert, and James Livingood. *A Different Valor.* Indianapolis: Bobbs Merrill, 1956.

Grimsley, Mark. "Learning to Say 'Enough.'" In *The Collapse of the Confederacy.* Edited by Mark Grimsley and Brooks D. Simpson. Lincoln: University of Nebraska Press, 2001.

Groom, Winston. *Shrouds of Glory.* New York: Atlantic Monthly, 1995.

Hamilton, J.G. *History of North Carolina.* Vol. 2. Chicago: Lewis, 1919.

Hendricks, Howard O. "Imperiled City: The Movements of the Union and Confederate Armies Toward Greensboro in the Closing Days of the Civil War in North Carolina." Master's thesis, University of North Carolina at Greensboro, 1987.

Hinshaw, Seth B., and Mary Edith Hinshaw, eds. *Carolina Quakers.* Greensboro, NC: North Carolina Yearly Meeting, 1972.

Hinshaw, Seth B. *Friends at Holly Springs.* Greensboro, NC: North Carolina Yearly Meeting, 1982.

Horn, Stanley. *Army of Tennessee.* Wilmington, NC: Broadfoot, 1987.

Hughes, Fred. *Guilford County, NC: A Map Supplement.* Jamestown, NC: Custom House, 1988.

Hughes, Nathaniel. *General William Hardee.* Baton Rouge: Louisiana State University Press, 1965.

Jordan, Paula S., and Kathy W. Manning. *Women of Guilford.* Greensboro, NC, 1979.

Jordan, Weymouth. *North Carolina Troops.* Vol. 8. Raleigh, NC: Department of Archives and History, 1981.

_____. *North Carolina Troops.* Vol. 15. Raleigh, NC: Department of Archives and History, 2003.

_____. *North Carolina Troops.* Vol. 4. Raleigh, NC: Department of Archives and History, 1973.

_____. *North Carolina Troops.* Vol. 14. Raleigh, NC: Department of Archives and History, 1998.

_____. *North Carolina Troops.* Vol. 6. Raleigh, NC: Department of Archives and History, 1977.

_____. *North Carolina Troops.* Vol. 10. Raleigh, NC: Department of Archives and History, 1985.

Joyce, Mary L., ed. *Clark's Collection of Historic Remembrances.* High Point, NC, 1950.

Leeper, Wesley. *Rebels Valiant.* Little Rock, AR: Pioneer, 1964.

Lindsley, John. *Military Annals of Tennessee.* Wilmington, NC: Broadfoot, 1996.

Lossen, Christopher. *Tennessee's Forgotten Warriors.* Knoxville: University of Tennessee Press, 1989.

Madaus, Howard. *The Battle Flags of the Confederate Army of Tennessee.* Milwaukee, WI: Milwaukee Public Museum, 1976.

Manarin, Louis H. *North Carolina Troops.* Vol. 1. Raleigh: Department of Archives and History, 1966.

Massey, Mary E. *Ersatz in the Confederacy.* Columbia: University of South Carolina Press, 1952.

McCaffrey, James M. *This Band of Heroes.* Austin, TX: Eakin Press, 1985.

McCurry, Stephanie. *Confederate Reckoning.*

Cambridge, MA: Harvard University Press, 2010.

McKean, Brenda C. *Blood and War at My Doorstep*. Vol. 2. Xlibris, 2011.

Mills, L.B., Jr. *Randolph County: A Brief History*. Raleigh: North Carolina Department of Archives and History, 2008.

Moore, Carol. *Images of Greensboro's Confederate Soldiers*. Charleston, SC: Arcadia, 2008.

Moore, Mark A. *The Battle of Bentonville*. Mason City, IA: Savas, 1997.

_____. *The Wilmington Campaign and the Battle for Fort Fisher*. Mason City, IA: Savas, 1999.

National Register Nomination. Stevens House, Salem, NC. North Carolina State Historic Preservation Office.

Pegg, William, Jr. *Something of the Story of Deep River*. Greensboro, NC: Guilford County Genealogical Society, 1999.

Perdue, Jack. "Part of Confederate Treasure Paid Out to Paroled Troops in Greensboro-Jamestown-High Point-Archdale Area." *Lt. F.C. Frazier Camp 668 SCV Newsletter* (October 1996).

Phillips, Robert L. *History of the Hospitals in Greensboro*. Greensboro, NC: Printworks, 1996.

Prokopowicz, Gerald. *All for the Regiment*. Chapel Hill: University of North Carolina Press, 2001.

Ragan, Henry B. *A Warrior and His Wife*. 1962.

Randolph County Historical Society. *Randolph County, 1779–1979*. Winston-Salem, NC: Randolph County Historical Society, 1980.

Reid, Richard. "A Test Case of the 'Crying Evil'": Desertion Among North Carolina Troops During the Civil War." *North Carolina Historical Review*, no. 58 (Summer 1981), 234–262.

Ridley, Bromfield. *Battles and Sketches of the Army of Tennessee*. Dayton, OH: Morningside, 1976.

Ridley, Bromfield, ed. *The Returned Battle Flags*. Redondo Beach, CA: Rank and File, 1995.

Robinson, Blackwell, and Alexander Stoesen. *History of Guilford County, North Carolina*. Greensboro, NC: Guilford Bicentennial Commission, 1971.

Rogers, Abbie. "Confederates and Quakers: The Shared Wartime Experience." *Quaker History* 99, no. 2 (Fall 2010), 1–19.

Roman, Alfred. *The Military Operations of General Beauregard in the War Between the States, 1861 to 1865: Including a Brief Personal Sketch and a Narrative of His Services in the War with Mexico, 1846–8*. New York: Da Capo, 1994.

Rose, Rebecca. *Colours of the Gray*. Richmond: Museum of the Confederacy, 1998.

_____. *The Confederacy's Last Hurrah*. New York: Harper Collins, 1992.

Schlosser, Jim. *The Beat Goes On*. Greensboro, NC: Greensboro Bicentennial Commission, 2008.

Smith, C. Alphonso, Mamie A. Richardson, and Mary Rawlins. *Annals of an American Family: A Chronicle of the Lives and Times of Successive Generations from Merging Pioneer Lines of the Richardson and Smith Families*. Greensboro, NC, 1953.

Sockwell, Helen P. *Life, Lore, and Legend of McLeansville*. Kernersville, NC: Sockwell, 2009.

Starnes, Gerald H. "'Tom Dooley'" and the 42nd North Carolina." *Confederate Veteran* (January-February 1994), 12–21.

Stokes, Samuel, et al. *Saving America's Countryside*. Baltimore: Johns Hopkins University Press, 1989.

Symonds, Craig. *Joseph E. Johnston*. New York: W.W. Norton, 1992.

Taylor, Darrell, "Research Leads to Glory Hole." *Treasure Search*, 58–61.

_____. "THer Uncovers Unknown Civil War Camp, *Treasure Search*, 16–18.

Thomas, Yvonne B. *Roads to Jamestown*. Fredericksburg, VA: Book Crafters, 1997.

Trotter, William B. *Silk Flags and Cold Steel*. Winston Salem, NC: John F. Blair, 1998.

Trudeau, Noah Andre. *Out of the Storm*. Boston: Little, Brown and Co., 1994.

Tucker, Phillip T. *The Final Fury*. Mechanicsburg, PA: Stackpole, 2001.

Tursi, Frank. *Winston-Salem: A History*. Winston-Salem, NC: J.F. Blair, 1994.

Vatavuk, William. *Dawn of Peace*. Bennett Place Support Fund, 1989.

Warner, Ezra. *Generals in Gray*. Baton Rouge: Louisiana State University Press, 1987.

Watford, Christopher M. *Civil War Roster of Davidson County, NC*. Jefferson, NC: McFarland, 2001.

Wharton, Don. *Smithfield as Seen by Sherman's Soldiers*. Smithfield, NC: Smithfield Herald, 1917.

Wiley, Bell. *Fourteen Hundred and 91 Days*

in the Confederate Army. Wilmington, NC: Broadfoot, 1987.
_____. *Life of Johnny Reb.* Baton Rouge: Louisiana State University Press, 1978.
Williams, Sue Vernon. *A Brief Diary of Events during the Last Months of the Civil War.*
Womack, Robert. *Call Forth the Mighty Men.* Bessemer, AL: Colonial, 1987.
Yates, Richard. "Governor Vance and the End of the War in North Carolina." *North Carolina Historical Review* 18, no. 4 (October 1941), 315–338.
Yearns, Buck W., and John G. Barrett, eds. *North Carolina Civil War Documentary.* Chapel Hill: University of North Carolina Press, 1980.

ARCHAEOLOGICAL REPORTS

Balicki, Joseph. "Defending the Capital: The Civil War Garrison at Fort C.F. Smith." In *Archaeological Perspectives on the American Civil War.* Edited by Clarence R. Geier and Stephen R. Potter. Gainesville: University of Florida Press, 2000.
Smith, Steven D., and James B. Legg. *The Best Ever Occupied: Archaeological Investigations of a Civil War Encampment on Folly Island, South Carolina.* Columbia: South Carolina Institute for Archaeology and Anthropology, 1989.
Smith, Steven, James B. Legg, Tamara S. Wilson, and Jonathan Leader. *"Obstinate and Strong": The History and Archaeology of the Siege of Fort Motte.* Columbia: South Carolina Institute for Archaeology and Anthropology, 2007.
Smith, Steven, James B. Legg, and Tamara S. Wilson. *The Archaeology of the Camden Battlefield: History, Private Collections, and Field Investigations.* Columbia: South Carolina Institute for Archaeology and Anthropology, 2009.
_____. *Understanding Camden: The Revolutionary War Battle of Camden as Revealed Through Historical, Archaeological, and Private Collections Analysis.* Columbia: South Carolina Institute for Archaeology and Anthropology, 2005.

INTERVIEWS AND CORRESPONDENCE

E-mails:
Adelson, Candace, to author: 27 May 2009.
Biggs, Greg, to author: 13 November 2010.
Brownlee, Ann, to author: 31 January 2010.
Burns, Jennifer, to author: 22 September 2009.
Curtis, Ed, and Sue Curtis, to author: 5 May 2011.
Graetz, Robert, to author: 4 August 2009.
Wright, Cathy, to author: 1 June 2009, 2 June 2009.
Interviews:
Lamberth, Boyd: 27 March 2010.
Moore, William: 22 April 2011.
Thompson, Timothy: 27 March 2010, 22 April 2011.
Miscellaneous:
Wright, Cathy, Museum Visit: 3 December 2009.

ARCHIVES AND MUSEUM COLLECTIONS

Alabama Department of Archives and History, Montgomery, AL
  Wheeler Family Papers
Atlanta Historical Society, Atlanta, GA
  Thomas, Lovie P., Papers
Bentonville Battlefield State Historic Site, Newton Grove, NC
  Bradley, Mark, Collection
  Unidentified Newspaper, "The Last Days of the Confederacy in Greensboro."
Duke University, Durham, NC
  Brent, George William, Papers
  Cheves, Rachel Susan, Papers
  Jenkins, Gertrude, Papers
  Jenkins, Robert Alexander, "Reminiscences of Robert Alexander Jenkins."
  Johnson, John, Diary
  Henry _____ Letter
  Tillinghast Family Papers
Eleanor S. Brockenbrough Library, Museum of the Confederacy, Richmond, VA
  Anderson, Archer, Collection
  Army of Tennessee Collection: Stevenson's Division (Box 1)
  Butler's Headquarters Flag File
    54th Virginia Flag File
    41st Georgia Flag File
    43rd Georgia Flag File
  Jones, Halcott P., Diary
  Mullen, Joseph, Diary
  Museum of the Confederacy Flag Collection
  Stevenson Collection
    3rd Florida Flag File
Emory University, Atlanta, GA
  Ash, John, Diary

Georgia Department of Archives and History, Atlanta, GA
Brown, James, Diary
McCorkle, Hezekiah, Diary
Moore, I.V., Diary
Greensboro Historical Museum, Greensboro, NC
Dantzler, Daniel D., *A Brief Diary of Events during the Last Months of the Civil War.*
Ferry, Albert, Letter
Foust, Mana D., Letter
Hale, Presley, Letter
Greensboro Public Library, Greensboro, NC
Bogart, Mary. "Refugees in Greensboro During the Sixties." Civil War File
Map, Greensboro, North Carolina, Sanborn Map Co., 1885
McLean, William C., Statement
Sloan, Mrs. Thomas, "Reminiscences, September 26, 1918," Civil War File
Walker, Letitia, "The Surrender in Greensboro," Civil War File
Kennesaw Mountain National Battlefield, Kennesaw, GA
Talley, William R., *An Autobiography of Reverend William Ralston Talley.*
Library of Congress, Washington, D.C.
Porter, Albert Q., Collection
Sherman, William T., Papers
Louisiana State University Archives, Baton Rouge, LA
Bringier, Louis, Papers
Mississippi Department of Archives and History, Jackson, MS
Jarman, Robert Amos, Papers
North Carolina Department of Archives and History, Raleigh, NC
Holland, J.Q., "Historical Sketch of Co. C, 71st Regiment."
Ray, Melinda, Diary
South Carolina Historical Society, Columbia, SC
Motte, John, Papers
Southern Historical Collection, University of North Carolina, Chapel Hill, NC
Albright, James W., Diaries and Reminiscences
Beatty, Taylor, Papers
Cleveland, Edmund J., Diary
Copeland, David T., Papers
Deans, Henderson, Reminiscences
Gordon, W.W., Diary
Hawks, Francis T., Papers
Heyward-Ferguson Papers, "Memoirs of S.W. Ferguson."
Hutson, Charles Woodward, Papers

Mallett, Charles Beatty, Papers
Mallory, Stephen, Diary
Smith, Jacob H., Diary
Smith, Kirby, Papers
Waring, Joseph Frederick, Diary
Wood, John Taylor, Papers
Tennessee State Library and Archives, Nashville, TN
Fielder, Alfred Tyler, Diary (Vol. 4)
Henderson, Carroll, Memoir
Pollard, William, Diary
Sloan, William E., Diary
Sullivan, Thomas L., Account Book
University of Michigan, Ann Arbor, MI
Stevens, William C., Correspondence
University of North Carolina-Wilmington, Wilmington, NC
Schenck, Nicholas, Diary (digital series)
Virginia Historical Society, Richmond, VA
Beckwith, Margaret Stanly, Reminiscences
McIntosh, Col. David G., Civil War Diary
Virginia Military Institute Archives, Lexington, VA
Crowther, Joseph W., Diary
Western Reserve Historical Society, Cleveland, OH
Walker Letters. Folder 6

ONLINE RESOURCES

http://www.historynet.com/an-eyewitness-account-of-the-evacuation-of-richmond-during-the-american-civil-war.htm/3.
http://www.uis.edu/newsreleases/2007/03/20070316.html.
www.armyhistory.org/ahf2.aspx?pgID=877&id=91&exComID=56
www.civilwar.nps.gov/cwss
www.flagspot.net/flags/it_rmemp.html#over.
www.fotw.vexillum.com/flags/us-csah.html.
www.geocities.com/bsdunagan/31st.htm.
http://jamestownnews.womacknewspapers.com/articles/2011/11/09/news/features/features61.txt.
www.ncmuseumofhistory.org/nca/search.html
www.ohsweb.ohiohistory.org/exhibits/fftc/about2/about_specs.apx?section=history&page.
www.oldstatehouse.org.
www.trading-ford.org/stoneman.html.

HISTORICAL MARKERS

"Army of Tennessee." Monument, Greensboro, NC.

"Johnston Moves West." North Carolina Civil War Trails Marker, Alamance County.

"Johnston Moves West." North Carolina Civil War Trails Marker, Alamance County.

"Johnston Moves West." North Carolina Civil War Trails Marker, Alamance County.

"Last Shots." North Carolina Civil War Trails Marker, Durham County.

"Last Review." North Carolina Civil War Trails Marker, Johnston County.

"Methodist Church." Marker on South Elm Street, Greensboro, NC.

Index

225